D1356426

United Nations University Series on Regionalism

Volume 19

The United Nations University Series on Regionalism, launched by UNU-CRIS and Springer, offers a platform for innovative work on (supra-national) regionalism from a global and inter-disciplinary perspective. It includes the World Reports on Regional Integration, published in collaboration with other UN agencies, but it is also open for theoretical, methodological and empirical contributions from academics and policy-makers worldwide.

Book proposals will be reviewed by an International Editorial Board.

The series editors are particularly interested in book proposals dealing with:

- comparative regionalism;
- comparative work on regional organizations;
- inter-regionalism;
- the role of regions in a multi-level governance context;
- the interactions between the UN and the regions;
- the regional dimensions of the reform processes of multilateral institutions;
- the dynamics of cross-border micro-regions and their interactions with supra-national regions;
- methodological issues in regionalism studies.

Accepted book proposals can receive editorial support from UNU-CRIS for the preparation of manuscripts.

Please send book proposals to: pdelombaerde@cris.unu.edu and lvanlangenhove@cris.unu.edu.

More information about this series at http://www.springer.com/series/7716

Irma Johanna Mosquera Valderrama •
Dries Lesage • Wouter Lips
Editors

Taxation, International Cooperation and the 2030 Sustainable Development Agenda

 Springer

Editors
Irma Johanna Mosquera Valderrama
Leiden University
Leiden, The Netherlands

Dries Lesage
Ghent University
Ghent, Belgium

Wouter Lips
Ghent University
Ghent, Belgium

ISSN 2214-9848   ISSN 2214-9856   (electronic)
United Nations University Series on Regionalism
ISBN 978-3-030-64856-5   ISBN 978-3-030-64857-2   (eBook)
https://doi.org/10.1007/978-3-030-64857-2

This Springer imprint is published by the registered company Springer Nature Switzerland AG.
The registered company address is: Gewerbestrasse 11, 6330 Cham, Switzerland

Preface

Taxation, International Cooperation and the 2030 Sustainable Development Agenda

Co-editors: Irma Johanna Mosquera Valderrama, Dries Lesage, Wouter Lips

Attaining the sustainable development goals (SDGs) as formulated by the United Nations is a challenge requiring collaboration and compliance at the level of both international and regional governance to be successful. Although not formulated explicitly as an SDG and less "visible" to many observers, international tax governance can be core to establishing fair financial and tax flows that prevent exploitation of weaker economies and societies globally.

The current volume, edited by Dr. Irma Johanna Mosquera Valderrama, Prof. Dries Lesage, and Dr. Wouter Lips, is a timely contribution to addressing various links between taxation and development. Its publication in a series related to UN academic background work is most suitable, not least given the linkages between the topic addressed and the 2030 Sustainable Development Agenda.

The themes addressed in this book—ranging from taxation and sustainable development to tax competition, tax incentives, and rules ensuring globally coherent policies—address frameworks for the growth path of several developing countries, covering topics that are central to sustainable development. Measures in global tax governance implicitly address biases in governance that could disadvantage weaker economies and increase instead of decreasing inequalities on the regional as well as the global level. The book is written from an interdisciplinary perspective, encompassing contributions by experts in domestic or international tax law, international relations, as well as international political economy. In addition to this, the book reflects different organizational perspectives, as it encompasses work by persons affiliated with international and regional organizations, think tanks, and governments as well as by academics. In this sense, the volume provides a comprehensive overview of several themes relevant to the link between global tax governance and development, not least in view of the status of the Base Erosion and Profit Sharing (BEPS) project, initiated by the OECD, with a political mandate by the G20, and the steps achieved so far.

Global tax governance is at the core of several challenges to reform and modernize the current international tax architecture. The BEPS project can be considered a milestone on the way to ensuring that economic activity—notably as conducted by multinational companies—is taxed in the jurisdiction in which it takes place. It was to provide a set of tools tackling challenges such as tax base erosion and profit shifting. It turns out, however, that different states across the globe have different perspectives on the BEPS and the implementation of its minimum standards, creating variation in policies and a lack of coherence in global policies. Moreover, the BEPS framework may need adaptation if it is to account more explicitly for the interests of developing countries and to strengthen implementation of the SDGs over time. Hence, this considerable first step toward new patterns of global tax governance might need revision and updates based on experiences as regards implementation and results obtained so far.

The current book provides an in-depth description of various elements of the BEPS, its minimum standards, and the ways they are addressed and implemented, providing a regional as well as global perspective on the topic. Clearly, based on the various chapters contained in the book, the volume offers a timely contribution to discussions on tax and development, not least in view of the challenges to implement the SDGs. While the COVID-19 pandemic is arguably slowing down the implementation of several of the SDGs—including reduction of poverty and of inequalities globally—it is of quintessential importance that other measures toward their implementation are taken; the economic recession resulting from the pandemic may present additional economic challenges to governments around the globe and put pressure on multinational companies in financial terms, but this may make new steps in global tax governance even more relevant in the years to come.

The book also helps demonstrating that global tax governance is not just a "technical" theme, relevant in the first instance for firms and for tax authorities, but that it has tangible effects "on the ground," as it addresses core issues related to equality, transparency, and fairness in terms of regional and global economic activity.

The three editors have compiled an impressive collection of contributions; the volume certainly has the potential to advance the agenda and discussion on global tax governance and on steps to be taken toward sustainable development.

Leiden, Netherlands   Madeleine O. Hosli
June 2020

Introduction

The purpose of this book is to address the link between international taxation and the 2030 Sustainable Development Agenda from a global and regional perspective. Its aims to identify how these linked areas can be studied and evaluated and how countries and international organizations could reinforce this link in light of the current international tax initiatives, including the Base Erosion and Profit Shifting (BEPS) Project initiated by the OECD with the political mandate of the G20.

The concept of this book came into fruition at a workshop held in Bruges, Belgium, on January 14, 2019, addressing *Tax and Development: The Link between International Taxation, the Base Erosion Profit Shifting Project and the 2030 Sustainable Development Agenda.*[1] This workshop was co-organized by the GLOBTAXGOV Project that investigates A New Model of Global Governance in International Tax Law Making[2] in close cooperation with Ghent University (Belgium) and the United Nations Institute on Comparative Regional Integration Studies (UNU-CRIS) (Belgium). This workshop itself was based on a 2018 working paper published by Mosquera, Lesage, and Lips at UNU-CRIS.[3] Several of the book chapters were presented there in their early forms.

---

[1]See Programme workshop and slides at https://globtaxgov.weblog.leidenuniv.nl/files/2019/01/Workshop-Programme-final-21-Dec-2018-with-slides2.pdf and report summary discussions https://globtaxgov.weblog.leidenuniv.nl/2019/01/18/tax-and-development-topics-for-discussion/

[2]The GLOBTAXGOV Project has received funding from the European Research Council (ERC) under the European Union's Seven Framework Programme (FP/2007–2013) (ERC Grant agreement n. 758671). Project (2018–2023). The GLOBTAXGOV Project investigates international tax law making including the adoption of OECD and EU standards by 12 countries. The GLOBTAXGOV Project has received funding from the European Research Council (ERC) under the European Union's Seven Framework Programme (FP/2007–2013) (ERC Grant agreement n. 758671).

[3]Mosquera Valderrama, I. J., Lesage, D., & Lips, W. (2018). Tax and development : the link between international taxation, the base erosion profit shifting project and the 2030 sustainable development agenda. UNU-CRIS Working Paper Series. Bruges: UNU-CRIS.

In light of the discussions that took place in this workshop, we invited scholars, officials working at international and regional organizations, and think tanks to contribute to this book. The result is a comprehensive book with 11 chapters addressing four overarching themes.

The *first* theme deals with "Global Tax Governance and Developing Countries" (Chaps. 1–3). These chapters address issues of global tax policy and the impact on developing countries. The *second* theme deals with "External Assistance for Tax Capacity Building" (Chaps. 4 and 5). These chapters identify issues that donors need to consider when granting external assistance. The *third* theme deals with "Tax Incentives and Attracting Sustainable Investment" (Chaps. 6–8). These chapters reflect on the dilemma between attracting investment and raising revenue from external sources. The *fourth* and final theme is "Harmful and Helpful Tax Practices for Sustainable Development" (Chaps. 9 and 10). These chapters research the impact and harmfulness of certain common tax practices in a systemic manner including a comparison with several countries.

Opening the book and the *first theme* is a chapter by Cassandra Vet, Danny Cassimon, and Anne Van de Vijver (UAntwerp, Belgium) titled "Distributive Justice in Transfer Pricing Governance: The impact of the G20-OECD-BEPS revision of Transactional Profit Split Method in Sub-Saharan Africa." This book is aimed at a diverse multidisciplinary audience, both in the academic and practitioner's world. We decided to put this chapter first because it is an excellent primer on all the issues to follow in the book. Vet, Cassimon, and Van de Vijver discuss the inherent distributional bias within the international tax regime and the marginalized role of developing countries. They offer a very thorough conceptual discussion on the different types of power and power resources countries can employ regarding international taxation. Furthermore, they argue for adding an additional criterion for output legitimacy in the BEPS project in the form of distributive justice. They strengthen their argument by employing a case study on the transactional profit split method and how it takes shape in sub-Saharan Africa.

The following chapter entitled "The Promise of Non-Arm's Length Practices—Is the Destination-Based Cash Flow Tax or Unitary Taxation the Panacea of which Developing Countries are in Search?" by Afton Titus (University of Cape Town, South Africa) discusses alternative paradigms for international tax allocation and how this would impact developing countries. It starts by evaluating the internationally entrenched transfer pricing regime, based on the arms'—length principle, and how it disadvantages developing countries in their capacity to collect revenue. She then discusses two alternative systems: unitary taxation and the destination-based cash flow tax. She specifically focuses on Kenya and South Africa when evaluating the potential benefits of both systems. Titus concludes with a call for an alternative to the arms'—length standard to improve the fairness and efficiency of taxing multinationals in Africa.

The third chapter in the book "The Suitability of BEPS in Developing Countries (Emphasis on Latin America and the Caribbean)" is written by Isaác Gonzalo Arias Esteban and Anarella Calderoni (Inter-American Centre of Tax Administrations, CIAT). Their chapter starts from the observation that implementing the BEPS actions may not be the most suited priority for developing countries, in light of the often-limited resources their tax policy administrations can muster. They argue that there needs to be an evaluation of the domestic circumstances within a country to help determine how good of a fit the BEPS recommendations, their needs, and their existing tax regimes are. They employ the brand-new BEPS Monitoring Database by CIAT to provide an overview of how Latin American and Caribbean countries are faring with implementing BEPS.

Moving on to the *second theme on* external assistance for tax capacity building is a chapter by Sathi Meyer-Nandi (GIZ, Germany, Private capacity). The chapter is titled "Policy coherence for Sustainable Development in International Tax Matters—A way forward for donor countries?" Meyer-Nandi argues for a holistic whole-of-government approach for assistance with achieving the SDGs, as aid donors should beware of competing policies. Specifically, in tax matters, she argues that next to technical assistance donor government should be mindful of how their tax policy and tax administration impact partner countries. Technical tax assistance should not be a matter of development agencies alone. She puts forth recommendations in three different areas: on tax treaties with developing countries, on transparency and sharing of aggregate financial data under the OECD exchange of information programs, and in international cooperation and administrative assistance between tax administrations.

The fifth chapter complements the previous chapter quite nicely. While the former deals with coordination within a donor country, the chapter by Wouter Lips and Dries Lesage (Ghent University, Belgium) tackles coordination within a partner developing country. "*Medium-Term Revenue Strategies (MTRS) as a coordination tool for DRM and tax capacity building*" handles a new concept by the Platform for Collaboration on Tax that is supposed to help developing countries design a whole-of-government country-owned approach on tax policy and administration reform and revenue goals and help technical assistance donors organize themselves around those needs. The authors first discuss the need for such a strategy and why the concept of medium-term revenue strategies can be valuable in the field of tax-related assistance aid. However, Lips and Lesage identify several potential pitfalls with the concept in terms of scope and ambition, democratic legitimacy, partners, and implicit standards and call for close scrutiny and country ownership when designing a medium-term revenue strategy.

Eleonora Lozano Rodríguez (Universidad de los Andes, Colombia) starts off the *third theme* on tax incentives and attracting sustainable investment with a chapter titled "*Tax Incentives in Pacific Alliance Countries, the BEPS Project and the 2030 Sustainable Development Agenda.*" This chapter starts from the observation that with the increase of international cooperation against base erosion, it has become more attractive to introduce tax incentives in order to attract investment. Lozano Rodríguez starts with a conceptual discussion on what tax incentives are and follows with a description of how the OECD's BEPS project aims to set a standard of good practice on preferential tax regimes and tax incentives. The author then discusses the state of tax incentives in Latin America, with a specific focus on the Pacific Alliance countries. She then concludes with a call to design monitor and follow-up processes in those countries to ensure that tax incentives are reaching their objectives, while contributing to, rather than diminishing, government revenues.

Chapter 7 is titled *"Tax Incentives In Developing Countries: A Case Study: Singapore And Philippines"* and is written by Irma Johanna Mosquera Valderrama (Leiden University, the Netherlands) and Mirka Balharova (King's College London, UK). Their chapter provides a case study of two countries: Singapore and the Philippines, belonging to the South East Asia region. Following the comparison of the tax incentives in these two countries, they offer several recommendations for best practices in the region. This chapter also evaluates tax incentives granted in Singapore and the Philippines in light of a newly proposed evaluative framework that takes into account the Sustainable Development Goals. This new evaluative framework can be also used by policy makers in developing and emerging countries.

The eighth chapter is written by Julien Chaisse and Jamieson Kirkwood (City University, Hong Kong). In *"Foreign Investors vs National Tax Measures: Assessing the Role of International Investment Agreements,"* the authors investigate the impact of the international law of foreign investment on tax issues and the interactions between the two regimes. Chaisse and Kirkwood offer a description of the convergences between both regimes and a quantitative and qualitative overview on recent tax disputes in investment arbitration. The latter is especially relevant since the 15 recent disputes where the host state lost the case were lost by only seven countries, all of which are developing countries. The chapter contributes to the book by investigating a link between two regimes that is currently underresearched.

The *fourth and final theme* on harmful and helpful tax practices for sustainable development offers two chapters that do a cross-country comparison to assess the international state of play on certain tax practices. Agustin Redonda (Council of Economic Policies, Switzerland), Christian von Haldenwang (German Development Institute, Germany), and Flurim Aliu (Council on Economic Policies, Switzerland) contribute the ninth chapter on "Tax Expenditure Reporting and Domestic Revenue Mobilization in Africa." Their chapter argues that tax expenditures are often overlooked in the public spending debate, while they can have significant revenue consequences. The authors examine the state of reporting and monitoring on tax expenditures in Africa and offer examples of (in)effective tax expenditures and why they sometimes stick around. The chapter is the first to make use of the innovative "Global Tax Expenditure Database" (GTED), an ongoing project aiming to increase transparency and boost research in the TE field.

The tenth chapter *"Negative Spillovers in International Corporate Taxation and the European Union"* by Leyla Ates (Altinbas University, Turkey), Moran Harari (Tax Justice Israel), and Markus Meinzer (Tax Justice Network) evaluates how the tax rules and tax rates of high-income countries impact the ability of other countries to pursue their preferred tax regime. The authors make use of the Corporate Tax Haven Index that assesses twenty key tax spillover indicators. Ates, Harari, and Meinzer offer evidence that indicates a clear requirement for EU member states to reform their tax systems in order to mitigate the negative spillover effects of their domestic tax rates and rules, both domestically, within the EU and beyond. Finally, the eleven chapter is a concluding chapter.

This book is the result of a collaboration between academics from laws, economics and political science practitioners, and think thanks from a diverse set of countries. Its setup was to build a bridge between the worlds of development policy and taxation. The editors believe we have succeeded in collecting a series of chapters that will appeal to both academics and people working in the field. This book should be interesting to people with a tax background who want to learn more on development policy and people who work professionally on development issues and wish to know more on how taxation relates to development. With this book, we hope to have contributed on the state of scholarship on tax issues in the Global South. We wish you pleasant reading and hope you find this volume useful in your professional and intellectual endeavors.

Leiden University, Leiden   Irma Johanna Mosquera Valderrama
The Netherlands
Ghent University, Ghent, Belgium   Dries Lesage
Ghent University, Ghent, Belgium   Wouter Lips

Contents

Part I
Global Tax Governance and Developing Countries

Chapter 1
Getting the Short End of the Stick: Power Relations and Their Distributive Outcomes for Lower-Income Countries in Transfer Pricing Governance

Cassandra Vet, Danny Cassimon, and Anne Van de Vijver

1.1 Introduction

Within the shadow of the G20-OECD Base Erosion and Profit Shifting (BEPS) Project, transfer pricing experts pack up their suitcases to go and assist developing countries in their efforts to implement a complex regime of transfer pricing auditing (Peters 2015; Tax Inspectors Without Borders 2018). At first glance, these efforts support the reduction of fiscal losses caused by "aggressive" transfer pricing practices, an important channel of corporate tax avoidance in Sub-Saharan Africa (Fuest and Riedel 2012). Yet, while these efforts strengthen the audit capacity of developing countries, the rules that guide these capacity development projects reinforce the distributional imbalance of the international tax regime (Magelhaes 2018). This chapter sheds light on the power relations at play during the G20-OECD reform of transfer pricing guidelines to highlight how these relations shape the distributional outcomes of the international tax regime.

Mosquera Valderrama (2015, 2018) already argued that the reform should not only offer a way out of the collective action problem developing countries face in the regulation of transfer pricing but also bring about solutions that are efficient and implementable within the tax culture and context of these countries. From this view, the legitimacy of the BEPS project depends on more than the sole representation of

C. Vet (✉) · D. Cassimon
Institute of Development Policy and Antwerp Tax Academy, University of Antwerp, Antwerp, Belgium
e-mail: Cassandra.vet@uantwerpen.be; danny.cassimon@uantwerpen.be

A. Van de Vijver
Faculty of Law and Antwerp Tax Academy, University of Antwerp, Antwerp, Belgium
e-mail: anne.vandevijver@uantwerpen.be

© The Author(s) 2021   3
I. J. Mosquera Valderrama et al. (eds.), *Taxation, International Cooperation and the 2030 Sustainable Development Agenda*, United Nations University Series on Regionalism 19, https://doi.org/10.1007/978-3-030-64857-2_1

lower-income countries throughout the reform process. If the BEPS project strives for developing country legitimacy, then both input and output legitimacy should be guaranteed. Here, in light of the embedded imbalance between source and resident jurisdictions in the tax regime (Magelhaes 2018; Christians 2017), we introduce an additional yardstick to evaluate the output legitimacy of the BEPS project, namely, distributive justice.

Moreover input and output legitimacy are not independent; the distribution and relations of power active during the BEPS reform shape the outcomes. Global institutional answers to corporate tax avoidance cannot be detached from their internal power distribution. Hearson (2018a), for instance, stressed that the multilateral institutional answers supported by most tax governance scholars will in all likelihood hold perverse effects for developing countries. History taught that the institutionalized outcomes of negotiations produced within a context of imbalanced power relations reflect this imbalance, a point Hearson (2018b) demonstrated through his empirical analysis of the distributional bias in Double Tax Treaties (DTT). Importantly tough, when we try to grasp power in global tax governance, we have to move beyond a one-dimensional view on power and its limited focus on the observable decision-making struggles that take place during political participation (Lukes 2005). To illustrate, even the institutions of the global tax regime tend to stabilize the regime's adherence to neo-liberalism (Lesage and Vermeiren 2011), an ideological base that preserves the unequal distribution of taxing rights as we will discuss later. In all, the historical underrepresentation of developing countries within the international tax regime is not simply readdressed by merely giving those previously marginalized a seat at the table.

This chapter maps out the power relations that molded the reform of the transactional profit split method (TPSM), one of the transfer pricing methods put forward in the OECD transfer pricing guidelines, to its specific distributional outcomes. As transfer pricing literally divides the profits of international corporate wealth into national tax baskets by pricing cross-border interactions, we use the material interests of developing countries in transfer pricing governance as our heuristic device to guide us through the multiple power relations. To start, we approach the private-public tug-of-war over authority in profit allocation as the struggle over the "size of the cake". Clearly, transnational corporations (TNCs) have an interest in maintaining their discretion in profit allocation maintain their leeway to engage in aggressive tax planning keep some of "calculated ambiguity" in their tax planning structures alive (Sharman 2010). Secondly, whereas each state has the fiscal objective to enlarge its tax base, the struggle over the slice of the cake represents the interstate struggle to bring the biggest share of TNCs' profits in the national tax base (Lips 2019). Finally, the third element touches upon Mosquera Valderrama's (2015, 2018) original discussion of the output legitimacy of the BEPS Project. Besides dealing with developing countries' stakes in having a bigger cake to share or getting a decent slice of the cake, the regime should also be efficient and implementable within the tax culture and context of these countries. Or rather, lower-income countries should also be able to actually eat their slice of the cake. The institutionalization of transfer pricing guidelines, and in this case specifically the revised guidance of the TPSM, reveals that even though the reform expanded the size of the overall cake of taxable profits, the criteria that authorize the use of the TPSM, along with the ongoing complexity of the regime, make it difficult for lower-income countries to obtain a decent slice of the cake and actually eat it.

Now, the question remains: "What are the power relations that produce these outcomes?" For this reason, we start off with a conceptual discussion on power in global tax governance. Afterward, a short discussion on the profit split method illustrates the appeal of the TPSM case study as it deals with the contentious issue of synergy or residual profits. In turn, we shed some light on the standard-setting process, highlight the key stakeholders involved, and elaborate on the collected data used for the qualitative content analysis. Afterward, we dive into the technicized discourse of the standard-setting process with our power goggles at hand to flesh out the distributional conflicts and power relations at play. Here, the analysis is organized along the three previously discussed developmental interests: the size of the cake, the slice, and whether or not these countries are actually able to eat their cake. In the end, we discuss our observations in light of the recent efforts to integrate lower-income countries and critique the pluralist expectation that proper representation of developing countries is a sufficient measure to make sure that the regime is also legitimate in the South.

1.2 The Different Faces of Power in Global Tax Governance

Foucault once said that "the conception of society that predominates is a hangover from an earlier social formation" (Kelly 2009, p. 43). This comment on the contingency of social order spells out the relation between the colonial context that gave rise to the international tax regime and the enduring bias of the regime to resident countries (Magelhaes 2018). From this angle, the bias of the regime toward resident taxation, the countries where the headquarters are located, and against source taxation, where the activities are taking place, is hardly surprising but nonetheless harmful. Yet, the distributional justice of the BEPS project in general, and specifically in transfer pricing, only recently gathered wider interest in academic circles (Magelhaes 2018; Christians 2017; Hearson 2018a; Christensen and Hearson 2019) and is rarely explicitly addressed within the reform agenda despite the distributive conflict over the allocation of profits between states (Lips 2019). This conflict would hardly come to light when one would solely focus on the observable expressions of interest and conflict during the initial BEPS policy process.

However, both Foucault and Lukes (2005, p. 90) drew attention to less visible displays of power and highlighted how power relations can be at their strongest when their workings remain hidden. The unpoliticization of the distributional impact, for instance, the technically insulated discourse of international tax experts, gave the distributive decisions an unpolitical aura, while these decisions did mold the regime further toward the interests of transnational corporations (Picciotto 2018a; Buttner and Thiemann 2017). Lukes (2005) described these exercises of power as power in the third dimension, power that secures consent without the presence of struggles and produces its results through the invisible constraints we put upon ourselves. To illustrate, the technical and expertise-led nature of the discourses during tax meeting insulated the standard-setting discussions from "political wrangling," a constraint that the stakeholders put on themselves.

Admittedly, some struggles did take place out in the open; Lukes (2005) refers to these power struggles as exercises of power in the first dimension. When policy advisors and tax advisors reframed civil society's claim for transparency into the policy goal to improve risk assessment capacity, the discursive struggle was visible (Christensen 2020). Still, while civil society did manage to get the topic on the agenda, their claim for transparency lost some of its scope as it fell outside of the ideational consensus on the limits of appropriate solutions. In other words, or in more Foucauldian terms, the claim for transparency as brought by civil society activists did not fit within "the regime of truths" upheld within the transnational tax sphere. These "truths" determine what may be held true in a particular discourse" and signal how different discourses relate to reality (Kelly 2009, p. 109). Basically, the demand for transparency challenged how the transnational tax discourse framed appropriate tax behavior of TNCs and governments. As a result, the professionals involved transformed the original demand into the need to improve risk assessment capacity while they made sense of the need for transparency (Christensen 2020), a goal that did fit within their view on reality. So, whereas Lukes (2005) tried to pull apart different forms or capacities of "having power," power is exercised within human and societal relations, and these power relations have manifold and overlapping characters.

Another display of power, power in the second dimension (Lukes 2005), is the use of power to shield the policy agenda from certain discussions and bring others to the fore of the debate. Indeed, it is important to reflect on not only what is discussed but also what is not and why. The refusal of the G20-OECD members to take up the demand of developing countries, their demand to reassess the allocation of taxing rights between source and resident countries, initially kept the topic out of the list of issues that needed to be resolved (Burgers and Mosquera Valderrama 2017, p. 31). That said, the mobilization of this bias in agenda setting clearly highlights how these forms of power shape the distributional outcomes of the project, but the counterpower within this relation strengthened and the topic now penetrates actions taken in light of the digitalized economy (Grondona 2019; Christensen and Hearson 2019).

As mentioned, both authors marked less visible forms of power relations and indicated that compliance not necessarily means a vacuum of power struggles. On the contrary, Foucault argues that power is not some kind of possession of people but rather always present in the relations that structure our social order (Kelly 2009, p. 37). Also, power tends to hide itself but can be found in its products, the social relations itself. According to Foucault power even has a strategic nature, a tendency to preserve itself and the relations it produced, that goes beyond intent of the agents involved (Kelly 2014, pp. 70–71). Though power cannot exist without people, the strategic nature and its organizing effect can be seen as a net effect of all the intentional exercises of power within the network of relations (Kelly 2009, p. 47). Lesage and Vermeiren (2011), for instance, discussed how the institutional pillar of neoliberal globalization provides resilience to neoliberal globalization even when ideational support for the free movement of goods and capital is in decline. In a way, the net effects of power relations in global tax governance gave rise to an institutional setting wherein "the material interests at the core of neo-liberal hegemony" are preserved through its horizontal governance setting amidst the collective action problems in international taxation (Lesage and Vermeiren 2011, p. 54).

Where Lukes (2005) drew attention to how power also has its effects when it puts constraints on ourselves and our rationality, Foucault sheds light on the power relations that produce these kinds of constraints or rationality (Kelly 2014). Here, his emphasis on discourses, the dialectical relation between knowledge and power and "regimes of truths", clarifies the strength of expertise networks and the problem of complexity in transfer pricing governance (Kelly 2014). The discourses of the experts and policymakers put forward in policy discussions on transfer pricing policy share a narrow and technical view on the meaning of transfer pricing and its relation to reality and the world economy. However, while the "regimes of truths" within this discourse were rarely challenged as the centrality of expert-led knowledge shielded the discourses from other "truths," policy-makers sought solutions to regulatory challenges within these narrow discourses and perspectives on reality. As a result, the complexity of the regime grew in response to the inability of policy-makers to come up with solutions outside of this technocratic consensus (Buttner and Thiemann 2017). Thereby the regime not only opened the door for tax advisors to capitalize on the indeterminacy created but also maintained the centrality of expert knowledge (Picciotto 2015; Sikka and Hampton 2005; Sharman 2010). These tax advisors grew so powerful within transfer pricing policy that Picciotto (2018a) even pointed out how these players shaped the regime in favor of private authority through regulatory arbitrage.

To some extent, this focus on less visible expressions of power might feel deterministic, undermining the agency of developing countries to turn the table around, or resist against the contingent distribution of taxing rights. Yet, Foucault underpins that power is always connected to resistance, or counterpower, as there would be no need for a power relation without the possibility of resistance (Kelly 2009, pp. 107–108). The networks of power in transfer pricing are emergent and would seize to exist without the regular production of those involved (Kelly 2009, p. 47). Consequently, these power relations also coincide with micro-resistances that can produce macro-resistances as the social order is always fluid and never fully stable. To illustrate, the regulatory fixes that added to the complexity of the regime are in part ways to stabilize the transfer pricing regime, its "regime of truths", and its associated social order within a shifting context. Nonetheless, these fixes also planted the seeds for the decay of this regime as the growing complexity and uncertainty of the transfer pricing rules undermined the authority of expert networks (Buttner and Thiemann 2017). The transfer pricing rules are now slowly politicizing (Grinberg 2016), and the distribution of taxing rights grew to be one of the contentious issues in the reform on the digitalized economy due to the mobilization of lower-income countries. In other words, the social order upheld in the international tax regime is shifting (Christensen and Hearson 2019).

1.3   The Profit Split Method and the OECD Standard-Setting Process

As said, the material interests of lower-income countries in transfer pricing governance are our heuristic device to analyze the power relations and their distributive outcomes of the TPSM. Important to know, the distributive conflict in transfer pricing materializes in the contentious nature of price requalifications by national revenue authorities. Where the current global tax regime still rests upon the separation of the TNC's tax base in different tax jurisdictions, transfer pricing or intracompany pricing is the everyday pricing technique to do so. However, the dominant principle governing this price-setting practice, the arm's length principle (ALP), is conceptually and practically flawed. This principle prescribes that unrelated party or rather market prices are the benchmark for related party transactions even though the nature of these transactions is different and reliable comparable transactions are difficult to come by (Picciotto 1992). Nevertheless, the authoritative standards of the OECD transfer pricing guidelines put forward methods to calculate the pricing range on the basis of these "comparable uncontrolled transactions" (CUP). The OECD guidelines started out as a manual for transfer pricing for TNCs; however, the distributional value of these guidelines lies in their use for the requalification of reported profits by revenue authorities. As many countries integrated these soft law standards (Grinberg 2016), these guidelines are the basis for profit requalification through transfer pricing auditing. Thereby, the content of these guidelines regulates when and how much tax authorities can adjust the division of profits by TNCs.

Importantly tough, the transactional profit split method (TPSM) changes the rules of the game set out above since it draws in residual profits. The profit split method is different from the CUP-based methods as it divides the combined profits earned from a transaction or transactions according to one or more "allocation keys" (Picciotto 2018b, p. 17). Therefore, the revision of the TPSM guidance brings in another layer in the distributive conflict, the struggle over residual profits. When the tax base is purely based on CUP-based transfer pricing methods, these profits often remain unregulated and vulnerable for aggressive tax planning (Cobham et al. 2019). On top of that, TNCs also have the tendency to locate their residual profits, besides in tax haven jurisdictions, in the jurisdictions where its top holdings are located (de Graaf et al. 2014, p. 309; Grondona 2019). The role of the TPSM guidance is to clarify when the method is most appropriate in comparison with the other methods. In other words, the revision of the guidance matters for countries as well as TNCs as it indicates the circumstances wherein revenue authorities can requalify the reported profits when they did not account for a part of the residual profits.

In addition to these distributional consequences, the reform of the TPSM opened the door to address the uncertain and costly implementation of the transfer pricing auditing in developing countries (Mehta and Siu 2016). The G20-OECD regime departs from a case-by-case logic, suggesting an in-depth investigation of the transaction or the "accurate delineation of the transaction," before comparing the relative suitability of different transfer pricing methods (Kadet et al. 2018). As a result, the BEPS Monitoring Group[1] and its affiliated scholars argue for the simplification and standardization of the transfer pricing regime so that developing countries are able to protect their corporate tax base (BEPS Monitoring Group 2018; Mehta and Siu 2016; Picciotto 2018b; Waris 2017). In fact, Mehta and Siu (2016) recommended lower-income countries to extend their use of profit split methods to protect their tax base through simplification and to avoid out of balance administration costs. However, the TPSM only brings incremental change to the current framework since it solely divides the profits of a certain group of transactions into different jurisdictions and not the global tax base of a TNC. Nonetheless, the method potentially simplifies the distribution of the tax base and could thereby help developing countries to actually perform the requalifications needed to protect its tax base (Greil 2017; Mehta and Siu 2016). This way, lower-income countries not only obtain their slice of the cake but are also able to eat it.

At the moment, the BEPS Monitoring Group (2018) describes the outcome of the revised guidance as the "lowest common denominator." Therefore, the Group continues their plea for simplification at the UN level and argues for standardized allocation, specific industry weights, objective measures, and industry-wide APAs (BEPS Monitoring Group 2018; Kadet et al. 2018). Meanwhile, the work on the revised nexus and profit allocation rules has been picked up by Action 1 (Tax challenges arising from digitalization). Since the Action 1 Report found that the whole economy was digitalizing (OECD 2015), this working program has a very wide scope. The ambition is to deliver a long-term and consensus-based solution in 2020 that reflects the right balance between precision and administrability for jurisdictions at different levels of development (OECD 2019).

Besides its clear distributional implications, the reform of the TPSM guidance has other advantages as a case study on developmental interests and power relations in global tax governance. Whereas the four BEPS minimum standards find their way to developing countries through the Inclusive Framework, Actions 8–10 on transfer pricing deserve our interest as a result of the strength and the implementation rate of the OECD transfer pricing rules (Grinberg 2016).

---

[1]The BEPS Monitoring Group (BMG) is a global network of independent researchers on international taxation, sponsored by tax justice organizations, concerned with the effects of tax avoidance by transnational corporations, especially on development. Its aim is to produce reports commenting on proposals for the reform of the international system for the taxation of transnational corporations.

Initially, the BEPS Working Parties failed to reach a consensus on the TPSM guidance, and therefore the guidance became part of the agenda for ongoing work published in the 2015 Final Report (Grinberg 2016, p. 1161). This not only indicates the contentious, and therefore politically interesting, nature of this guidance; it also gave rise to the involvement of developing countries. To clarify, the Inclusive Framework notes that all members are invited to participate on equal footing in the ongoing work on transfer pricing that followed the 2015 Final Report (OECD 2017a). Therefore, this chapter discusses how the power relations found in the micro-level interactions within the policy-making environment shaped the distributional outcomes for developing countries, starting from the 2015 agenda for ongoing work until the 2018 published Revised Guidance on the Application of the TPSM.

Throughout the reform process, the G20-OECD worked with public discussion drafts and publicly recorded stakeholder discussions to gather feedback for Working Party 6 (WP6). This working party is the G20-OECD working group in charge of the policy reform process that consisted of state representatives and OECD experts. Thus, this group prepared, along with the OECD secretariat, the different discussion drafts (see dark grey boxes Fig. 1.1) and processed the written and oral feedback given during the public stakeholder consultation sessions (see light grey boxes Fig. 1.1). The process depicted in Fig. 1.1 thereby depicts the process wherein new pieces of discourse, draft documents, working party meetings, or stakeholder discussions feed into the subsequent ones. The data for this analysis exists out of the recordings of the different stakeholder consultation sessions, the discussion drafts, and the final revised guidance. Unfortunately, the insights on the positions of the state representatives are solely based on their interventions during the stakeholder meetings and the content of the policy documents. As a result, we based our analysis on a qualitative content analysis of the different policy papers[2] on the TPSM guidance and the recorded stakeholder discussions while paying specific attentions to the interaction between the different pieces of discourse. In addition, we also calculated the speaking time divided over the different participants to highlight who is most vocal during the stakeholder meetings and has or feels authorized to speak (Figs. 1.1, 1.2, 1.3, 1.4, and 1.5).

Despite the lack of data on the WP6 discussion, we were able to illustrate (see Fig. 1.2) the number of interventions made by state representatives during the stakeholder meetings as these are part of the recorded sessions. Here it is clear that the USA together with Japan were most active during the stakeholder discussions.

One of the common critiques on the legitimacy of the BEPS project is the lack of integration of lower-income countries in the agenda- and standard-setting process (Mosquera Valderrama et al. 2018). However, stakeholder involvement is also

---

[2]2015 Final Report action 8–10 section on the transactional profit split, the Public Discussion Draft Revised Guidance on Profit Splits 4 July 2016, the Public Discussion Draft Revised Guidance on Profit Splits 22 June 2017, The Revised Guidance on the application of the transactional profit split June 2018

Fig. 1.1 Institutionalization of the TPSM guidance

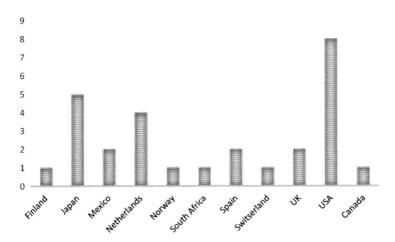

Fig. 1.2 Number of interventions from WP6 members during the stakeholder discussions (WP6 2016a, b, 2017a, b)

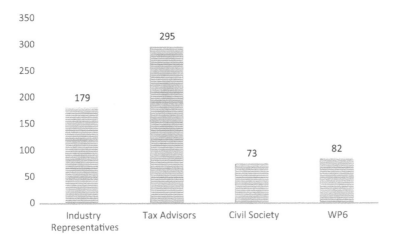

Fig. 1.3 Speaking time during stakeholder discussions (number of minutes) (WP6 2016a, b, 2017a, b)

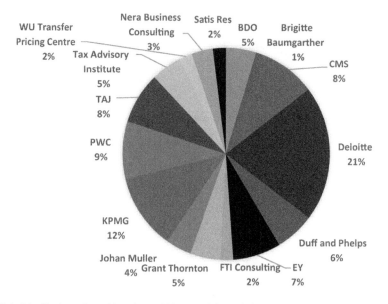

Fig. 1.4 Distribution of speaking time within tax advisory industry (WP6 2016a, b, 2017a, b)

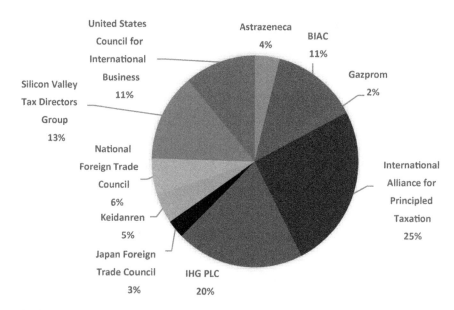

Fig. 1.5 Distribution of speaking time of business representatives (WP6 2016a, b, 2017a, b)

unevenly divided among the different groups of stakeholders as is shown by the distribution of speaking minutes over the different groups during the public discussions (see Fig. 1.3). An observation that supports the argument explained above on the role of expert knowledge and how experts have the authority to decide on what is important in terms of transfer pricing policy. Although the BEPS Monitoring Group, part of civil society (see Fig. 1.3), was the most active participant in terms of spoken minutes (70 min), this group is, besides the University of Lausanne (part civil society Fig. 1.3), the only non-business representative that took part of the stakeholder discussions. A second important observation on authority in standard-setting is the dominant presence of the tax advisory industry (see Fig. 1.3).

When taking a closer look at the internal allocation of minutes within the tax advisory sector, it becomes evident that the Big Four companies mostly took the floor, along with Taj, a specialized Deloitte network entity in international tax, and CMS, an international tax law firm (see Fig. 1.4). Deloitte is further the clear front-runner in terms of minutes spoken, especially when we add up Taj's speaking time as TAJ is actually Deloitte network entity. From this view Deloitte's discourse took up about 30% of the debate (see Fig. 1.4).

A second hint on the uneven power relations in standard-setting is the distribution of time among the business representatives. Firstly, within this group the International Alliance for Principled Taxation (IAPT) leads the discussions while representing a group of multinationals in search of predictable tax rules and the end of double taxation. Although the group clearly represents business interests, it is the Baker McKenzie law firm, a firm active in the tax advisory industry, that pleads in the name of this group. On a regional level, business councils of the USA and Japan follow a similar high level of engagement as their state representatives. Finally, BIAC is the overall representatives for business interests at the OECD, and in sectoral terms we observe the presence of the pharmacy industry (AstraZeneca), the hotel industry (IHG PLC), and a Russian gas exporter (Gazprom). Overall, the presence of business from lower-income countries is lacking, but the same can be said on the representation of small- and medium-sized businesses.

1.4   The Cake

Similar to the academic debate, as shown again from our analysis of the debates, the stakeholders spend a great deal of their time and energy scrutinizing the ALP principle during the public TPSM discussions. However, in contrast to the negative viewpoint on the ALP often shared by acadamics, most representatives defended and expanded the role of the ALP in transfer pricing. To illustrate, tax advisors from TAJ and a representative from BIAC argued for the limited use of the TPSM as unrelated parties only use a profit split method in extremely rare circumstances (WP6 2016a, b). This way, they discursively expanded the interpretation of the ALP by arguing that the ALP is not just a benchmark for price setting but also a benchmark for selecting the appropriate transfer pricing method. In all, the majority of tax advisors and business representatives struggled with the revised guidance on the TPSM as they felt that it expands the application of the method beyond "arm's length circumstances" (WP6 2016a).

To some degree, this observation is correct as the TPSM guidelines challenge the application of the ALP in transfer pricing matters. First of all, the G20-OECD wrote in 2015 that "the main strength of the method is that it can provide solutions for highly integrated operations for which a one-sided method would not be appropriate" (OECD/G20 2015, p. 57). A one-sided method essentially comes down to a method whereby you price the transaction of the local affiliate and a related party with the help of a CUP. These CUPs or comparables are the cornerstone for the implementation of the ALP in transfer pricing, and by acknowledging that these can be inappropriate, WP6 opened the door to the wider ALP debate. Two years later, WP6 continues this train of thought and recognized that certain related party transactions have "specific, possibly unique, facts and circumstances of the associated enterprises that are not present in independent enterprises" (OECD 2017b, p. 5). Further, WP6 bridges the ideational controversy by taking on a language of "arm's length outcomes." And in the end, the final guidance defensively excludes the private sector's interpretation by stating that "It is sometimes argued that a transactional profit split method is rarely used among independent enterprises, and thus its application in controlled transactions should be similarly rare. However where such a method is determined to be the most appropriate, this should not be a factor since transfer pricing methods are not necessarily intended to replicate arm's length behavior, but rather to serve as a means of establishing and/or verifying arm's length outcomes for controlled transactions" (OECD 2017b, p. 5, 2018, p. 13).

Now, what are the interests at stake in this tug-of-war on the role of the ALP in the revised TPSM guidance? Basically, the private and public sector both struggle for control over residual profits, the profits beyond arm's length that TNCs create through their decision to integrate activities in their value chain. One-sided or CUP-based methods do not account for profits beyond arm's length. In the case that an affiliate prices all related party transactions on the basis of one-sided methods, then, all residual profits fall outside of that affiliate's tax base (Cobham et al. 2019). Therefore, the TPSM lends its attractiveness for public authorities from its two-sided character wherein the full profits related to the transaction are part of the profits to be split among the associated jurisdictions.

This clarifies the business representatives' concern on the "subjective application" of the TPSM by revenue authorities (WP6 2017a). For instance, CMS signals that certain criteria could end up in "opening Pandora's box of requalifications," and Ernst and Young discuss the perverse effect of the risk-sharing criterion as revenue authorities could claim that risk is shared and demand their part of the residual profits (WP6 2016a, b). Similarly, the Silicon Valley Tax Directors Group worries about revenue authorities bundling transactions to end up with the right amount of integration to apply the TPSM (WP6 2016b), and BIAC notes the enthusiasm of revenue authorities to use the TPSM in case of significant profits (WP6 2017a). In a way, the tax advisors and industry representatives try to skew the interpretation of the central principle of taxation in their interest to freely plan where to file the residual profits.

Clearly, the declining ideational power of the ALP, or the resistance against the ALP as one of the upheld "truths" in the transfer pricing discourse, threatens TNCs' political power to plan their financial and fiscal operations freely. The existence of Global Wealth Chains (GWCs) explains the role of the ALP in maintaining private authority over global tax governance in the form of transfer pricing (Seabrooke and Wigan 2014). Seabrooke and Wigan (2014, p. 257) conceptualize GWCs as the wealth chains that "hide, obscure and relocate wealth to the extent that they break loose from the location of value creation and heighten inequality." Tax planning structures wherein TNCs plan the location of their residual profits to minimize taxation are an example of such a GWC. The ALP then plays a crucial role in preventing regulatory interference as it essentially does not acknowledge the existence of residual profits (Greil 2017). Ylonen and Teivainen (2018, p. 445) describe the role of the ALP herein as the principle that offers a basis for assuming the existence of markets in non-market circumstances. Yet, the TPSM challenges the assumption of market circumstances and in way recognizes that "transacting within an MNC as opposed to on the market suggests MNC formation provides benefits for the firm, which cannot readily be market sourced" (Bryan et al. 2017, p. 75). As a result, the private sector loses some discretion in managing where these profits touch down and become part of a jurisdiction's tax base (Biggins in Bryan et al. 2016, p. 949).

The opening up of the discourse around interpretation of the ALP signals the changing power relations within the expert networks in which the tax advisory industry for long had the upper hand (Buttner and Thiemann 2017; Picciotto 2018a). Although this study misses information on internal WP6 meetings, the sharp dismissal of the private sector's interpretation of the ALP by the US representative sharp dismissal by the US representative of the private sectors indicates that some state representatives and policy-makers no longer fully accept this interpretation as a "truth" within the transfer pricing discourse (WP6 2017a). The USA representative claimed that he basically "tunes out" when he hears the argument that the TPSM only should be used in circumstances where non-related parties would use this method to price their transactions. To some extent, the more skeptical position of WP6 towards the expert network's interpretation signals the politicization of transfer pricing and the decreasing power of the tax advisory industry to set the limits of the transfer pricing discourse.

In addition, the BEPS Monitoring Group actively challenges the private sector consensus (see Fig. 1.3). For instance, the Group's representative, Sol Picciotto, combines expert-based and moral authority to challenge the ALP as he underlines that several of their group members worked in the tax advisory sector but that these members only now, after leaving the industry, are at liberty to denounce the ALP "for obvious reasons" (WP6 2016a). Prof. Picciotto refers to the interests of the tax advisory industry to maintain inefficient concepts as these concepts are essential for the industry to advise TNCs on how to maximize their creative compliance within a complex regulatory framework (Shah 2017; Sharman 2010). Lately, certain civil society organizations became effective in challenging the technocratic consensus in international taxation through their use of different "languages" to politicize tax justice issues (Dallyn 2017). This way, alternative discourses entered insulated policy settings and created uncertainty around the previously upheld "regimes of truth." Nonetheless, these civil society advocates needed to combine expertise-based and moral authority to make sure that their claims actually became part of the policy discourse (Seabrooke and Wigan 2016). That said, one thing is clear. The discursive struggles of the private industry on the ALP illustrate that the veneer of market behavior around intra-group planning activities is under threat. Thereby, the discourse of non-interference in market circumstances might not for long ring-fence tax planning behavior from public regulation.

1.5 The Slicing of the Cake

A bigger cake brings benefits to all when the slices are shared equally among all participants. While the growing recognition of residual profits in international taxation is a crucial step to retrieve the untaxed profits in tax havens, it is the tax model in combination with the worldwide distribution of foreign direct investment (FDI) that determine whether lower-income countries benefit from these recaptured profits (Cobham et al. 2019). Within a unitary tax regime, the residual profits are part of the cake that is distributed; however, this is not the case under a transactional method within the confines of the separate entity principle as we explained above. The TSPM does not bundle the related party interactions between two or more parties but rather divides the profits related to a specific transaction among the concerned parties. Therefore, developing countries need to make the "right" contributions in their FDI sectors to be part of these "concerned parties" and actually get access to the table where the cake is shared. In this vein, the criteria that justify the application of the TPSM under the most appropriate framework determine the share of the residual profits that potentially strengthens the tax base of lower-income countries. These countries then have a clear material interest to make sure their value chain contributions fall under the criteria that justify the application of the TPSM under the most appropriate framework.

But in Foucault's terms, power shaped the categories, institutions, and discourses of the transfer pricing practice (Kelly 2009). Similar to the historical power relations that formed the source-resident distinction in international taxation, the transfer pricing regime implicitly applies a hierarchy between different value chain contributions. One powerful distinction within the transfer pricing discourse is the difference between "routine," "simple," or "replicable" contributions and "non-routine" functions that create rents or profits above the regular return on capital (Cobham et al. 2019, p. 9). The use of this distinction within the TPSM guidance risks strengthening the power of advanced economies over developing economies in international taxation, especially now that the source-resident debate gains momentum in the Action 1 agenda (Grondona 2019).

Throughout the standard-setting process, WP6 decided that the lack of comparable transactions or CUPs is not a sufficient condition to apply the TPSM, a powerful decision with implications for lower-income countries as these are the ones that struggle the most with the lack of available comparables. This decision is that responds to concerns on the use of the TPSM "in the absence of reliable comparables, without considering whether the profit split method was itself appropriate" (OECD/G20 2015, p. 58). In reality, the concern was that TPSM would be applied for "simple functions," and within the transfer pricing discourse, this was seen as "inappropriate" (OECD 2018, p. 14).

de Graaf et al. (2014) already noted the uneven distribution of residual profits between headquarter and basic value chain functions. This exclusion of simple functions for the application of the TPSM adds to this discrepancy and strengthens the imbalance in taxing rights, the right to tax residual profits, between developing countries and advanced economies. Developing countries are still mostly integrated in the initial parts of value chains, by providing primary resources or performing basic manufacturing goods. WP6's exclusion of simple functions thereby creates the situation wherein tax jurisdictions that primarily make "simple" contributions to integrated value chains only receive a marginal share of the overall synergy profits. This way, the allocation of value along the global value chain in the current global tax regime reproduces the uneven patterns of economic development in the world economy, and for this reason others criticized the G20-OECD for its lack of a transparent and inclusive theory on value creation (Quentin and Campling 2018; Wolfram 2019).

The TPSM guidance speaks of an appropriate application when parties share economically significant risks and make unique and valuable contributions to the transaction (OECD 2018). Despite the fact that these contributions are indeed difficult to value under CUP-based methods, the project hereby allocates the weight of synergy profits to the higher or headquarter functions of the TNC. What does this then mean for the project's credo "realign profits with value creation"? Basically, the TPSM guidance neglects a horizontal interpretation of value creation within the GVC wherein "the starting point is the horizontal progression of the GVC from raw materials to the point of consumption, with 'value added' arising at each node along the chain" (Quentin and Campling 2018, p. 47).

From this more horizontal perspective on value creation, captive distributors[3] also add value that legitimizes a share of the residual profits. Nonetheless, when we listen to the discourse of certain stakeholders on captive distributors, it is clear that these experts underwrite a different interpretation of value, one that diminishes the contribution of the primary nodes in the value chain. The discussion on captive distributors spiraled out of the debate on the presumption of synergy profits in integrated global value chains. Here, CMS questioned the assumption that captive distributors bring in contributions to the global value chain that result in the creation of residual profits, since the contributions of these dependent distributors are similar to unrelated parties (WP6 2017b). In response, the BEPS Monitoring Group pointed

---

[3]"Captive value chains. In these networks, small suppliers are transactionally dependent on much larger buyers. Suppliers face significant switching costs and are, therefore, 'captive'. Such networks are frequently characterized by a high degree of monitoring and control by lead firms" (Gereffi et al. 2005, p. 84).

out that captive distributors do bring in additional profits through integration as their relationship is different from unrelated parties in terms of preferential access (WP6 2017b). The US Council for International Business went further and stated that "even if these profits exist, they should be allocated where the strategic decisions responsible for the integration are made" (WP6 2017b). From this perspective, the headquarter functions harvest all the benefits from integration, and the international tax system further re-embeds its bias toward resident-based taxation.

Precisely for this reason, Quentin and Campling (2018) argue that the current interpretation of value creation aligns with a logic of money creation, or value added, instead of a horizontal interpretation of value creation. To illustrate, the reasoning of the US Council follows the pattern of price setting wherein the headquarter would get the residual profits as a result of the relations of control and risk. Conversely, Quentin and Campling (2018) suggest that the current regime lacks a theory on value creation beyond price determined money flows. For this reason, "tax reforms intended to ameliorate global inequalities 'must refocus' to elsewhere in the value chain where the value captured by 'lead firms' is actually created" (Quentin and Campling 2018, p. 52).

Similar to Ylonen and Teivainen (2018), these authors cast a critical light on the role of the ALP and business power in taxation. However, instead of a public-versus-private logic, Quentin and Campling (2018) bring in a geopolitical dynamic in international taxation. In brief, the authors make a distinction between a vertical and a horizontal logic of value creation wherein the vertical logic follows the pattern of exchange values from the perspective of asset owners. The ALP then suggests that "exchange values between unconnected parties accurately reflect value creation" and thereby excludes a horizontal interpretation of value creation wherein "the starting point is the horizontal progression of the GVC from raw materials to the point of consumption, with 'value added' arising at each node along the chain" (Quentin and Campling 2018, p. 47).

Consequently, the focus on exchange values as a basis for splitting up the profits reproduces the global pattern of extracting surplus value through chains of capital ownership. Therefore, Quentin and Campling (2018) conclude that an international tax regime without a horizontal theory on value creation reproduces global inequalities. In turn, the TPSM guidance judgment on the "inappropriateness" of compensating "simple functions" for synergy profits in fact relates to the inappropriateness of this allocation within a vertical logic of value creation. In contrast to a more horizontal interpretation, a vertical interpretation relates to the actual relations of market power and control in global value chains wherein the dependent producer would not have sufficient bargaining power to share in the residual profits.

Throughout the discussions, the BEPS Monitoring Group brought in the statement that every related party transaction that takes place within a TNC adds to the creation of residual profits as the existence of these profits is the 'raison d'être' of integration in the first place (WP6 2016b, 2017a). Yet, they do not contest the criteria that justify the TPSM as the most appropriate method on the basis of their geopolitical bias, nor push for a more horizontal interpretation of value creation. In general, proposals designed to strengthen tax auditors in BEPS-related challenges fail to recognize their geographical redistributive impact (Cobham et al. 2019). For instance, destination-based taxation wins popularity because of its ability to curb tax planning as consumers are less mobile than capital (Auerbach et al. 2017). Nonetheless, these proposals push the benefits of value creation, in terms of taxation, further away from the initial nodes of GVCs, where, for instance, the necessary natural resources are extracted. Cobham et al. (2019) actually simulated the distributive impact of different tax reform packages with the use of data on the global distribution of profits made by American-owned TNCs in the year 2016. Different reform packages, from the OECD, IMF, and the Independent Commission for the Reform of International Corporate Taxation (ICRICT), investigate the option of relocating profits out of tax havens by allocating part of the taxing rights, and especially in terms of residual profits, to market jurisdictions, there where the sales take place. Despite the fact that the location of sales are less vulnerable to manipulation, and therefore an effective route to shift profits out of tax havens, the sole focus on market jurisdictions would be detrimental for lower-income countries (see Table 1.1). First of all, the simulation of Cobham et al. (2019) highlights that the absolute gains of the OECD reform package would bring the least amount of absolute gain to lower-income countries, and the global formulary apportionment (GFA) reforms proposed by ICRICT the most. Importantly, the ICRICT reform does not rely on the strict application of the ALP to calculate the routine profits. But secondly, notwithstanding the potential of these reforms to redirect residual profits out of tax havens, Table 1.1 indicates that sole use of sales as a criterion for the allocation of residual, or surplus profits, favors high-income countries. To highlight the geopolitical dimension of this criterion, Cobham et al. (2019) contrasted these results with the absolute gains of models that use both sales and employment as criteria for profit allocation. Not surprisingly, and especially not when we take in mind the arguments in favor of a more horizontal logic of value creation, these models would bring higher absolute gains to lower-income countries and a more even distribution of the profits in general (see Table 1.1).

At the moment, contestation of the logics of value creation in transfer pricing is still limited (Cobham et al. 2019; Quentin and Campling 2018; Wolfram 2019), and discourses within policy circles regularly reproduce the vertical interpretation of value creation without contention. Here, the unbalanced presence of stakeholders during these stakeholder discussions sets the range of discourses and restricts perspectives from the global south and civil society. For instance, the business representatives that took part in the debate represented the capital owners of TNCs and their headquarter interests. Some of the business representatives seemed especially vocal in the protection of residual profit allocation towards the end of the global value chain and openly protected this distribution during the discussions. For instance, IAPT stated that WP6 needs to be really clear in who takes part in sharing these profits as it does not make sense to give a part of these profits to "some routine manufacturer" (WP6 2017a). On the other, the distinctions between simple and non-routine functions, routine profits, and residual profits are produced through power relations but also part of the knowledge upheld in the discourses on international tax.

Table 1.1 Profit distribution under different models (absolute gain/$bn) (reworked table Cobham et al. 2019, p. 16)

Absolute gain, $bn	Current allocation	GFA sales	GFA sales EMP	IMF sales	IMF sales EMP	OECD (20%) sales	OECD (20%) sales + EMP	OECD sales	OECD sales + EMP
High income	1010.4	110.2	88.2	120	105.2	14.8	11.8	74	59.2
Upper middle income	45.7	28.4	86.1	27.4	66.1	3.8	11.6	19.1	57.8
Lower middle income	20.2	−4.6	32.8	−0.2	24.9	−0.6	4.4	−3.1	22
Low income	−0.3	0.6	1	0.9	1.2	0.1	0.1	0.4	0.7
Tax havens	344.5	−134.6	−208	−148.1	−197.4	−18.1	−28	−90.4	−139.8
Total	1420.5								

Despite WP6 implicit consensus, Hearson and Prichard (2018) and Picciotto (2018b) illustrate that certain emerging economies have sufficient political cloud to challenge the status quo in international taxation and in the logics on value creation. Specifically, a handful of emerging economies have taken unilateral action and pursue their own interests in transfer pricing. China's, and to some extent India's, practice of using location-specific advantages to decide on how to share the residual profits reeks of a horizontal interpretation of value creation. Basically, the logic of location-based advantages supports the idea that the contribution tax jurisdiction in terms of access to infrastructure, resources, and cheap labor should also be rewarded when splitting up the tax base (Hearson and Prichard 2018).

1.6 Capturing the Slice and Eating It

Until now, this discussion focused on the distributional impact of the material rules. However, Van de Vijver et al. (2020) revealed the shortcomings of the BEPS reforms in fostering responsible tax behavior of TNCs. Therefore, countries rely on transfer pricing audits to requalify the reported profits and claim their "rightful" share of the cake. The difficult shift from aggressive tax planning to more responsible tax behavior is even more problematic for lower-income countries as transfer pricing audits are complicated and costly procedures. As a result, the TPSM guidance could also readdress the distribution of the global tax base in favor of lower-income countries by simplifying the regime (Picciotto 2018b; Greil 2017; Mehta and Siu 2016). At first, the policy reform of the TPSM was applauded for its potential to simplify the regime (Mehta and Siu 2016; Greil 2017). However to this date, the current outcomes do not contain any steps toward standardization in terms of sectoral approaches or in terms of profit splitting factors, and the initial enthusiasm of these scholars faded way (Kadet et al. 2018).

Whereas the BEPS Monitoring Group argued for standardization throughout the discussion, the private sector representatives, and in particular the tax advisory sector, stipulated the non-prescriptive character of the TPSM guidance. These advisors defended the "correct sequence" in transfer pricing, wherein the decision on both the most appropriate method and the choice of the profit splitting factors follows the accurate delineation of the transaction (WP6 2016b, 2017a). This is in the interest of the tax advisory sector as the complexity and length of transfer pricing procedures are fundamental to part of their profit-making activities (Sikka and Hampton 2005). In the end, the advisory sector's discourse was at winning end of this struggle, and the final guidance explicitly stated its non-prescriptive character (OECD 2018).

Essentially, the primacy of the accurate delineation of the transaction underlines the case-by-case logic in the TPSM guidance. This accurate delineation of the transaction comes down to an in-depth analysis of the transaction through the functions, risks, and assets involved. By adhering to this case-by-case approach in transfer pricing, the G20-OECD project maintains an information and a capacity bias against the interests of developing countries (Kadet et al. 2018). First of all, the selection of the most appropriate method builds on this analysis. Inevitably, TNCs have access to more in-depth information on their operations than any revenue authority, and revenue authorities therefore have to play a game of catch-up while auditing the adequacy of TNCs' functional analysis that underpins the method and the transfer price.

Secondly, revenue authorities are in need of very specialized and complex expertise to perform this analysis and revenue authorities in the global south struggle to build this capacity, TNCs employ tax advisors part of transnational expert community focused on transfer pricing (Kadet et al. 2018). The tax advisory industry is invested in keeping the case-by-case logic in place as this approach maintains the complexity and discretion in the application of the regime (Picciotto 2018a), a complexity needed to continue the profitable business of advising on tax planning strategies and strategic compliance (Shah 2017; Sikka and Hampton 2005). On the other, the advisory industry protects its almost epistemic and existential position in transfer pricing, as both business and regulators need these experts to make the current regime work. Accordingly, it is no surprise that the industry was most active in preserving the case-by-case logic in transfer pricing and dominated most of this overall debate (see Fig. 1.3).

Similar to the tug-of-war over the size of the cake, the struggles over standardization inhabit a public-versus-private authority logic, but, in contrast to the discussion on the existence of residual profits, private interests prevail this time around. In part, the difference in capacity bias between low- and high-income countries explains the weakness of the standardization plight as revenue authorities within advanced economies are well resourced with tax auditors part of the transnational network of transfer pricing experts (BEPS Monitoring Group 2018).

Finally, Ylonen and Teivainen (2018)'s thesis on the role of the ALP clarifies the importance of the ALP discourse to prevent standardization as this discourse supports the idea of market relations in non-market circumstances. In fact, the ALP slows down the demand for regulatory intervention through standardization, as it supports the ideology of non-intervention in intra-company planning. One tax advisor's statement captures this discourse perfectly, as he stated that "the guidance should not interfere with the TNC's ability to independently decide on its capital structure" (WP6 2017a). In a way, this discourse, in favor of a case-by-case logic, supports the idea that public authorities are not supposed to decide how these prices should be set or mediated within a capital chain of a TNC. Instead, price setting should follow "the market," and TNCs should have the prerogative to structure its capital as they see fit.

1.7 Conclusions

Mosquera Valderrama et al. (2018) pointed out that the BEPS Inclusive Framework, designed to expand the reach of the G20-OECD BEPS project, emphasizes integration through implementation but neglects integrating these countries in the negotiation of these standards. That said, in this chapter we argued through our analysis of power relations during the TPSM process that the underrepresentation of the material interests of lower-income countries cannot be solely addressed by giving these countries a seat at the table. After a critical look of dynamics at play, we conclude that the pure participation of developing countries in the standard-setting forums is not sufficient to guarantee output legitimacy for these countries. The discourses and "truths" upheld in the negotatiated outcomes maintain a distributive imbalance between low- and high-income countries and hand out higher rewards to jurisdictions that host the higher value chain functions of the global value chain. Specifically, discourses built on the arm's length principle and a vertical interpretation of value creation work in favor of this status quo.

Throughout our discussion, the uneven distribution of residual profits was our topic of interest as developing countries are generally excluded from participating in these profits. Therefore, we added another layer to Mosquera Valderrama (2018)'s discussion on output legitimacy, namely, distributive justice. Distributive justice requires collective action as developing countries cannot solve the lack of distributive justice in the current status quo "through individual action, through market exchanges, or through voluntary cooperation in civil society" (Scharpf in Mosquera Valderrama 2015). In the case of the revised TPSM guidance, the distributional outcome of the BEPS process undermines the output legitimacy of the regime for lower-income countries. Specifically, the guidance only reshuffles the authority on the allocation of residual profits from private to public authority but neglects to integrate criteria that take into account the contributions from lower-income countries and fails to take steps toward a more implementable regime. As a result, the standard-setters decided on a bigger cake, but lower-income countries only got the crumbs of this cake without the tools to actually eat it.

This observation raises some questions on the demand for transfer pricing assistance and the rollout of capacity building projects wherein these guidelines are a point of reference in terms of "appropriate" transfer pricing governance. Hereby we shed a critical light on the distributional consequences of the capacity-based approach toward the integration of lower-income developing countries. The problem of administrability of the TPSM in lower-income countries clearly captures the different modalities of integrating developing countries within the international tax regime. On one hand, the regime acknowledges the problem of a capacity bias against lower-income countries and invests in technical assistance and capacity building. In turn, the strengthened expertise and capacity within tax administrations should make lower-income countries more likely to effectively participate in the current regime (Mosquera Valderrama et al. 2018). On the other hand, lower-income countries are expected to take a seat at the table and take part in the transfer pricing discourse without the acknowledgement or an open discussion on the distributional bias of this knowledge.

Yet, the current framework is not set in stone as the continuous discussion on taxing rights in the work on the digitalized economy illustrates. Maybe the revised guidance of the TPSM did not bring solace for developing countries, but it did reveal that order in international taxation is shifting. In other words there is a momentum to commit and make sure that the lower-income countries will not yet again end up with the short end of the stick.

References

Auerbach, A. J., Devereux, M. P., Keen, M., & Vella, J. (2017). International tax planning under the destination-based cash flow tax. *National Tax Journal, 70*, 783–801.

BEPS Monitoring Group. (2018). *Submission to the subcommittee on article 9 (associated enterprises) on the revision of the UN practical manual on transfer pricing for developing countries.* United Nations Committee of Experts on International Cooperation in Tax Matters.

Bryan, D., Rafferty, M., & Wigan, D. (2016). Politics, time and space in the era of shadow banking. *Review of International Political Economy, 23*(6), 941–966. https://doi.org/10.1080/09692290. 2016.1139618.

Bryan, D., Rafferty, M., & Wigan, D. (2017). Capital unchained: Finance, intangible assets and the double life of capital in the offshore world. *Review of International Political Economy, 24*(1), 56–86. https://doi.org/10.1080/09692290.2016.1262446.

Buettner, T., & Thiemann, M. (2017). Breaking regime stability? The politicization of expertise in the OECD/G20 process on BEPS and the potential transformation of international taxation. *Accounting Economics and Law-a Convivium, 7*(1). https://doi.org/10.1515/ael-2016-0069.

Burgers, I., & Mosquera Valderrama, I. J. (2017). A fair slice for developing countries. *Erasmus Law Review, 10*(29), 767–783.

Christensen, R. C. (2020). Transparency. In L. Seabrooke & D. Wigan (Eds.), *Global wealth chains: Asset strategies in the world economy.* Oxford: Oxford University Press.

Christensen, R. C., & Hearson, M. (2019). The new politics of global tax governance: Taking stock a decade after the financial crisis. *Review of International Political Economy, 26*(5), 1068–1088. https://doi.org/10.1080/09692290.2019.1625802.

Christians, A. (2017). BEPS and the new international tax order. *Brigham Young University Law Review, 2016*(6), 1603–1647.

Cobham, A., Faccio, T., & FitzGerald, V. (2019). Global inequalities in taxing rights: An early evaluation of the OECD tax reform proposals. *SocArXiv.* https://doi.org/10.31235/osf.io/j3p48

Dallyn, S. (2017). An examination of the political salience of corporate tax avoidance: A case study of the tax justice network. *Accounting Forum, 41*(4), 336–352. https://doi.org/10.1016/j.accfor. 2016.12.002.

de Graaf, A., de Haan, P., & de Wilde, M. (2014). Fundamental change in countries' corporate tax framework needed to properly address BEPS. *Intertax: International Tax Review, 42*(5), 306–316.

Fuest, C., & Riedel, L. (2012). Tax evasion and tax avoidance: The role of international profit shifting. In P. Reuters (Ed.), *Draining development* (pp. 109–142). Washington, DC: World Bank.

Gereffi, G., Humphrey, J., & Sturgeon, T. (2005). The governance of global value chains. *Review of International Political Economy, 12*(1), 78. https://doi.org/10.1080/09692290500049805.

Greil, S. (2017). The dealing at arm's length fallacy: A way forward to a formula-based transactional profit split? *Intertax: International Tax Review, 45*(10), 624–630.

Grinberg, I. (2016). The new international tax diplomacy. *Georgetown Law Journal, 104*(5), 1137–1196.

Grondona, V. (2019). *The dangers if the residual profit split*. Retrieved from https://www. taxjustice.net/2019/10/03/the-dangers-of-the-residual-profit-split/

Hearson, M. (2018a). The challenges for developing countries in international tax justice. *Journal of Development Studies, 54*(10), 1932–1938. https://doi.org/10.1080/00220388.2017.1309040.

Hearson, M. (2018b). When do developing countries negotiate away their corporate tax base? *Journal of International Development, 30*(2), 233–255. https://doi.org/10.1002/jid.3351.

Hearson, M., & Prichard, W. (2018). China's challenge to international tax rules and the implications for global economic governance. *International Affairs, 94*(6), 1287–1307. https://doi.org/ 10.1093/ia/iiy189.

Kadet, J. M., Faccio, T., & Picciotto, S. (2018). *Profit-split method: Time for countries to apply a standardised approach*. Institute of Development Studies, International Centre for Tax and Development.

Kelly, M. G. E. (2009). *The political philosophy of Michel Foucault. Routledge studies in social and political thought* (Vol. 61, 1st ed.). New York: Routledge.

Kelly, M. G. E. (2014). *Foucault and politics: A critical introduction. Thinking politics*. Edinburgh: Edinburgh University Press.

Lesage, D., & Vermeiren, M. (2011). Neo-liberalism at a time of crisis: The case of taxation. *European Review, 19*(1), 43–56. https://doi.org/10.1017/S1062798710000372.

Lips, W. (2019). Great powers in global tax governance: A comparison of the US role in the CRS and BEPS. *Globalizations, 16*(1), 104–119.

Lukes, S. (2005). *Power: A radical view* (2nd ed.). Basingstoke: Palgrave Macmillan.

Magelhaes, T. D. (2018). What is really wrong with global tax governance and how to properly fix it. *World Tax Journal, 10*(4), 499–536.

Mehta, K., & Siu, E. D. (2016). Ten ways developing countries can take control of their own tax destinies. In T. Pogge & K. Mehta (Eds.), *Global tax fairness* (pp. 339–356). Oxford: Oxford University Press.

Mosquera Valderrama, I. J. (2015). Legitimacy and the making of international tax law: The challenges of multilateralism. *World Tax Journal, 7*(3), 344–366.

Mosquera Valderrama, I. J. (2018). Output legitimacy deficits and the inclusive framework of the OECD/G20 base erosion and profit shifting initiative. *Bulletin for International Taxation, 73*(3), 1–11.

Mosquera Valderrama, I. J., Lesage, D., & Lips, W. (2018). *Tax and development: The link between international taxation, the base erosion profit shifting project and the 2030 sustainable development agenda*. UNI-CRIS Working Paper Series. UNU-CRIS.

OECD. (2015). *Addressing the tax challenges of the digital economy, action 1. 2015 final report*. OECD/G20 base erosion and profit shifting Project. Paris: OECD.

OECD. (2017a). *Background brief inclusive framework on BEPS*. Paris: OECD. Retrieved from https://www.oecd.org/tax/beps/background-brief-inclusive-framework-for-beps-implementa tion.pdf

OECD. (2017b). *Public discussion draft BEPS action 10 revised guidance on profit splits*. Paris: OECD. Retrieved from https://www.oecd.org/tax/transfer-pricing/Revised-guidance-on-profit-splits-2017.pdf

OECD. (2018). *Revised guidance on the application of the transactional profit split method: Inclusive framework on BEPS: Action 10*. Paris: OECD. Retrieved from www.oecd.org/tax/ beps/revised-guidance-on-the-application-of-the-transactional-profit-split-method-beps-action-10.pdf

OECD. (2019). *Programme of work to develop a consensus solution to the tax challenges arising from the digitalisation of the economy*. OECD/G20 Inclusive Framework on BEPS. Paris: OECD. Retrieved from www.oecd.org/tax/beps/programme-of-work-to-develop-aconsensus-solution-to-the-tax-challenges-arising-from-the-digitalisation-of-the-economy.htm

OECD/G20. (2015). *BEPS project: Aligning transfer pricing values with value creation—Actions 8–10*. Final reports. Paris: OECD.

Peters, C. (2015). Developing countries' reactions to the G20/OECD action plan on base erosion and profit shifting. *Journal International Taxation, 69*(6/7), 1–11.

Picciotto, S. (1992). International taxation and intrafirm pricing in transnational corporate groups. *Accounting Organizations and Society, 17*(8), 759–792. https://doi.org/10.1016/0361-3682(92)90003-B.

Picciotto, S. (2015). Indeterminacy, complexity, technocracy and the reform of international corporate taxation. *Social and Legal Studies, 24*(2), 165–184. https://doi.org/10.1177/0964663915572942.

Picciotto, S. (2018a). *International tax, regulatory arbitrage and the growth of transnational corporations*. Institute of Development Studies, International Centre for Tax and Development.

Picciotto, S. (2018b). *Problems of transfer pricing and possibilities for simplification*. ICTD working paper 86:61.

Quentin, D., & Campling, L. (2018). Global inequality chains: Integrating mechanisms of value distribution into analyses of global production. *Global Networks—A Journal of Transnational Affairs, 18*, 33–56. https://doi.org/10.1111/glob.12172.

Seabrooke, L., & Wigan, D. (2014). Global wealth chains in the international political economy. *Review of International Political Economy, 21*(1), 257–263. https://doi.org/10.1080/09692290.2013.872691.

Seabrooke, L., & Wigan, D. (2016). Powering ideas through expertise: Professionals in global tax battles. *Journal of European Public Policy, 23*(3), 357–374. https://doi.org/10.1080/13501763.2015.1115536.

Shah, A. K. (2017). *The politics of financial risk, audit and regulation: A case study of HBOS*. Abingdon: Routledge.

Sharman, J. C. (2010). Offshore and the new international political economy. *Review of International Political Economy, 17*(1), 1–19. https://doi.org/10.1080/09692290802686940.

Sikka, P., & Hampton, M. P. (2005). The role of accountancy firms in tax avoidance: Some evidence and issues. *Accounting Forum, 29*(3), 325–343. https://doi.org/10.1016/j.accfor.2005.03.008.

Tax Inspectors Without Borders. (2018). *Annual report 2017/2018 tax inspectors without borders*. Retrieved from http://www.tiwb.org/resources/publications/tax-inspectors-without-borders-annual-report-2017-2018-web.pdf

Van de Vijver., A, Cassimon., D, & Engelen., P.-J. (2020). A real option approach to sustainable corporate tax behavior. *Sustainability, 12*(13), 5406, 1–17.

Waris, A. (2017). *How Kenya has implemented and adjusted to the changes in international transfer pricing regulations: 1920–2016*. ICTD working paper 69. Institute of Development Studies, International Centre for Tax and Development.

Wolfram, F. R. (2019). *Aligning profit taxation with value creation*. Munich: CESifo Group.

WP6, B. (2016a). *WP6 public consultation—Revised guidance on profit splits—First session*. Paris: OECD.

WP6, B. (2016b). *WP6 public consultation—Revised guidance on profit splits—Second session*. Paris: OECD.

WP6, B. (2017a). *Public consultation: Revised guidance on profit splits—First Session*. Paris: OECD.

WP6, B. (2017b). *Public consultation: Revised guidance on profit splits—Second Session*. Paris: OECD.

Ylonen, M., & Teivainen, T. (2018). Politics of intra-firm trade: Corporate price planning and the double role of the arm's length principle. *New Political Economy, 23*(4), 441–457. https://doi.org/10.1080/13563467.2017.1371124.

Chapter 2
The Promise of Non-arm's Length Practices: Is the Destination-Based Cash Flow Tax or Unitary Taxation the Panacea of Which Developing Countries Are in Search?

Afton Titus

2.1 Introduction

Africa is at an unprecedented precipice of continental unity with the signing of the African Continental Free Trade Area Agreement (AfCFTA). At a time when some Western countries are implementing measures to move away from other countries, African countries are working toward greater unity. The signing of the AfCFTA heralds the eventual formation of a continent-wide single market. While the extent of integration under the AfCFTA currently involves the removal of tariffs and the cooperation on intellectual property, investment, and competition policies, the time seems opportune to speculate as to the direction of a continental-wide, unified approach to transfer pricing. It is estimated that Africa loses approximately US$50 million annually through illicit financial flows (United Nations Economic Commission for Africa (UNECA) and the African Union Commission (AUC) 2015), of which transfer pricing is cited as one of the main contributors to such losses (UNECA and AUC 2014; Readhead 2016).

Transfer pricing is understood as determining the "remuneration for the transfer of goods, intangibles and the provision of services among related enterprises" (Hamaekers 2001). As more than 70% of all global trade occurs between related parties, transfer pricing concerns are of primary relevance to multinational enterprises and revenue authorities alike (ibid.).

The reason for determining transfer prices arises from the fear that multinational enterprises with several branches in foreign countries may shift profits into low tax jurisdictions (ibid). In such low tax jurisdiction, the further fear is that such profits

A. Titus (✉)
University of Cape Town, Cape Town, South Africa
e-mail: afton.titus@uct.ac.za

© The Author(s) 2021
I. J. Mosquera Valderrama et al. (eds.), *Taxation, International Cooperation and the 2030 Sustainable Development Agenda*, United Nations University Series on Regionalism 19, https://doi.org/10.1007/978-3-030-64857-2_2

29

either may not be subject to tax at all or may be subject to only a nominal tax. It would seem then that the fears that transfer pricing is meant to allay are not so much that the country of residence may not get to tax the profits but rather that the source country will not levy the necessary taxes.

Over time, the arm's length principle became the standard agreed by the Organisation of Economic Co-operation and Development (OECD) members in determining transfer prices for the purposes of corporate income taxation (Russo 2005). As the OECD grew in influence internationally, this standard became the international standard. The arm's length standard deems dealings between associated enterprises to be controlled transactions which have to be adjusted to reflect the uncontrolled transactions which would have been concluded between independent parties in comparable circumstances to the associated enterprises (Rogers-Glabush 2015). The arm's length principle was initially designed to apply to intra-company dealings between the head office and branch of a company (Russo 2005). Its scope was later broadened to also apply to the transactions concluded between separate entities, such as the subsidiary and the parent company (ibid.).

It has been noted that the essence of the arm's length principle is to ensure that related enterprises deal with each other as they would with independent parties (Hamaekers 1997). The overarching rationale for this is to guarantee the equal tax treatment of multinational enterprises and independent companies and, in so doing, to avoid the distortive effects of competition (OECD 2017).

Overall then, transfer pricing was designed to ensure that the profits of multinational enterprises are subject to corporate income tax somewhere and, in so doing, minimize the competitive edge multinationals enjoy so as to make the playing field level for independent companies. In seeking to achieve this end through the arm's length principle, the drawbacks and challenges arising from the implementation of this principle have become apparent, especially as it applies in the developing country context. This has led to a call for developing countries to question whether the arm's length principle is suited for their particular context (Waris 2017).

This chapter responds to that call by undertaking such an evaluation under the auspices of the AfCFTA and its potential to create unity across Africa. While the time for fiscal unity in Africa may not yet be upon us, it is nonetheless useful to begin thinking about the direction Africa may one day possibly take with respect to transfer pricing.

This chapter therefore evaluates whether non-arm's length standards, such as unitary taxation and the destination-based cash flow tax (DBCFT), may be suitable alternatives to the arm's length standard for African developing countries when calculating the taxable profits of multinational companies. In considering this context, the author has selected two African developing countries—Kenya and South Africa—by which to provide this context.

As two of Africa's biggest economies and equally ranked in terms of the attractiveness to investors according to Ernst and Young's 2017 Africa Attractiveness Index, the corporate income tax policies adopted by these two African countries are likely to attract the attention of investors and other African countries alike. Moreover, Kenya and South Africa are two African countries who have had the

longest-standing transfer pricing departments within their respective revenue authorities (UNECA and AUC 2015; Waris 2017). This means that these two countries are
best placed to make an informed decision regarding a possible move away from the
arm's length standard. As such, Kenya and South Africa serve as useful contexts.

In doing so, this chapter is presented in the following order: First, the arm's length
standard is analyzed together with its advantages and disadvantages. This is
followed by similar analysis of the unitary taxation and DBCFT models before the
possible application of these non-arm's length models to the developing country
context of Kenya and South Africa is then discussed. Thereafter, this chapter
concludes.

2.2 An Evaluation of the Varying Models

2.2.1 The Arm's Length Principle

The arm's length principle first made its appearance in the "Draft Convention for the
Allocation of Business Profits between States for the purposes of Taxation" prepared
in 1933 by the Fiscal Affairs Committee of the League of Nations (see Appendix to
Carroll 1934). Article 3 dealt with determining the profits of permanent establishments as follows:

> If an enterprise with its fiscal domicile in one contracting State has permanent establishments
> in other contracting States, there shall be attributed to each permanent establishment the net
> business income which it might be expected to derive if it were an independent enterprise
> engaged in the same or similar activities under the same or similar conditions. Such net
> income will, in principle, be determined on the basis of the separate accounts pertaining to
> such establishment. Subject to the provisions of this Convention, such income shall be taxed
> in accordance with the legislation and international agreements of the State in which such
> establishment is situated. The fiscal authorities of the contracting States shall, when neces-
> sary, in execution of the preceding paragraph, rectify the accounts produced, notably to
> correct errors or omissions or to re-establish the prices or remunerations entered in the books
> at the value which would prevail between independent persons dealing at arm's length. If an
> establishment does not produce an accounting showing its own operations, or if the
> accounting produced does not correspond to the normal usages of the trade in the country
> where the establishment is situated, or if the rectifications provided for in the preceding
> paragraph cannot be effected, or if the taxpayer agrees, the fiscal authorities may determine
> empirically the business income by applying a percentage to the turnover of that establish-
> ment. This percentage is fixed in accordance with the nature of the transactions in which the
> establishment is engaged and by comparison with the results obtained by similar enterprises
> operating in the country. If the methods of determination described in the preceding
> paragraphs are found to be inapplicable, the net business income of the permanent estab-
> lishment may be determined by a computation based on the total income derived by the
> enterprise from the activities in which such establishment has participated. This determina-
> tion is made by applying to the total income coefficients based on a comparison of gross
> receipts, assets, number of hours worked, or other appropriate factors, provided such factors
> be so selected as to ensure results approaching as closely as possible to those which would be
> reflected by a separate accounting.

From this extract it can determined that the profits of the permanent establishment were to be established through the following methods:

1. Adjusting the accounting books of the permanent establishment in order to deem arm's length transactions.
2. Applying a fixed percentage to the turnover of the permanent establishment, such percentage is to be determined to produce the results that would have been produced had a comparable resident company undertaken transactions of a similar nature.
3. Creating a simulation of separate accounting through determining the total income of the permanent establishment. This is done by creating coefficients from comparisons of the gross receipts, assets, number of hours worked, and other suitable factors of other businesses.

As Langbein (1986) has argued, these are essentially accounting or bookkeeping methods to determine an accounting profit that governments want to subject to tax. Moreover, the arm's length principle relies on the separating accounting approach to determining such profits (Sadiq 2001). Despite the fact that the arm's length principle rests on a non-legal methodology, the proponents of this standard argue that the following advantages may be gained from applying the principle as a legal standard:

1. It is a norm of international tax that is widely accepted in the international community (ibid.; Green 1993).
2. It creates an equality in the tax treatment of related and unrelated companies (Sadiq 2001; Green 1993).
3. It most accurately determines the "true" source of income (McLure and Weiner 2000).

Commentators, however, doubt the veracity of the above. Hellerstein (2005) argues that it is not at all clear that the arm's length principle is an internationally accepted norm, a point made by Langbein (1986) decades earlier. Moreover, De Graaf et al. (2014) question the feasibility of an "equal" treatment of related and unrelated companies when in doing so the arm's length standard ignores the synergies arising from corporate integration, a state of affairs which is in fact an economic reality. Economic reality is further ignored when the arm's length principle takes into account interim profits as they arise in the group context before the profits are actually realized and when losses within the group cannot be balanced against the profits of other group members (Hertzig et al. 2010). Finally, Hellerstein (2005) questions whether determining the "true" source of income is a worthwhile endeavor. Instead, it is argued that income should be allocated to countries which have a claim to it based on an equitable distribution of such income (ibid.; McIntyre 2003).

Notwithstanding the purported advantages of the arm's length principle, the numerous difficulties encountered in applying the arm's length principle to determine transfer prices are well documented (Avi-Yonah 2007; Avi-Yonah and Benshalom 2011; Sadiq 2004; Turina 2018). These difficulties have made the implementation of the principle "extraordinarily complex" (Hellerstein 2005).

Moreover, it has been noted that the arm's length principle does not adequately address abuses while at the same time allowing revenue authorities to maximize their tax collections through taking advantage of the uncertainties in implementing the arm's length principle (Avi-Yonah and Musselli 2019).

In the light of these challenges, Brooks (2009) suggests that the time may be opportune for developing countries to devise an alternative means by which to equitably allocate income between countries.

2.2.2   Unitary Taxation

Unitary taxation works from the premise that the financial performance of companies whose businesses are integrated, such as in the case of a group of companies, should be combined in order to capture the synergies arising from such integration (Hellerstein 2005). While formulary apportionment complements unitary taxation, unitary taxation may be implemented without it (ibid.; Weiner 1999). Formulary apportionment envisages that the profits of multinational companies should be allocated across the countries in which such companies operate on the basis of a formula which accounts for where the income-producing activities are conducted (ibid.). While the choice of factors which are to make up this formula is ultimately a political choice (Hertzig et al. 2010), the prevailing formula is one based on an equal weighting of the three factors of production (labor, capital, and assets) and sales as a representation of demand (Kobetsky 2008).

Unitary taxation differs from the arm's length principle in that it is not applied to every transaction in order to produce a profit or loss on that transaction which then cumulatively becomes the taxable profit (Hertzig et al. 2010). Instead, unitary taxation produces a single, consolidated profit for the entire integrated business. In doing so, one of the advantages of a unitary tax system is that it eliminates the need for transfer pricing as the transactions occurring between the components of the integrated business are ignored (ibid.; Kobetsky 2008). Proponents of unitary taxation argue that a further advantage of the system is that it more accurately reflects economic reality (Bird 1986; Sadiq 2001; Weiner 1999). Economic reality is reflected by the fact that no interim profits within the group of companies are generated; the synergies arising from an integrated business are accounted for; and losses are set off against profits of companies belonging to the same group (Hertzig et al. 2010). Furthermore, unitary taxation would allow for greater certainty. This is especially as every step of applying the unitary taxation system would have to be legislated (Langbein 1986). These steps would encompass the rules for consolidation and the factors in terms of which the consolidated profits are to be allocated across countries. Langbein (1986) notes that such legislative measures would ensure that very little room is left for manipulation and would necessitate effective taxpayer information disclosure.

It has also been argued that a unitary taxation system would result in greater efficiency and fairness (Sadiq 2001). Efficiencies are created through a tax system which recognizes the efficiencies achieved by the integration of businesses (ibid.) and through resource saving as taxpayers and revenue authorities alike are freed from the complexities of transfer pricing determinations and the resultant disputes (Kobetsky 2008). Fairness is fostered through a tax system which uses the actual financial performance of the integrated business and not that of comparables which effectively attributes the business acumen and decisions of others onto the taxpayer (Kauder 1993). Formulary apportionment also creates fairness by allowing the tax system to follow the economic choices made by the taxpayer itself as profits are allocated to countries based on the economic decisions of the taxpayer (Sadiq 2001). Finally, it is argued that a benefit of unitary taxation is that it reduces the incidence of tax evasion and avoidance due to the extent of the reorganization that would be required from integrated businesses when seeking to evade or avoid taxes (ibid.).

Unitary taxation is not without its disadvantages. First, it has been argued that difficulties may be encountered in defining the level at which businesses will be considered to be integrated (Hertzig et al. 2010). If the threshold is set too low, it may overstate the synergies arising from integration (ibid.). If the threshold is too high, it may not properly reflect the economic realities of an integrated business (ibid.). Secondly, the prospect of having a consolidated profit subject to tax presents different tax planning opportunities (ibid.). The third criticism relates to formulary apportionment in that the arbitrariness of the factor selection may lead to inappropriate results in so far as income may be allocated to low-tax countries despite the absence of significant income-generating activities located there (ibid.).

Moreover, Fargas Mas (2018) argues that while the concept of a unitary tax system is attractive, the difficulty lies in determining who is to be responsible for drawing up the rules for such consolidation. It was suggested that this could be done by relying on the International Financial Reporting Standards (IFRS) (ibid.). However, Fargas Mas (2018) points out the criticisms of such an approach in that this would allow the accounting bodies who draw up the IFRS to effectively decide the taxable base and become legislators.

Despite its flaws, many have strongly advocated for the global adoption of unitary taxation coupled with formulary apportionment, arguing that such a system is more equipped to deal with the challenges of taxing an integrated business (Bird 1986; Sadiq 2001; Kobetsky 2008).

2.2.2.1   Feasibility in an African Developing Country Context

Both Kenya and South Africa currently adopt the arm's length principle as a means of allocating profits arising from the transactions concluded between components of an integrated business (Kenya: Income Tax Act, Chapter 470, section 18(3) and South Africa: Income Tax Act, No. 58 of 1962, section 31). In this regard, both countries closely follow the OECD Guidelines (2017). It would therefore constitute a major shift for both countries to implement unitary taxation along with formulary apportionment.

Having said that, recent studies have indicated that perhaps Kenya and South Africa should seriously consider making such a shift (Waris 2017; Wier and Reynolds 2018). At the moment, transfer pricing cases take up an extraordinary amount of resources for both the Kenya Revenue Authority (KRA) and the South African Revenue Service (SARS). Both the KRA and SARS have dedicated transfer pricing units with the KRA having grown their staff complement to 34 members recently (Okuth 2018), while SARS has had long-standing plans to do the same (PWC 2012). Despite dedicating staff to transfer pricing issues, transfer pricing cases take an extraordinarily long time to be finalized in both countries. A transfer pricing case takes on average between 1½ and 4 years to be completed in South Africa (OECD 2019). In Kenya, the average transfer pricing case takes approximately 4–5 years to be completed (Waris 2017). Moreover, in order to deal effectively with transfer pricing issues, staff have to be exceptionally well trained. Kenya was one of the first recipients of transfer pricing training by the OECD in 2009 (Waris 2017), and the KRA now boasts members of its transfer pricing units who are experts in analyzing the various disclosures to be made in transfer pricing documentation (KPMG 2015). Thus, the KRA has experts in functional analysis, asset analysis, risk analysis, and economic analysis, for instance (KPMG 2015).

Notwithstanding these measures, Kenya and South Africa are still losing substantial revenues as a result of transfer pricing. While a 2018 report indicated that Kenya lost US$907 million in 2013 (Global Financial Integrity 2018), this number may be much higher today given the number of multinational companies operating in Kenya whose annual turnover exceeds 750 million euros (Initiative for Global Development and Dalberg Global Development Advisors 2011; Waris 2017). Similarly, South Africa loses approximately US$475 million annually as a result of transfer pricing (Donnelly 2019; Wier and Reynolds 2018).

These losses may be attributed to the problems experienced by Kenya and South Africa in implementing the arm's length standard in their respective countries. The arm's length standard is particularly problematic in Kenya and South Africa because both these countries deal with many large multinational companies that effectively operate as monopolies in their industries (Waris 2017; Wier and Reynolds 2018). This issue is particularly significant in South Africa where a report recently concluded that 80% of the income earned by foreign-owned firms in South Africa were earned by only 10% of the largest of those firms (Wier and Reynolds 2018).

Furthermore, implementation of the arm's length standard requires the availability of a large database of comparables. This is difficult to construct in Kenya because the digitization of company records is still incomplete (Waris 2017). Similarly in South Africa, the availability of comparable data is hampered by the fact that it is only public companies who are required to make their financial records available to the public (Companies Regulations 2011; Deloitte 2015).

If Kenya and South Africa were to implement unitary taxation, it would immediately free up the government resources and time as discussed above. This would result in the administrative capacity to retrain staff in a new system.

Kenya and South Africa, however, would have to make the decision at which level to define when a business has a sufficient degree of integration to bring about unitary taxation. While this would be a difficult decision, the author is of the view that South Africa has already laid the groundwork for this sort of discussion when deciding at which stage parties would be affiliated or related to each other in applying the arm's length principle under its existing laws. In this regard, it is suggested that perhaps this discussion should begin with whether South Africa's definition of a "group of companies" in Section 1 of its Income Tax Act is adequate in capturing what is meant by an "integrated business."

A unitary taxation system would allow the taxation of multinationals' profits to be more closely aligned with economic reality while also providing the concomitant benefits of a fair and efficient system.

In the light of the above, it would seem that perhaps it would not be too onerous for Kenya and South Africa to consider implementing a unitary taxation system. In a similar vein, the adoption of a formulary apportionment system may also be beneficial to these countries.

Kenya is a unique position in that it is home to both foreign and resident multinationals (Kelley 2011). Moreover, Kenya and South Africa are preferred destinations for multinationals (EY Attractiveness Africa 2019). As such, Kenya and South Africa would be more likely than other African countries to have the factors of production housed within their borders. It may therefore be beneficial for Kenya and South Africa to adopt the equally weighted factors of assets, capital, labor, and sales.

Aside from the difficult decision of deciding on which factors are to make up the formula, once this decision is made, it is noted that a legislative approach to how profits of multinationals are to be allocated across countries may benefit Kenya and South Africa in that it would allow greater certainty for both taxpayers and revenue authorities while also allowing for less room for discretion within may result in fewer disputes.

Moreover, if Kenya and South Africa were to reach consensus on which factors they would use in their formulas, as two of the biggest economies in Africa, it may pave the way for other countries in Africa to adopt similar formulas—and perhaps this process may be facilitated by the AfCFTA. Historically, such natural cooperation has occurred before.

It has been noted that in the United States when Iowa unilaterally adopted a sales-based apportionment with respect to corporate income tax, this triggered a "spontaneous coordination" as other states followed suit while pursuing their own best interest (De Wilde 2016). De Wilde argues that it is not inconceivable for a similar "spontaneous cooperation" to occur on a global level (ibid.). Similarly, the author argues that the AfCFTA could allow for a similar "spontaneous cooperation" to happen in Africa at the impetus of two of the biggest economies in Africa, Kenya and South Africa—if such a move were in the best interest of the individual countries. It is submitted that a move to unitary taxation combined with formulary apportionment may well be in the best interest of African countries.

In this way, the necessary political consensus among African countries may be reached on such a scale that it may minimize the likelihood of double or non-taxation arising from differences in approaches to formulary apportionment between African countries.

In respect of the rest of the world, however, it is noted that Kenya and South Africa have concluded a number of double taxation agreements. Their obligations under these treaties would have to be factored in when making the decision to move away from the arm's length standard. The Independent Commission for the Reform of International Corporate Taxation (ICRICT) suggests that countries considering such a shift should implement unitary taxation and formulary apportionment as a minimum alternative tax to the arm's length standard (ICRICT 2018). In terms of this approach, the multinational company's tax liability would be calculated both in terms of the arm's length standard, as required by most double taxation agreements, and in terms of unitary taxation with formulary apportionment (ibid.). Only in the event that liability under the arm's length standard is less than the result under unitary taxation with formulary apportionment would the amount as determined under the non-arm's length standard apply (ibid.).

While this methodology would be time-consuming, it may serve as a transitional measure for African countries wishing to adopt unitary taxation with formulary apportionment as a standard until (and if) this becomes a uniform position across African countries.

In considering the above, the author is of the view that a unitary taxation system coupled with formulary apportionment may be a viable alternative to the arm's length principle for Kenya and South Africa on a principled basis. Significant administrative challenges would have to be addressed by both countries in implementing such a change, a discussion of which would be beyond the scope of this chapter. However, these challenges would not diminish the fact that unitary taxation and formulary apportionment would hold great promise if it were implemented in Kenya and South Africa.

2.2.3 Destination-Based Cash Flow Tax

The DBCFT was first proposed by Bond and Devereux in 2002 (Bond and Devereux 2002) and has more recently been the subject of discussion (Auerbach 2017; Auerbach et al. 2010, 2017a, b; Avi-Yonah and Clausing 2017). The DBCFT basically envisages that tax on corporate income or profits should be levied at "destination," that is, the country in which the final sales to customers are made should be allowed to levy the tax (Cui 2017). This prospect produces an alternative to "residence" and "source" paradigms (ibid.).

It has been noted that there are two versions of the DBCFT currently in the literature (ibid.). The first is the taxation of corporate income through a sales-only formulary apportionment (Auerbach et al. 2010; De Wilde 2018). The second is a destination-based value added tax (VAT) with deductions for labor costs and refundable losses (Auerbach and Devereux 2013). Each of these shall be analyzed in turn.

2.2.3.1 Sales-Only Formulary Apportionment

Some of the advantages of shifting to this method of taxing corporate profits lies in its movement away from the residence/source paradigm with all its known problems (Cui 2017); its potential to remove known profit-shifting opportunities should the DBCFT be adopted globally (Hebous et al. 2019); and its potential to make the tax rate irrelevant to firms deciding on the location of their operations (ibid.).

The sales-only formulary apportionment method of taxing corporate income is a new element to the international tax melting pot. This method envisages that the corporate income should be divided among the countries where the goods or services are sold (Cui 2017). This method was initially proposed by Auerbach, Devereaux, and Simpson (2010) before being discussed by De Wilde (2018) in the context of the EU's CCCTB proposal. De Wilde (2018) suggests that the EU should abandon the CCCTB proposal altogether in favor of adopting a unitary tax system based on sales-only formulary apportionment. De Wilde (2018) argues that this system with its worldwide tax consolidation of multinational companies would allow economic profits to be taxed while moving away from the flawed and vulnerable residence and source paradigms. De Wilde (2018) further argues that a sales-only formulary apportionment would allow EU Member States to once again obtain control of the tax policy function of corporate income tax as the control of the location of corporate profits would be taken away from companies.

This method, however, is not without its criticisms. Fargas Mas (2018) argues that the reliance on a sales-only formulary apportionment method would effectively exclude most developing countries from participating in the allocation of taxing rights. This is because most sales typically take place in a developed country (ibid.).

Further criticism of the sales-only formulary method lies in the fact that it would be ineffectual to apply in the case of intermediary or business-to-business sales (Cui 2017). Cui (2017) argues that if the destination-based, sales-only factor should be applied in intermediary sales, this would allow the parties to the sale agreement to decide on the location of the sale (and where tax is levied) in the same way as is the case now with respect to the manipulation of the production factors, assuming that there is collusion between the purchaser and seller. It has been noted that sales to actual final customers are evident in only a very small percentage of cases, and therefore the potential for manipulation of the sales-only formulary method is great (ibid.).

A further complication of implementing this method is that it is not customary for sellers to gather information on the purchasers (ibid.). The sales-only formulary apportionment method would therefore require the seller to undertake information-gathering activities, a new cost which would have to be absorbed by sellers (ibid.). Similar information-gathering complications would play out on an international level. Cui (2017) argues that the sales-only formulary apportionment method would require multilateral cooperation from all the countries involved—residence, source, and destination. Costs still need to be allocated to the sales which means that the country of destination would require the country of production to provide such information (ibid.). Cui (2017) therefore questions whether a sales-only formulary apportionment method is really different from the current system.

With respect to information-gathering, the author notes that perhaps it would be worthwhile to consider the mechanisms employed under the VAT system to keep track of the destination of the sales and to acquire the necessary customer information.

2.2.3.2 Destination-Based VAT Adjusted for Wages

The second form of the DBCFT is a destination-based VAT with deductions for labor costs and refundable losses. In terms of this destination-based VAT method, no interest or depreciation would be deductible, while investment expenses would be deductible (Auerbach 2017). In this way, this method seeks to exclude the normal return on investment and only tax economic rents (ibid.). Moreover, a border adjustment is to be made such that income arising from exports is exempted while no deduction is allowed for imported inputs (ibid.).

Advantages of this method lie in the more balanced tax treatment of the returns of debt and equity capital; the simplification of the tax system in removing the need to calculate income; and the fairness involved in not taxing the normal return on investments (ibid.).

Hebous et al. (2019) speculate that this method would benefit developing countries. They argue that revenues in developing countries should increase because developing countries are generally capital importers with big trade deficits. Moreover, they opine that developing countries would benefit from replacing tax incentives with a cash flow tax in that such a decision would likely broaden the tax base in developing countries and in so doing bring in more revenue. However, Hebous et al. (2019) do acknowledge that developing countries who rely on location-specific rents and revenue from natural resources would probably lose out upon implementing this method. Moreover, they note that this method would be more volatile than corporate income tax as a consequence of investments varying more than depreciation allowances (ibid.). Such volatility would be exacerbated in developing countries with the immediate tax refund function of the destination-based VAT system (ibid.).

Immediate tax refunds would be a reality, Auerbach (2017) notes because the adoption of this method would see the increase of net operating losses of taxpayers—especially for taxpayers with large amounts of export sales. Auerbach et al. (2017b), however, suggest that perhaps the loss should be allowed to be offset against other taxes such as payroll taxes. Should this be implemented instead of an immediate release of a refund, perhaps the volatility of this method could be reduced. A further drawback of this method is the difficulties arising from taxing financial institutions (ibid.). In this respect, Auerbach (2010) suggests that the current system of allowing for a deduction of interest and the taxation of interest received should be retained while now also allowing for the taxation of amounts borrowed and the deduction of amounts lent. Moreover, concerns have been raised that this method would not be compatible with the World Trade Organization agreements (ibid.).

Grinberg (2017), however, argues that adjustments may be made to this method to make it compatible with the World Trade Organization agreements. According to Grinberg (2017), first the tax base should be clearly defined as being a tax on domestic consumption such that the normative parameters of the tax are evident. Next, all businesses operating within the domestic market must be registered as DBCFT taxpayers, while non-resident businesses may choose not to be so registered (ibid.). DBCFT taxpayers would be allowed to deduct all wages paid to resident taxpayers, while wages paid to non-resident aliens would not be deductible (ibid.,). Moreover, DBCFT taxpayers would be entitled to deduct non-financial payments made to other DBCFT taxpayers (ibid.). Should a business choose not to register as a DBCFT taxpayer, other DBCFT taxpayers would not be allowed to deduct the payments made to that non-registered business (ibid.). Grinberg (2017) argues that the World Trade Organization case law provides that World Trade Organization-compliant tax systems are to treat imported products and domestic products similarly unless the importer does not adhere to defensible administrative rules.

A major concern of this method, however, is that it introduces nothing new to the international tax arena (Cui 2017). Instead, this method may only serve to create significant trade distortions while failing to tax what is intended—corporate profits (ibid.; Shaviro 2018). This is because this method would only change the amount of the corporate's inputs and outputs while it would leave the profits that ultimately accrue to the shareholders unaffected (Cui 2017). In the light of this, Shaviro (2018) questions whether a country would effectively have two VAT systems if it were to adopt this form of the DBCFT when it already has a VAT system. Shaviro (2018) further questions whether the adoption of this form of DBCFT in conjunction with a VAT system would have any utility.

A further concern is that this DBCFT method only serves to allocate revenue to where shareholders reside and not where customers reside (ibid.). This is because the labor compensation is excluded which results in the taxation of only consumption financed by domestic profits—the domestic economic rent on capital (ibid.). A pure tax on consumption would tax all domestic consumption irrespective of whether it is generated by labor or economic rent and regardless of where such elements are generated (ibid.). This method would not do this (ibid.). Finally, Cui (2017) opines that the immediate loss refund feature is not administratively feasible for most countries.

From a substantive point of view, commentators agree that the DBCFT proposals do not introduce anything new to international tax. As such, it is unlikely to be a serious contender to replacing the arm's length principle.

2.2.3.3   Feasibility in an African Developing Country Context

Both Kenya and South Africa currently implement a classical corporate income tax system. A switch to a DBCFT system would therefore constitute a major overhaul. In considering whether such an overhaul would be worthwhile, it is sobering to consider the transitional costs that such a change would incur. It was estimated that if the United States were to implement a DBCFT, it would result in a US$5 trillion loss in the value of foreign assets held by US residents, while non-residents would realize a US$8 trillion gain on the value of US-held assets as the US$ would appreciate against foreign currencies (Graetz 2017). Such transitional costs would be prohibitive in an African developing country context.

Notwithstanding the transitional costs, the sales-only formulary apportionment method may be attractive, but only in so far as the sales actually were to take place within Kenya or South Africa. Should the sales take place elsewhere, Kenya and South Africa would stand to lose its taxing rights—rights which it otherwise may have had if the production factors of the multinational company were actually housed in their countries. More importantly, the complications which would arise from intermediate sales and the administrative difficulties involved in keeping track of where the final consumers are located would be an additional administrative burden on the respective revenue authorities. It is therefore doubtful whether it would be worth Kenya and South Africa making the normative and administrative leap to adopt a sales-only formulary apportionment method of taxing corporate income.

Similarly, adopting a destination-based VAT method with a deduction for labor and allowing for immediate loss refunds would probably not be feasible for Kenya and South Africa. Administratively, allowing for the immediate refund of losses would create too great a risk for fraud, especially when both countries are already plagued with VAT-related fraud. Moreover, given the questionable normative difference between this method and VAT regarding who and what is ultimately subject to tax, and given that both Kenya and South Africa already have VAT systems in place, the destination-based VAT method would not hold much promise for Kenya and South Africa.

The author is of the view that the only real advantage these two African developing countries may possibly gain from a switch to a DBCFT system—in whatever form—would be to capitalize on the "novelty" aspect of such a change. The two countries could possibly benefit from mobile capital attracted by the shift in method of taxation. However, if the spillover effects would be as significant as some suggest, this "novelty" would be short-lived as other countries adopt similar methods. Once this happens, Kenya and South Africa would be exactly in the same position as it is now—competing with other countries and regional blocks on the basis of non-tax-related factors.

Moreover, if Kenya and South Africa were to adopt a destination-based VAT system adjusting for labor and while allowing for immediate loss refunds, they may end up in a worse position at that future point than they currently are. In such future situation, they would be constrained in taxing non-resident resource-exploiting companies; they would be dealing with a method that is volatile on account of investment cycles; the method would be heavily reliant on domestic sales; and they would be dealing with the increased risk of fraud arising from the immediate loss refund aspect.

Aside from the initial gains arising from being one of the first to implement a DBCFT system, it would not be feasible or wise for Kenya or South Africa to change to a DBCFT system.

2.3 Conclusion

Kenya and South Africa have adopted the arm's length principle in their respective domestic legislations as a mechanism to determine and allocate the profits of multinationals across different countries. While this is in keeping with international practice, it is not at all clear whether this is best suited for these two African developing countries.

In considering whether alternatives to the arm's length principle may be viable in the context of these two countries, this chapter has outlined the advantages and disadvantages to adopting either a unitary taxation system coupled with formulary apportionment or a DBCFT system—either in the form of a sales-only formulary apportionment or a destination-based VAT adjusted for wages.

While the implementation of a DBCFT (in either form) would not be suited for either Kenya or South Africa given the concern that its design would not effectively tax corporate profits and the prohibitive transitional costs involved in such a change, this chapter argues that a unitary taxation system with formulary apportionment holds promise. Unitary taxation would allow for the Kenyan and South African corporate income tax systems to more effectively reflect the economic realities of the many multinationals currently operating in these countries, would allow more efficiencies and fairness into the operation of the tax system, and would allow for government resources to be freed from transfer pricing issues to implementing unitary taxation. Moreover, the factors which make up the prevailing formula for formulary apportionment may be feasible in Kenya and South Africa given that they are both favorable destinations to host multinationals.

It has also been noted that should Kenya and South Africa succeed in agreeing on a formula, there is a strong likelihood that this may act as a catalyst for other African countries to reach consensus on the use of such a formula in their own jurisdictions—similar to what has occurred in the United States historically.

While it has often been noted that it is unlikely that global unitary taxation and formulary apportionment would take hold any time soon, such viewpoint in no way relieves countries from the necessity of making difficult decisions regarding which rules to follow in allocating income across jurisdictions. Amid the ever-growing calls for the fair allocation of income among countries, perhaps the time has come for African developing countries to take the path less travelled and to develop rules which would make the most economic sense for them. It is submitted that adopting a system of unitary taxation coupled with formulary apportionment may be a step in that direction.

References

Treaties

Agreement Establishing the African Continental Free Trade Area Agreement. (Signed 21 March 2018).

Legislation

Companies Regulations, 2011 (Government Gazette No. 34239) to the Companies Act, 71 of 2008, regulation 30 read with regulation 28 (South Africa).
Income Tax Act, Chapter 470, section 18 (Kenya).
Income Tax Act, No. 58 of 1962, section 31 (South Africa).

Articles

Auerbach, A. J. (2010). *A modern corporate tax*. Washington, DC: Center for American Progress and Hamilton Project.
Auerbach, A. J. (2017). Demystifying the destination-based cash-flow tax. *Brookings Papers on Economic Activity, 48*(2), 409–432.
Auerbach, A. J., & Devereux, M. P. (2013). Consumption and cash flow taxes in an international setting. NBER Working Paper No. 19579. National Bureau of Economic Research.
Auerbach, A. J., Devereux, M. P., & Simpson, H. (2010). Taxing corporate income. In A. Stuart et al. (Eds.), *Dimensions of tax design: The Mirrlees review* (pp. 837–913). New York: Oxford University Press.
Auerbach, A., Devereux, M. P., Keen, M., & Vella, J. (2017a). International tax planning under the destination-based cash flow tax. *National Tax Journal, 70*, 783–802.
Auerbach, A., Devereux, M. P., Keen, M., & Vella, J. (2017b). Destination-based cash-flow taxation. Working Paper no. 17/01, Oxford University Centre for Business Taxation, pp. 1–92.
Avi-Yonah, R. S. (2007). The Rise and fall of arm's length: A study in the evolution of U.S. international taxation. Law & Economics Working Papers Archive: 2003–2009. Retrieved September 6, 2019, from https://repository.law.umich.edu/law_econ_archive/art73
Avi-Yonah, R. S., & Benshalom, I. (2011). Formulary apportionment: Myths and prospects—Promoting better international policy and utilizing the misunderstood and under-theorized formulary alternative. *World Tax Journal, 3*(3), 371–398.
Avi-Yonah, R. S., & Clausing, K. (2017). Problems with destination-based corporate taxes and the Ryan blueprint. *Columbia Journal of Tax Law, 8*(2), 229–255.
Avi-Yonah, R. S., & Musselli, A. (2019). Amazon Goldcrest project and the relevance of comparability analysis under the arm's length Principle. *International Transfer Pricing Journal, 26*(3), 159–166.

Bird, R. M. (1986). The interjurisdictional allocation of income. *Australian Tax Forum, 3*(3), 333–353.

Bond, S., & Devereux, M. P. (2002). Cash flow taxes in an open economy. C.E.P.R. Discussion Papers, No. 3401, Centre for Economic Policy Research.

Brooks, K. (2009). Tax sparing: A needed incentive for foreign investment in low-income countries or an unnecessary revenue sacrifice? *Queen's Law Journal, 34*(2), 505–564.

Carroll, M. B. (1934). Allocation of business income: The draft convention of the League of Nations. *Columbia Law Review, 34*(3), 473–498.

Cui, W. (2017). Destination-based cash-flow taxation: A critical appraisal. *University of Toronto Law Journal, 67*(3), 301–347.

De Graaf, A., De Haan, P., & De Wilde, M. (2014). Fundamental change in countries' corporate tax framework needed to properly address BEPS. *Intertax, 42*(5), 306–316.

De Wilde, M. F. (2016). Taxation of multinational enterprises in a global market: Moving to corporate tax 2.0? *Bulletin for International Taxation, 70*(3), 182–187.

Donnelly, L. (2019, January 11). Giants cost SA billions in lost taxes. *Mail and Guardian.* Retrieved November 5, 2019, from https://mg.co.za/article/2019-01-11-00-giants-cost-sa-billions-in-lost-taxes

Graetz, M. J. (2017). The known unknowns of the business tax reforms proposed in the house republican blueprint. *Columbia Journal of Tax Law, 8*(2), 117–170.

Green, R. A. (1993). The future of source-based taxation of the income of multinational enterprises. *Cornell Law Review, 79*(18), 18–86.

Grinberg, I. (2017). A destination-based cash flow taxation can be structured to comply with World Trade Organization rules. *National Tax Journal, 70,* 803–818.

Hamaekers, H. (1997). Can the free negotiation of prices within a multinational enterprise serve as an arm's length method? *International Transfer Pricing Journal, 4*(1), 2–4.

Hamaekers, H. (2001). Arm's length—How long? *International Transfer Pricing Journal, 8*(2), 30–40.

Hebous, S., Klemm, A., & Stausholm, S. (2019). Revenue implications of destination-based cash-flow taxation. International Monetary Fund. IMF Working Paper, No. 2019/7. https://doi.org/10.5089/9781484392935.001

Hellerstein, W. (2005). Income allocation in the 21st century: The end of transfer pricing. *International Transfer Pricing Journal, 12*(3), 103–111.

Hertzig, N., Teschke, M., & Joisten, C. (2010). Between extremes: Merging the advantages of separate accounting and unitary taxation. *Intertax, 38*(6/7), 334–349.

Kauder, L. M. (1993). Intercompany pricing and section 482: A proposal to shift from uncontrolled comparables to formulary apportionment now. *Tax Notes, 58,* 485–493.

Kelley, K. (2011, November 5). Kenya hosts 3 of Africa's top multinationals. *The East African.*

Kobetsky, M. (2008). The case for unitary taxation of international enterprises. *Bulletin for International Taxation, 62*(5), 201–215.

Langbein, S. I. (1986). The unitary method and the myth of arm's length. *Tax Notes, 30,* 625–683.

Okuth, E. (2018, November 18). KRA unearths tricks foreign firms use to dodge paying taxes. *Daily Nation.* Retrieved November 5, 2019, from https://www.nation.co.ke/news/How-foreign-firms-dodge-paying-taxes/1056-4856874-7brxkxz/index.html

Russo, R. (2005). Application of arm's length principle to intra-company dealings. *International Transfer Pricing Journal, 12*(1), 7–15.

Sadiq, K. (2001). Unitary taxation—The case for global formulary apportionment. *Bulletin for International Taxation, 55*(7), 275–286.

Sadiq, K. (2004). The fundamental failing of the traditional transfer pricing regime—Applying the arm's length standard to multinational banks based on a comparability analysis. *Bulletin for International Taxation, 58*(2), 67–81.

Shaviro, D. N. (2018). Goodbye to all that? A requiem for the destination-based cash flow tax. *Bulletin for International Taxation, 72*(4/5), 248–258.

Turina, A. (2018). Back to grass roots: The arm's length standard, comparability and transparency—Some perspectives from the emerging world. *World Tax Journal, 10*(2), 295–348.

Waris, A. (2017). How Kenya has implemented and adjusted to the changes in international transfer pricing regulations: 1920–2016. ICTD Working Paper 69. Institute of Development Studies.

Weiner, J. M. (1999). Using the experience in the U.S. states to evaluate issues in implementing formula apportionment at the international level. OTA Paper 83, U.S. Department of the Treasury.

Books and Chapters

De Wilde, M. F. (2018). Chapter 2: The CCCTB relaunch: A critical assessment and some suggestions for modification. In P. Pistone (Ed.), *European tax integration: Law, policy and politics* (pp. 35–84). Amsterdam: IBFD.

Fargas Mas, L. M. (2018). Commentary on chapter 2: CCCTB relaunch: Why a destination-based model would not work. In P. Pistone (Ed.), *European tax integration: Law, policy and politics* (pp. 85–98). Amsterdam: IBFD.

McIntyre, M. J. (2003). The use of combined reporting by nation states. In B. J. Arnold, J. Sasseville, & E. M. Zolt (Eds.), *The taxation of business profits under tax treaties* (pp. 245–298). Toronto: Canadian Tax Foundation.

McLure, C. E., & Weiner, J. M. (2000). Deciding whether the European Union should adopt formulary apportionment of company income. In S. Cnossen (Ed.), *Taxing capital income in the European Union: Issues and options for reform* (pp. 243–292). New York: Oxford University Press.

Rogers-Glabush, J. (2015). *IBFD international tax glossary* (7th ed.). Amsterdam: IBFD.

Organization Documentation

Draft Convention Adopted for the Allocation of Business Income between States for the Purposes of Taxation, adopted by the Fiscal Committee at its last meeting, June 15th to 26th, 1933, and published as an annex to its report to the Council of the League. Document C.399.M.204.1933. II.A. F./Fiscal 76.

OECD. (2017). *OECD transfer pricing guidelines for multinational enterprises and tax administrations 2017*. Paris: OECD.

OECD. (2019). Mutual agreement procedure statistics. South Africa.

United Nations Economic Commission for Africa and the African Union Commission. (2014). *Progress report on illicit financial flows: Why Africa needs to "track it, stop it and get it."* UNECA.

United Nations Economic Commission for Africa and the African Union Commission. (2015). *Report of the high level panel on illicit financial flows from Africa*. UNECA.

Reports and Studies

Deloitte. (2015). *Transfer pricing in South Africa' presentation to the Portfolio Committee on Trade and Industry*. Retrieved November 5, 2019, from https://www.thedti.gov.za/parliament/2015/Deloitte.pdf

Ernst & Young. (2019). *How can bold action become everyday action?* EY attractiveness program Africa.

Global Financial Integrity. (2018). *Kenya: Potential revenue losses associated with trade misinvoicing*. GFI.

Independent Commission on the Reform of International Corporate Taxation. (2018). *A roadmap to improve rules for taxing multinationals a fairer future for global taxation*. ICRICT.

Initiative for Global Development and Dalberg Global Development Advisors. (2011). *Pioneers on the frontier: Sub-Saharan Africa's multinational corporations*. IGD and DGDA.

KPMG. (2015). *Global transfer pricing review*. Kenya: KPMG International Cooperative.

PricewaterhouseCoopers. (2012). *Spotlight on Africa's transfer pricing landscape*. Transfer Pricing Perspectives: Special Edition. PwC.

Readhead, A. (2016). *Preventing tax base erosion in Africa: A regional study of transfer pricing challenges in the mining sector*. Natural Resource Governance Institute.

Wier, L., & Reynolds, H. (2018). *Big and 'unprofitable': How 10% of multinational firms do 98% of profit-shifting*. WIDER working paper 2018/111. United Nations University World Institute for Development Economics Research.

Chapter 3
The Suitability of BEPS in Developing Countries (Emphasis on Latin America and the Caribbean)

Isaác Gonzalo Arias Esteban and Anarella Calderoni

3.1   Introduction

This chapter attempts to analyze some of the potential implications that the OECD/G20 Base Erosion and Profit Shifting (BEPS) Project could have on member countries of the Inter-American Centre of Tax Administrations (CIAT) in the Latin America and Caribbean (LAC) region. This includes strategic considerations for deciding whether to implement BEPS; tactical aspects regarding the manner and extent to which the proposals could be implemented; and operational aspects relating to the current implementation. It is important to note that CIAT countries from this region present extensive differences in their size, context, tax regulations, and levels of experience. Information taken from CIAT's Transfer Pricing Database shows us that some of the countries in the region have a limited treaty network with only one or two countries while others have over 30 treaties in force (CIATData 2016). Most LAC countries have transfer pricing legislations, albeit only a few countries have an extensive level of practice with them (CIATData 2018b). Some countries have efficient risk assessment tools that help them identify when to apply anti-abuse rules, while other countries are only beginning to introduce these rules (CIATData 2018a).

When the BEPS project first started in 2013, the OECD/G20 and the international tax community had many challenges ahead of them. The technical concepts dealt with in each of the action points had to be explained and understood clearly by authorities and technical officials, thereby building the momentum and support necessary to drive forward a discussion of these issues on an international scale. The Inclusive Framework (IF) on BEPS was created for interested countries to join

I. G. Arias Esteban (✉) · A. Calderoni
Inter-American Centre of Tax Administrations (CIAT), Panama City, Republic of Panama
e-mail: garias@ciat.org; acalderoni@ciat.org

© The Author(s) 2021
I. J. Mosquera Valderrama et al. (eds.), *Taxation, International Cooperation and the 2030 Sustainable Development Agenda*, United Nations University Series on Regionalism 19, https://doi.org/10.1007/978-3-030-64857-2_3

the initiative and participate in the discussions under an "equal footing" criteria, with the goal of reaching a general consensus regarding proposed solutions (OECD 2019). Many of the BEPS objectives need adoption on a global scale to be most effective; this implies persuading the domestic political will of countries toward mutual agreement and compliance with the BEPS proposals. In this regard, the BEPS discussions have helped to attract the support and justification needed to pass tax reforms, close legislative gaps, and occasionally increase the disposition of available resources for the tax administrations. Moreover, it is necessary to recognize that in practical terms, developing countries acted as observers in this process. Nevertheless, it may be expected that the future influence of developing countries on BEPS will be proportional to the experience they have gained in their interactions with BEPS.

3.2 Strategic Aspects: Why Implement BEPS?

This section will attempt to identify how the BEPS proposals may fit into the tax vision of a developing country and the elements to be evaluated prior to or during its implementation. In order to assess the feasibility of BEPS, a country must first understand the issues in each BEPS Action: the objectives, the potential impact on tax compliance, and other expected results (including the potential impact on international relations). The decision to adopt BEPS proposals may be influenced by internal and external forces. Internally, the tax administration may wish to attain better results, increase the scope of the tax base, or reduce base eroding activities. Prior to BEPS, it may have been more difficult for countries to impose taxation on a corporation that creates value in their jurisdiction but does not declare it or provide fair remuneration for it; however, BEPS Actions 8–10 and the substance requirements in Actions 5 and 6 contain proposals that may help retain the value and corresponding taxable base generated in the country. For example, a new assessment mechanism allocates the value and control over intangible assets to the entities that perform the Development, Enhancement, Maintenance, Protection, and Exploitation (DEMPE) functions related to that intangible (OECD/G20 Base Erosion and Profit Shifting Project 2015a). Externally, motivations to implement BEPS could stem from the wish to avoid international sanctions. For example, amending or derogating a "harmful tax regime" (as per the criteria of Action 5) could lead to the country's name being removed from a blacklist. Similarly, from the point of view of the ministry of finance, the commercial impact of BEPS and its effect on foreign direct investments should be analyzed (e.g., the impact on the economy of implementing actions related to tax transparency or exchange of information).

If a country considers that the BEPS recommendations are feasible and could contribute to achieve the objectives of the tax administration, then decisions must be taken to outline the path toward their implementation. To ascertain the highest benefits, a certain level of international harmonization is required. For this, the government may want to consider joining the IF (although this could be an overwhelming commitment for a developing country as it requires a budget to cover the annual membership fee, the travel expenses associated with the country's attendance at meetings and events, and the technical capacity to participate in the "international decision-making process"). The IF dictates that all countries must implement the "BEPS package" minimum standards, regardless of their individual characteristics (OECD 2019). However, not all countries have the ready capacity (or the interest) to implement some of the recommendations (e.g., a small country without transfer pricing legislation having to implement Action 13). From this domestic point of view, the mandatory element of the IF may be perceived by some as unreasonable. Nevertheless, international harmonization and increased alignment of the tax regimes are necessary to further progress, foment cooperation, and reduce loopholes found throughout the various tax systems.

A country's political system will also influence their participation in the IF. For example, the commitments of a country's leadership position may be debilitated by frequent changes in government. It follows that, when the current government commits to the IF and makes BEPS a part of their fiscal strategy, their efforts may be backtracked once a new political party is elected. This situation hasn't happened yet at the political level in the LAC region. However, it has been observed at an operational or technical level (e.g., resources were allocated and then retracted; laws were repealed or stopped somewhere along the legislative process). A similar plight follows the opposing scenario; if the leadership role has been in the same hands for an extended period of time, ministers and high-ranking government officials may be resistant to foreign commitments or any changes in the tax code, consequently blocking the decision to join the IF and inhibiting the prospective implementation of BEPS.

One factor to keep in mind when joining the IF (or when unilaterally implementing BEPS) is the potential for disruption in key economic sectors. Taxpayers may be hesitant and resistant toward any measures that they perceive could violate their tax certainty. Furthermore, taxpayers in sectors that enjoy preferential tax treatment or benefit from tax incentive programs are likely to protest as there is a chance these could be dissolved under the BEPS proposals. A country should contemplate the potential resulting impact on these sectors when making their decisions. Furthermore, it is important for the administration to uphold neutrality and build trust in the eyes of the taxpayers. Maintaining clarity and strong communication can be an important tool to get everyone on board with the changes. Moreover, the tax administration may offer certain concessions such as the possibility to reveal assets or transactions, without punitive consequences, during the months prior to the BEPS proposals coming into effect (i.e., a grace period).

In summary, the advantages of implementing BEPS may include increased efficiency of the tax system, improving the country's international reputation, association with a sweeping global initiative, and the opportunity to motivate political will and knowledge on issues which—in the LAC experience—countries have been generally apathetic toward. On the other hand, the barriers or challenges may include the allocation of scarce resources in the face of competing priorities and the feasibility to comply in due course with the stringent IF commitments, among others.

3.3   Tactical Aspects: How to Implement BEPS?

Once the strategic aspects have been analyzed, a country must decide on the tactical plans to achieve its successful and sustainable implementation. This analysis takes into account the country context and the available resources and infrastructure in place. In general, the main barriers that developing countries often experience include the lack of necessary information and technology, insufficient control processes and risk analysis tools, slow or inefficient juridical infrastructure and administrative processes, lack of expertise or trained officials for high-level technical functions, and others depending on individual country characteristics. Tactical considerations also include decisions on the technical aspects of BEPS: whether to sign the MLI, which treaties to list, what reservations to make, which optional clauses to choose within the minimum standards, and to what extent the elective action points will be implemented. These decisions require studies, research, discussions with domestic stakeholders, etc. to forecast the potential effects. Decisions regarding technical aspects may require an investment in human resources as those officials involved in the process should fully understand the issues dealt with in each of the BEPS Actions and how these will interact with the current tax legislations. If necessary, capacity building workshops or training events could be provided. Similarly, post-implementation, the country will need tax experts who understand and are able to sustain the objectives of the regulations in order to make and try cases relating to BEPS abuse. It is not enough for the rules to merely exist; there needs to be the tools and human capacity to process, understand, and enforce them. Otherwise, without the perception of consequences, taxpayer behaviors will remain unchanged.

Sustainability is key as implementation is only the first stage in the process; countries need to ensure subsequent capacity and political stability to enforce the changes. For the tax administrations of developing countries, where juridical and administrative resources may be lacking, technical assistance can play a fundamental part. The role of organizations such as CIAT is to coordinate and provide support for tax administrations, aiming to strengthen their ability to evaluate the strategic, tactical, and operational aspects surrounding BEPS. As a counterpart to the efforts provided by international organizations and donors, tax administrations should prioritize the infrastructure and personnel needed to generate an optimal environment that capitalizes on the benefits from this technical assistance. In this regard, the performance indicators of Action 11 are useful to follow up on the progress. Action 11 tries to overcome the difficulties that arise from a lack of information regarding corporate taxation by creating datasets and analytical tools to better monitor the economic impacts of tax avoidance and BEPS-related changes (OECD/G20 Base Erosion and Profit Shifting Project 2015d). Thus, keeping authorities and peers informed on the progress of BEPS motivates its continual support. Going one step further, Action 11's range of attributes could be expanded by including risk assessment indicators that allow tax administrations not just to monitor BEPS but also to identify risks for better applying the BEPS recommendations.

Choosing the specific Actions to be implemented will depend on the characteristics of the tax regime and the domestic political circumstances. Even those Actions which a country has not chosen to implement yet can serve to guide long-term objectives and shed light on future policies. A country may want to provide its taxpayers with clarification on the BEPS modifications with reference to the corresponding BEPS documents published by the OECD (e.g., "For further understanding of the documentation requirements see the OECD's Action 13: 2015 Final Report"). However, it is advisable to make clear whether any future changes or updates to the referenced BEPS/OECD documents will assert influence on the interpretation of the legislation as this could lead to legal uncertainty.

3.3.1 The Minimum Standards

As previously mentioned, joining the IF or signing the MLI is a strategic option that requires adherence to the four BEPS minimum standards (encompassed in Actions 5, 6, 13, and 14). This section will analyze, in consecutive order, their potential implications.

The minimum standard of Action 5 requires the review of preferential tax regimes and the implementation of a transparency framework for tax rulings (OECD/G20 Base Erosion and Profit Shifting Project 2015b). This relies on the country's acquiescence toward the OECD criteria that deems a regime as "harmful." This could cause major disruptions in the functioning of the tax systems for many LAC countries that use incentives and safe harbor regimes to attract foreign investment, entice voluntary compliance, and attempt to increase short-term collection. However, in the long term, these measures may prove beneficial as it has often been found that tax incentives result in unsustainable effects, many times losing the country more revenue than they bring in. These incentives can be especially unfavorable when dealing with sectors that have high exit barriers or with companies that need the natural resources in that specific location.

The minimum standard found in Action 6 includes the addition of an anti-abuse rule: the principal purpose test (PPT) and/or a limitation on benefits (LOB) rule depending whether it is simplified or detailed, as well as the inclusion of a paragraph in double tax treaties that defines the purpose of the treaty as being "for the evasion of double taxation without creating opportunities for non-taxation" (OECD/G20 Base Erosion and Profit Shifting Project 2015e). In the LAC region, there may be less initial attention paid to this minimum standard as there are only a few countries that count on an expansive treaty network. As of 2016, the LAC CIAT member countries had an average of 20 treaties per country (CIATData 2016).[1]

Regardless of their treaty network relevance, the concepts touched upon in Action 6 may be used to fortify domestic regulations (e.g., requiring taxpayers to meet substance-over-form, economic reality, or principle purpose tests). However, for a developing country where the tax administrations' resources and expertise are limited, it could be difficult to apply and defend an anti-abuse rule, such as the PPT, especially when arguing against corporations with unlimited resources. Tax courts can look forward to gaining experience on this and other BEPS developments in the forthcoming years.

Arguably, one of the most adopted BEPS proposals is the Country-by-Country (CbC) report, the minimum standard of Action 13. The CbC allows information from multinational enterprises to be reported and exchanged through a standardized format (OECD/G20 Base Erosion and Profit Shifting Project 2015f). The OECD further assists countries to implement this minimum standard by offering to join the CbC Multilateral Competent Authority Agreement (CbC MCAA) and other legislative proposals. For developing countries with a restricted information regimes or limited access to databases, this Action is especially useful to increase the administrations' knowledge regarding taxpayer activities. As with any information regime, continual improvements are necessary to identifying the best procedures for evaluating the veracity of the information presented and avoiding undesired results in the risk assessment process.

The minimum standard of Action 14 consists of 21 elements dealing with preventing disputes, availability and access to mutual agreement procedures (MAP), resolution of MAP cases, and the implementation of MAP agreements (OECD/G20 Base Erosion and Profit Shifting Project 2015c). Although quite comprehensive, LAC countries may perceive its impact to be less consequential due to the lack of treaties and the general inexperience of MAP usage in the region (see Fig. 3.1).

Hesitation to implement the Action 14 standard stems from the possibility for a country to lose a portion of its tax base as a result of the dispute resolution or arbitration. Further hesitation arises when contemplating the optional "mandatory arbitration clause" that requires a level of commitment and compromise in terms of sovereignty. This Action requires extensive training of MAP experts that can present and defend their arguments (especially when negotiating with more experienced countries). In order to comply with the main intention of objectivity, arbitration (mandatory or not) requires some minimum neutrality conditions that may be hard to achieve in the LAC context. Nevertheless, this Action is highly relevant in an arena where disputes are imminent in several cases.

---

[1]For comparison, the European Union countries with the least number of treaties signed, Croatia, Malta, and Slovenia, had an average of 67 treaties in 2018 (Hearson 2018).

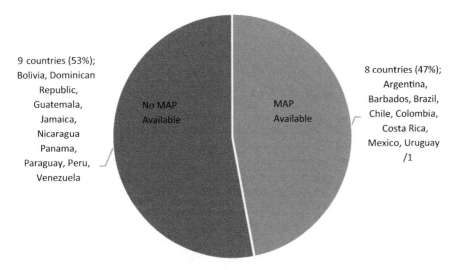

9 countries (53%);
Bolivia, Dominican
Republic,
Guatemala,
Jamaica,
Nicaragua
Panama,
Paraguay, Peru,
Venezuela

8 countries (47%);
Argentina,
Barbados, Brazil,
Chile, Colombia,
Costa Rica,
Mexico, Uruguay
/1

Fig. 3.1 Availability of map in the region as of 2018. 1) Uruguay is in the process of resolving their first mutual agreement procedure started in 2018. Source: CIATData (2019)

3.4   Operational Aspects: What Is Happening with BEPS?

It follows that, once the BEPS proposals have been implemented, they must be enforced using adequate tools and processes. One of the biggest challenges is first to detect the BEPS risks and then to know how to manage it, applying the correct measure in a timely manner following its identification. As mentioned above, some countries have observed positive results from the use of concessions or tax benefits that motivate taxpayers to regularize their tax positions prior to applying BEPS measures or tax transparency rules. Another challenge involves maintaining fluidity and not overwhelming the judicial system in this new context where disputes are likely to arise. Thus, the elements found in Action 14 and/or other mechanisms for avoiding disputes are imperative.

Through domestic and international cooperation on tax matters, the administration can attain more information with which to prepare and defend their assessments. In this regard, CIAT has created a database on harmful tax planning, providing a forum for countries to share their experiences, specifically emphasizing how they were able to identify the taxpayers' risky behavior and which tools where used to justify their contentions. As can be seen in the database, domestic rules similar to the general anti-avoidance rule seen in Action 6 give an option for countries to denunciate taxpayer behaviors (acting as a sort of "blanket clause"). The Availability of Public Information tool (DIP) is another CIAT product for tax administrations that facilitates the identification of public information, useful for verifying the taxpayers' situation (through a database of withholding agents, real estate registry, company registry, etc.).[2]

3.4.1 Findings from the CIAT BEPS Monitoring Initiative

The OECD/G20 have been consistent in their efforts to promulgate the BEPS proposals, and—based on the quantity of countries that have joined the IF—their efforts have paid off. Nevertheless, the project is only 6 years old which is a short amount of time for proposals to be presented, adopted, implemented, and applied. Thus, an analysis of the long-term effects that the BEPS project has on a developing country's administrative and judicial processes is yet unavailable. In the LAC region, many countries find themselves in the stage of capacitating their administration and judicial system to better handle the issues in the newly adopted regulations. Moreover, a few of the countries have begun to report positive results pertaining to the exchange of information, the elimination of preferential regimes, and the fortification of their transfer pricing regimes.

To this extent, in 2018–2019 CIAT carried out a study relating to the adoption of BEPS Actions across its member countries. Representatives from the tax administrations of these countries indicated which of the recommendations from each Action had been implemented and whether they were "totally implemented" (including all of the recommendations found in the Action report) or if they were "partially implemented" (including only some of the recommendations). The detailed information as to which specific recommendations were implemented by each country is available in the resulting "BEPS Monitoring database" available at CIATData.[3] It must be noted that CIAT merely tallied the statements made by the tax administrations relating to their level of adoption of the BEPS recommendations. Therefore, CIAT does not pretend for this to be an official measure or review on the level of implementation such as that done by the IF.

For the purposes of this chapter, we have extracted the information relating only to the CIAT member countries from the LAC region. Figure 3.2 shows the "popularity" of each Action as determined by their implementation.

It should be noted that the Actions which encompass the minimum standards (5, 6, 13, and 14) have an inherent bias that thrusts forward their implementation. The highest levels of total adoption are seen in Actions 5 and 13 (in which all of the recommendations were included as part of their implementation). Action 6 is shortly behind along with Actions 3 and 7 which, notably, are not minimum standards. The actions which have not been adopted to their full extent by any country are Actions 1, 2, 11, and 14. Moreover, the potential issues relating to Action 14 mentioned in

---

[2]Access to the database of harmful cases, as well as the DIP tool, is only available to officials of CIAT member country tax administrations.

[3]https://www.ciat.org/beps-monitoring-database/?lang=en

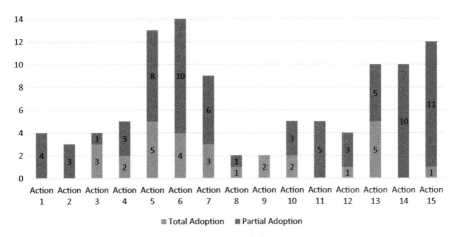

Fig. 3.2 General adoption of each BEPS action by 29 LAC CIAT member countries (segregated between partial and total adoption), as of June 2019. Source: Author elaboration using information from the CIAT Data BEPS Monitoring database, accessed on June 2019

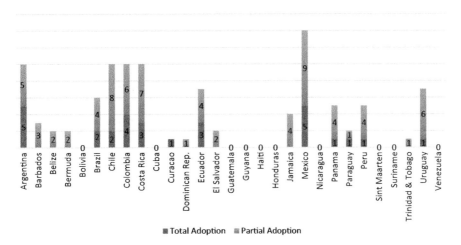

Fig. 3.3 Number of BEPS actions adopted per country by 29 LAC CIAT member countries as of June 2019 (segregated between partial and total adoption). Source: Author elaboration using information from the CIAT Data BEPS Monitoring database, accessed on June 2019

the section above (i.e., the concession of sovereignty) could explain why there has not been a country that has totally adopted all of the recommendations related to this action.

In opposition, Fig. 3.3 shows the quantity of BEPS Actions implemented by each country without identifying which of the 15 Actions were implemented, only how many.

Those countries with a total level of implementation demonstrate a strong adherence toward the BEPS proposals. That being said, for a developing country, the

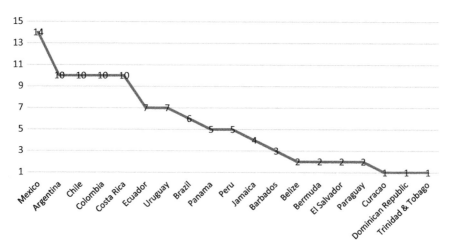

Fig. 3.4 Total number of BEPS actions adopted per country in 19 LAC CIAT member countries (without differentiating between partial and total implementation), as of June 2019. Ten CIAT member countries that did not report any level of BEPS implementation are missing from this graph. Source: Author elaboration using information from the CIAT Data BEPS Monitoring database, accessed on June 2019

attainment of even partial implementation shows strong commitment and potential (depending on the context). Through this disposition, it may be acceptable to disregard the difference between them, considering partial and total implementation together to enhance the visual accessibility of the information. Thus, the amalgamation provides us with the total quantity of Actions being implemented, as seen in Fig. 3.4.

Mexico has considered, at least partially, some of the recommendations from 14 Actions (93%), all except for Action 4. Furthermore, Argentina, Chile, Colombia, and Costa Rica have considered the recommendations suggested in ten of the Actions (67%), while Ecuador and Uruguay are closest behind with seven Actions (46%).

3.5 Opportunities to Improve BEPS Suitability in Developing Countries

As is the case with most innovative approaches, at the start of the OECD/G20 BEPS Project, it was impossible to predict the globally felt ripple effects that would result from this initiative. It is irrefutable that the BEPS project has provided substantial support for governments and tax administrations in the creation of new policies, promoting capacity building, enhancing international cooperation initiatives, and others. Although these BEPS issues are important, a developing country must weigh their various competing demands against their limited resources. For example, the administration may want to prioritize items necessary to control taxpayers such as a taxpayer registry, information systems, collection tools, a transfer pricing regime, and risk analysis tools, among others.

Many developing countries had only general knowledge or limited experience in these topics at the moment when the BEPS Action Plan was being discussed; therefore, their needs may have been underrepresented in this first stage. Nevertheless, all of the topics have an important impact for developed and developing countries whose focus is now on attaining the capacity to achieve effective implementation. For less developed countries, the more prescriptive or "simpler" measures could generate the biggest impact. It will be interesting to see the developments that BEPS continues to inspire as it provides a guided path for advancements in the international tax arena.

The OECD is actively taking measures to overcome any representational bias as countries continue to learn and share their experiences in the groups and international forums provided by them. We expect that, as their experience continues to grow, developing countries will gradually have more influence on the BEPS initiative. Bearing this in mind, the following observations (especially relating to developing country needs) are presented for the evolution and further integration of the BEPS project.

- A stronger focus on Action 11 and complementary concepts that aim to sustain and enhance BEPS in the developing world. For example, by promulgating opportunities for capacity building and technical assistance with the aim to increase domestic expertise.
- Continual training and development programs for all levels (e.g., authorities, tax officials, and those in the judiciary) to improve the decision-making process and the effective implementation of legislations pertaining to BEPS.
- Evaluation of alternatives for the BEPS recommendations that are not feasible in small or low-income developing countries. For example, offering a more simplified approach for administrations who find it difficult to justify spending limited resources on the application of complex measures and costly information regimes.
- A stronger focus on tools that help to increase the effective collection of tax payable. This could allow developing countries to reduce the quantity of tax that has become uncollectible due to the statute of limitations period running out or the onset of a tax holiday.
- Further analysis is necessary in relation to the impact of tax exonerations or holidays that may be found to cause tax base erosion. For example, it could be that Country A does not impose taxation on Company A because they are being taxed on that income in Country B (thereby Country A is avoiding juridical double taxation). However, if Country B then decides to provide a concession to Company A, this could be seen by Country A as an erosion of their tax base.
- A stronger focus on integrated risk management processes would assist tax administrations to determine which taxpayers have a higher risk of BEPS and put the corresponding measures in place to pre-emptively desist such behavior.

- More research in Actions 8–10 regarding the financial industries. This information could assist countries in furthering their understanding of the potential abuses that may arise from the use of inflated remuneration rates for financing services; financing entities; in-house banks; and potential permanent establishment thresholds when a lending entity has a certain share of the national debts.

References

CIATData. (2016). *Double taxation agreements DTA's*. Retrieved from data base on transfer pricing rules and practices in Latin American and Caribbean countries: https://ciatorg. sharepoint.com/sites/cds/_layouts/15/Doc.aspx?sourcedoc=%7Bd447a547-6d55-4cc1-9603-f9659d7d6f31%7D&action=default&slrid=0e2a5a9f-5049-a000-f817-25bf91bf2707& originalPath=aHR0cHM6Ly9jaWF0b3JnLnNoYXJlG9pbnQ uY29tLzp4Oi9zL2Nkcy9FVWVsUjlSVmJJjR
CIATData. (2018a, April). *Anti-abuse rules*. Retrieved from data base on transfer pricing rules and practices in Latin American and Caribbean countries: https://ciatorg.sharepoint.com/:x:/s/cds/ Ec1sSRrEGLxIs5Cxi-Zii3gBh110QfB2Rlo_XTRiQuAHhA?e=pqo1Iu
CIATData. (2018b, April). *General aspects*. Retrieved from data base on transfer pricing rules and practices in Latin American and Caribbean countries: https://ciatorg.sharepoint.com/:x:/s/cds/ ET2u9Wm_Y95DjpyRNCAKRu8BkbEeCAwcAcFOoyp5aouQxg?e=X23CpE
CIATData. (2019). *Transfer pricing in Latin America and the Caribbean: A general overview based on CIATData*. https://biblioteca.ciat.org/opac/book/5689
Hearson, M. (2018). *The European Union's tax treaties with developing countries*. Brussels: GUE/NGL.
OECD. (2019). *About—OECD BEPS*. Retrieved from Organisation for Economic Co-operation and Development: https://www.oecd.org/tax/beps/about/#:~:text=The%20OECD%2FG20% 20Inclusive%20Framework,needed%20to%20tackle%20tax%20avoidance
OECD/G20 Base Erosion and Profit Shifting Project. (2015a). *Aligning transfer pricing outcomes with value creation, actions 8–10—2015. Final reports*. Paris: OECD. Retrieved from https:// doi.org/10.1787/9789264241244
OECD/G20 Base Erosion and Profit Shifting Project. (2015b). *Countering harmful tax practices more effectively, taking into account transparency and substance, action 5—2015. Final report*. Paris: OECD.
OECD/G20 Base Erosion and Profit Shifting Project. (2015c). *Making dispute resolution mechanisms more effective, action 14—2015. Final report*. Paris: OECD.
OECD/G20 Base Erosion and Profit Shifting Project. (2015d). *Measuring and monitoring BEPS, action 11—2015. Final report*. Paris: OECD. Retrieved from https://doi.org/10.1787/ 9789264241343-en
OECD/G20 Base Erosion and Profit Shifting Project. (2015e). *Preventing the granting of treaty benefits in inappropriate circumstances, action 6—2015. Final report*. Paris: OECD.
OECD/G20 Base Erosion and Profit Shifting Project. (2015f). *Transfer pricing documentation and country-by-country reporting, action 13—2015. Final report*. Paris: OECD.

Part II
External Assistance for Tax Capacity Building

Chapter 4
Policy Coherence for Sustainable Development in International Tax Matters: A Way Forward for Donor Countries?

Sathi Meyer-Nandi

4.1 Introduction

4.1.1 Background

The Addis Ababa Action Agenda (AAAA) puts taxation distinctively into the spotlight of the Sustainable Development Goals (SDGs). The mobilization and effective use of domestic resources (DRM) are seen as vital to financing and achieving the SDGs. Efforts by developing countries to improve their DRM capabilities are supported by targeted international assistance (UN 2015, Action area II, A.).The rationale is to help developing countries ultimately help themselves—as more domestic resources gradually lead to less foreign aid dependency. More domestic resources in developing countries also lead to a more stable State, which is capable of providing basic public services, such as health care, infrastructure, and education. Accordingly, large amounts of public resources are allocated to DRM support, covering various areas to broaden and secure the tax base of developing countries. There is additional consensus that low-income countries are disproportionately affected by tax avoidance strategies of multinational corporations [a practice known as "Base Erosion and Profit Shifting" (BEPS)] and tax evasion through undeclared offshore accounts. Tackling BEPS and participating in the global transparency framework (hereafter referred to as "international tax matters") are hence of particular relevance for enhancing revenues in developing countries and a focus area of donor support with enhanced technical assistance [either bilaterally

All opinions expressed in the paper are those of the author in her private capacity.

S. Meyer-Nandi (✉)
GIZ GmbH, Bonn, Germany

I. J. Mosquera Valderrama et al. (eds.), *Taxation, International Cooperation and the 2030 Sustainable Development Agenda*, United Nations University Series on Regionalism 19, https://doi.org/10.1007/978-3-030-64857-2_4

between donor and partner country or through supporting capacity building programs from international organizations[1] (e.g., OECD, UN, World Bank, or IMF)].

To put the political commitment of donors into perspective, or even better, into numbers, 20 donor countries alone have explicitly declared to double their 2015 support for DRM of over USD215 million until 2020. The commitment amounts to over USD430 million by 2020 of gross disbursements for DRM support (ATI 2019, p. 12). These commitments for spending public money are not insignificant in scale but well justified if it constitutes the catalyst to create self-sufficiency. However, given this scale, enhanced policy coherence can go a long way, ensuring that public money is well spent.

4.1.2 What Is Policy Coherence for Sustainable Development (PCSD)?

PCSD requires a holistic evaluation of all national policies—including the tax policy—concerning their impact on the achievement of the SDGs for all stakeholders. Many countries consider PCSD as a critical means to manage potential trade-offs, promote synergies, and reduce inefficient spending. Hence, all countries explicitly agreed to incorporate the enhancement of PCSD as a focal point for implementing the 2030 Agenda [as inter alia enshrined in Target 17.14 of the AAAA and in Commitment 3 in the Addis Tax Initiative (ATI)].

This commitment ensures that aid spending is not "wasted" by competing policies as it presupposes that government considers development goals working toward all other national policies. The whole government, beyond foreign affairs, development ministries, and aid agencies, needs to be engaged in this endeavor to manage tensions and synergies between different sectoral, domestic, and international policies. Other relevant stakeholders such as civil society and private sector should ideally also be included in this dialogue.

One should bear in mind that PCSD does not prescribe full coherence, an impossible endeavor anyway. Nor, does the rule dictate that development objectives trump every other national policy. It should rather be seen as a mechanism to facilitate dialogue for informed weighing and balancing of different policy decisions with the goal that public money is spent prudently.

---

[1]See, for instance, the OECD's technical assistance projects on international tax issues: OECD (2019).

4.1.3 Why Is PCSD so Important in the Area of International Tax Matters?

PCSD in international tax matters helps to ensure that the vast amount of resources allocated to helping developing countries mobilize more revenues are supported and not de facto cancelled out by national tax policy choices of donor countries. Some choices on tax policy and tax administration of donor countries create strong interactions with these international tax matters in developing countries (IMF 2014, p. 1). These choices have ramifications on the tax base in developing countries as well as the cooperation modalities between the tax administrations. This is why technical assistance alone should not be the only means to increase DRM in developing countries. Donor countries need to review their own national tax policy and administrative practices to better identify negative or positive spillovers on the tax base of developing countries.

4.1.4 Rational and Structure of the Chapter

In practice, the genuine implementation of PCSD in the area of international tax matters has some room for improvement. Though civil servants agree that giving with one hand but taking with the other is inefficient and that seeking synergies between different policy areas is a good thing to do, the holistic dialogue between all relevant ministries and stakeholders is often missing.

Different ministries and stakeholders speak different languages, which can be a big obstacle for a holistic dialogue particularly in such a technical subject matter, such as international taxation. Additionally, the different stakeholders have different understandings on what benefits sustainable development. This is why PCSD is often lost in translation. It stays a concept which—despite being internationally endorsed—constitutes the neglected hot potato civil servants do not want to touch.

What is however often forgotten is that PCSD is not a zero-sum game. Adjusting policies more toward development objectives can also be beneficial for other policy goals. Accordingly, having mechanism in place for inclusive dialogue among all stakeholders on international tax matters can bring useful ideas, which go beyond "do no harm to developing countries" but can also be beneficial for the national industry of the donor country.

Against this backdrop, this chapter is devoted to potential measures of donor countries to better align their tax policy with their development effort in the area of international tax. These measures aim at raising the revenues in developing countries while also contributing to a positive investment climate. Accordingly, Part II will primarily focus on establishing a policy for tax treaties with developing countries, which enhance source taxation and tax certainty. Part III includes domestic measures to enhance transparency in developing countries which go beyond the internationally agreed standards on exchange of information. Part IV elaborates on mechanisms to enhance cooperation between the tax administration of the donor and partner country, to provide better skill transfer while boosting tax certainty for companies.

4.2 Donor's Tax Treaty Policy Toward Developing Countries

4.2.1 Background

In principle the rationale of Double Tax Treaties (DTTs) is to increase tax certainty and avoid double taxation for cross-border activities of taxpayers. They foster bigger certainty as they set limits to the taxation of cross-border investments through allocating taxing rights between the foreign direct investment (FDI) recipient country—generally in fiscal terms referred to as the source country—and the residence country of the investor. DTTs are responsible for mitigating double taxation by "harmonizing tax definitions, defining taxable bases, assigning taxing jurisdictions, and indicating the mechanisms to be used to remove double taxation when it arises" (Baker 2012, p. 2 referring to UNCTAD 2011).

However, an important feature of DTTs is that they have a bias in favor of the residence state. They tend to shift taxing powers from the source state to the residence state. This bias does not have to be problematic if two treaty partners are involved with largely symmetrical investment pattern (Braun and Zahler 2017, p. 2). However when two countries have an asymmetrical investment position—as is generally the case between developing and industrialized country—this shift in taxing powers implies a significant loss of tax base for the source country (Rixen and Schwarz 2009).

Developing countries are mainly net capital importing countries, with the capital streaming predominantly from industrialized countries into their economy and capital income flowing the other way around. Hence, the limitation on source country taxing powers to the benefit of the residence country brings about the disadvantage of revenue foregone from restricted source country taxation next to the cost of treaty negotiation and administration (Keen and Mullins 2017, pp. 11–41).

Hence, the question is does the DTT realize sufficient net gains from increased FDI to neutralize the revenue losses? The answer is one does not know. Conclusive empirical evidence on the investment effects of treaties is missing, since identifying causality (between the conclusion of the treaty and the resulting increased FDI) is inherently problematic (Hearson 2018).[2] However what has become increasingly prevalent and perceived as problematic is the issue of developing countries losing tax revenues due to the conclusion of tax treaties.

---

[2]Also Appendix V of the IMF (2014) paper provides an analysis of different studies undertaken on the correlation of treaties and the increase of FDI.

Additionally, next to the reduction of tax revenues due to the limitation of source taxation, DTTs also limit the policy space of developing countries to legislate feasible measures against BEPS. Due to administrative capacity restraints, potential responses against base erosion and profit shifting, which resulted out of the OECD BEPS project, might not be administrable for some developing countries.

For instance, excessive use of deductible payments to foreign affiliated companies in form of interest, service charges, insurance premiums, management fees, and royalties has been identified as one of the key base erosion causes in developing countries (G20 2014; Oguttu 2017, pp. 35–36). Although not being officially addressed in the BEPS Project, withholding taxes have often been considered the most suitable means for developing countries against this tax avoidance technique (IMF 2014, pp. 33–34; UN Report 2013, p. 11).

Withholding taxes do not compensate entirely the loss of income stripping since mostly the withholding tax rates are lower than the corporate income tax rate. They should also not be excessive, since they are levied on gross basis and can increase the cost of capital. However, they constitute a workable backstop and tax base protection mechanism, which should not be neutralized via the tax treaty (Shay 2017, pp. 65–66).

4.2.2 Domestic Measures of Donor Countries

4.2.2.1 Create a Policy for Tax Treaties with Developing Countries

When DRM is a priority area of donor countries, it is desirable that their tax treaty policy toward their partner countries reflects this aim—if coherence is an aspiration. Accordingly, donor countries should create a formal policy; they openly pledge to adhere to when entering into tax treaty negotiations with developing countries and when reviewing existing ones.

When designing the policy, it is important to engage the whole government, significant players in the economy, civil society, academia, and developing countries which constitute a particular focus of the donor's aid program. Accordingly, the ministry of finance, treasury—or whoever is responsible for tax treaties—should engage foreign affairs, the development ministry, and aid agency in the dialogue. Other relevant stakeholders such as civil society, academia, and the private sector should share their viewpoints on how the policy should look like and the expected effect on DRM and the investment climate.

The policy should go beyond a mere communication of a country's willingness to accept broader permanent establishment concepts, higher withholding tax rates at source, parts of the UN Model, as well as anti-abuse measures for tax treaties with developing countries which receive aid.[3] In a holistic forum of communication among all relevant stakeholders, the tax policy strategy should have the aim to provide for higher source-based taxation, foster tax certainty, and avoid double taxation through fully crediting the higher source-based taxation and stronger cooperation between both tax administrations.

Accordingly, the box below depicts contemplations regarding source taxation, tax certainty, and the avoidance of double taxation, which should be considered by donor countries in their endeavor to create a tax treaty policy toward developing countries.

More Source Taxation

- Tax treaty should be customized to the domestic legal framework of the developing country, with the aim to make sure that the treaty uphelds domestic source taxation to the biggest extent possible.
- As a practical anti-base erosion measure, when domestic law provides withholding taxes on deductible payments, such as on services fees and insurance premiums, the treaty should not inhibit this fiscal space. More nuanced withholding tax policy can rather be adressed via domestic law (supported by technical assistance of donor countries) and not through restrictions on treaty level.
- Customize your treaty to the specific circumstances of the country. For instance, if the country often provides tax holidays, including higher dividend withholding taxes, which only apply, when the distributed income has been subject to a tax holiday, could be an option. Also tax sparing provisions should be considered when appropirate.

Tax Certainty

- Are domestic law provisions, such as the permanent establishement definitions, outdated and hence result in uncertainty in their application, especially in connection with their interplay with the tax treaty? In such cases technical assistance could be provided to update domestic law to better reflect international standards.
- What is the experience of business regarding the tax framework of the country and its administration? What were the main challenges, which could be adressed via the treaty to provide more tax certainty?
- Strenghten the cooperation modalities between both tax administrations through enhanced cooperation arrangements (establishing bilateral safe harbours, bilateral APA programmes, enhanced knowledge sharing, simultansous tax audits, etc.).

No Double Taxation

- Donor countries should try to provide a full tax credit on the higher source taxation, so that it does not have a negative effect on the investment climate.
- Donors need to calculate whether the resulting tax expenditure on their side is sustainable and maybe need to coordinate between ministry of finance and the development ministry to credit some of these expenses to the development budget if necessary.

---

[3]These communications are mostly directed at countries which appear on the Development Assistance Committee (DAC) List as countries and territories eligible to receive official development assistance (ODA). The list consists of all low- and middle-income countries based on World Bank data on gross national income per capita.

4.3 Transparency

4.3.1 Background

The late US Justice Louis Brandeis famously stated, "sunlight is the best disinfectant." Correspondingly, an important mechanism for the elimination of tax avoidance and evasion is transparency. Transparency through the exchange of information on a global scale helps to avoid information asymmetries though enhancing a more transparent global tax footprint. Particularly for developing countries, it constitutes an important tool to inhibit the loss of revenues from assets held offshore or misrepresented cross-border activities. The G20 and the OECD's Global Forum on Transparency and Exchange of Information for Tax Purposes (the Global Forum) were the driving force to improve transparency through setting global standards for information sharing around the world. The OECD has developed two complementary international standards: the Exchange of Information on Request (EOIR) and the Automatic Exchange of Financial Account Information (AEOI).

- The EOIR standard calls for exchange of information to the widest extent possible. Subject to having the respective legal basis in place, information that is "foreseeably relevant" for tax purposes is made available and accessible between tax authorities. The exchangeable information includes the identity of the beneficial owners of companies and other legal entities; arrangements such as partnerships and trusts; accounting information; and bank account information.[4]
- AEOI standard takes the cooperation a step further. It requires the systematic and periodic transmission of "bulk" taxpayer information by the source country to the residence country in a common reporting format or standard. Local banks and financial institutions of participating countries are required to obtain information on financial accounts, which they make available to the local tax authorities; they, in turn, provide that information on an automatic basis to other countries in a standardized format (without the need for sending a specific request) (OECD 2014b).

The OECD's Global Forum provides customized technical assistance programs to help developing countries implement both standards to counter tax evasion. The technical assistance is offered in various forms delivered on-site and off-site and in collaboration with other partners (e.g., other international organizations, development banks, or donor countries). The assistance is targeted to establishing the required legal framework (domestic law and treaties) and the practical organizational arrangements to be able to make use of the international transparency standards.[5]

---

[4]For more information on the EOIR, please consult OECD (2016).

[5]More information on the different technical assistance programs can be found in the OECD's work on tax and development under OECD (2019).

4.3.2 Domestic Measures of Donor Countries

4.3.2.1 Review the Domestic Transparency Framework

The first measure of donor countries is to make sure that their network of exchange relationships covers all relevant developing countries (at least those developing countries, which are recipients of aid programs by the donor). The legal framework in place can either be based on bilateral instruments [DTTs or Tax Information Exchange Agreements (TIEA)] or multilateral mechanisms, such as the Mutual Administrative Assistance Convention. Hence, a gap analysis could first be conducted to see whether the coverage is sufficient and if not how to close these gaps in the most resource efficient way for the developing country.

Additionally, detecting hidden offshore wealth through exchange of information requires the availability of relevant information. This is why, also from a policy coherence perspective, it is vital that donor countries have domestically all required information available. The identity of legal and beneficial owners of bank account, relevant entities, and arrangements, as well as the accounting information for these entities, needs to be at disposal. It requires effective enforcement provisions to make sure that those responsible for collecting this information do the relevant due diligence. The accuracy of the information and the compliance need to be monitored with penalties in place, which sufficiently deter non-compliance.

4.3.2.2 Disclosing Aggregate Data

It will still take time, and a multitude of assistance before AEOI becomes viable for developing countries. Until then, the EOIR will be the instrument to obtain cross-border information. The disadvantage of EOIR is that tax authorities need to be aware of a tax evader and link the evasion to a specific jurisdiction to request the missing information from this jurisdiction. However, obtaining this preliminary evidence when one has limited resources available can be difficult. This is where the sharing of de-identified aggregate data about financial accounts held in donor countries can be beneficial. Such information could be published each year depicting totals by country of origin held in the donor country (Knobel and Meinzer 2017, pp. 37–39).

To date, many countries have spontaneously shared aggregate data with their treaty partners on various types of income, such as the existence and amount of foreign-owned accounts in their jurisdiction. The Global Forum stated that G20 and other developed countries may consider spontaneously sharing aggregate data with a specific developing country. The purpose of this would be:

> to build awareness of AEOI, to demonstrate possible revenue benefits and increase the prioritisation of AEOI, and to obtain political commitment to AEOI. (G20 2014, p. 22)

One step further to the spontaneous sharing of aggregated data with treaty partners is to simply publish de-identified aggregated information about accounts held in the country (as Australia and Switzerland are already doing).[6] Given that only totals by country of origin would be published, no confidentiality rules would be breached. The big advantage of such measure is that it allows both countries not constituting treaty partners as well as civil society to find out basic information about their residents' holdings abroad. Such a measure helps developing countries to allocate their scarce resources more effectively. It gives tax administrations in developing countries directly the information in which countries their residents held the biggest amount of offshore assets. This is helpful to channel the attention of a tax authority to a certain jurisdiction to request information from.

It can also increase political pressure on government in developing countries to more effectively fight against tax evasion, as it provides more transparency on the scale of offshore assets. The increased pressure on politicians can be especially beneficial in developing countries, in which the political or economic elite opposes the introduction of AEOI, due to their own exposure to undeclared offshore money. Transparency in general also helps the population of a developing country to estimate whether the tax rules and administration in their country are functional or need revision.

4.4 International Cooperation/Administrative Assistance

4.4.1 Background

Base erosion through abusive transfer pricing is considered a major risk for developing countries. The limited capacity and the lack of information in order to apply adequate transfer pricing rules have been identified as a key BEPS issue in developing countries (G20 2014, p. 10). Many resources are allocated to strengthening transfer pricing capacity. For instance, the Platform for Collaboration on Tax and Tax Inspectors Without Borders all have activities in place to improve the transfer pricing regimes in developing countries and to enhance their audit capacity.[7] However, the World Bank pointed out that building transfer pricing expertise is not a short-term endeavor and that country experience suggests that institution building for effective transfer pricing audit skills takes a minimum of 3–5 years (Cooper et al. 2016, p. xix).

Next to the base erosion in developing countries, also tax uncertainty on behalf of business is exacerbated by the tax administration's limited experience in transfer pricing. This often leads to highly unpredictable tax outcomes, which have a negative impact on the investment climate in the country.

More agile mechanisms for collaboration between tax administrations of donor and developing country can play an important role to firstly rectify the information

---

[6]For more information on Australia's amended bill, see Tax Justice Network (2016).

[7]For more information see the progress report of the Platform For Collaboration on Tax (2019).

asymmetry of some auditors in developing countries, increase industry-specific know-how, and transfer pricing (TP) capacity. At the same time, tax certainty can be boosted for businesses of the donor country, which want to invest in the developing country. The legal basis for this enhanced cooperation can already be found in most current tax treaties—if they include the international standard of exchange of information, TIEAs or the Mutual Administrative Assistance Convention.

4.4.2 Domestic Measures of Donor Countries

While ensuring that all exchanges of information are in accordance with the provisions of an effective bilateral or multilateral tax convention, agile and enhanced modalities for cooperation between tax administrations should be created. In the process of designing these modalities, again the whole government, significant players in the economy, civil society, academia, and developing countries which constitute a particular focus of the donor's aid program should be included in the design process. In an inclusive dialogue, these modalities should feed into the aim to enhance DRM in developing countries and increase technical capacity as well as tax certainty for businesses for a better investment climate. Some modalities are suggested below.

4.4.2.1 Specific Working Agreements Between Tax Administrations Including Joint Tax Audits and Safe Harbors

Donor countries could conclude a special working agreement or memorandum of understanding (MoU) with the tax administration in a developing country treaty partner, setting forth the details for enhanced cooperation and discussion (Meyer-Nandi 2018, p. 54). Donor countries could agree to periodically share generic industry knowledge (e.g., information concerning whole economic sectors, such as the oil or pharmaceutical industry, the banking sector, etc.) if this is helpful for the partner country to better understand value chains in specific sectors.[8] It should enable a platform to intensify and facilitate practical discussion on transfer pricing methods or comparability analysis between the tax administration of the developing country and the donor. To avoid disputes from arising, joint tax audit programs can be created, to jointly determine the facts and circumstances of cross-border cases.

These MoUs can also include bilateral safe harbors acceptable for both tax administrations. A safe harbor is a simplified regime that applies to a defined category of taxpayers or transactions. It enables eligible taxpayers to establish transfer prices by applying, for instance, a simplified transfer pricing approach

---

[8]Para. 6.1 OECD Model: Commentary on Article 26 (2014).

provided by the tax administration.[9] In the case of bilateral safe harbors, two or more[10] tax administrations by means of competent authority agreements define together a category of taxpayer and/or transactions and establish pricing parameters (i.e., the safe harbor) that would be acceptable to both countries.[11] This bilateral agreement largely reduces the risk of potential double taxation or double non-taxation, which could arise under unilateral safe harbors. The OECD created a sample agreement for common categories of transfer pricing cases involving low-risk distribution functions, low-risk manufacturing functions, and low-risk research and development (R&D) functions.[12] These sample safe harbors can be used as a starting point and modified to the specific country context and relationship between donor and developing country.

The "development-friendly" safe harbors should be established in close collaboration with business and civil society for specific transactions and functions, particularly relevant in the country context of the developing country. Ultimately, the rational of the bilateral safe harbors should be to provide a means of protecting the local tax base in the developing country in common transfer pricing fact patterns without a burdensome enforcement effort. At the same time, they need to reduce the compliance cost of the taxpayer and increase tax certainty.

4.4.2.2 Bilateral Advanced Pricing Agreements (APAs)

Bilateral APA programs between donor and developing countries could be a practical solution to enhance tax certainty for business while also speeding up the capacity building process of tax administrations (Meyer-Nandi 2018, pp. 57–59). Additionally, having the donor's tax administration present would provide more checks and balances during the negotiations and neutralize the knowledge asymmetry potentially present in unilateral APA negotiations only between multinational enterprises and a developing country tax administration. These bilateral negotiations, interactions, and cooperation between two tax administrations alleviate double taxation of the multinational taxpayer's income. It also provides an avenue for countries to quickly get up to speed on international practices while defending their tax base and increasing bilateral cooperation.[13]

In the course of the negotiation, the two tax administrations obviously have an incentive to opt each for a point of view that maximizes their revenue collection. In bilateral APAs with developing countries, a policy could be adopted by the donor to be more beneficial to developing countries. Tax administrations from the donor

---

[9]Sec. E.2. OECD Transfer Pricing Guidelines (2017).

[10]Then the safe harbor is called "multilateral safe harbor."

[11]Para. 4.117., OECD Transfer Pricing Guidelines (2017).

[12]Annex I to Chapter IV, OECD Transfer Pricing Guidelines (2017).

[13]More information on the advantages of bilateral APAs in comparison to unilateral ones can be found in Cooper et al. (2016, p. 321).

could, for instance, heed so-called location-specific advantages in the allocation of profit to attribute a bigger share of profit to the developing country.[14]

4.5 Concluding Words

The aim of this chapter is to provide civil servants with some food for thought how to improve PCSD in the area of international tax matters and to demonstrate that PCSD is not a zero-sum game. Adjusting the tax policy of a donor country more toward development objectives can foster DRM in developing countries while also being beneficial for the industry of the donor country itself. The aspiration of the author is that donor countries will create the necessary platform for an inclusive dialogue on this neglected topic. Engaging all relevant ministries and stakeholders (business, civil society, and academia) to work on a domestic strategy how to better increase PCSD in the area of international tax matters can bring new ideas, promote informed decision making, and aid effectiveness. Having an inclusive dialogue on such a technical subject matter is not an easy endeavor indeed. However, it is necessary to start it, as it does not only affect the taxes in developing countries but also the taxpayers in donor countries. The taxpayer in the donor country is the financier of civil servants and their policies. Against this background, civil servants owe a genuine dialogue on PCSD in the area of international tax matters to their taxpayers, as it improves prudent public spending.

References

G20 Sources

G20. (2014). *Two-part report to G20 developing working group on the impact of BEPS in low income countries* (p. 43). Retrieved from http://www.oecd.org/tax/tax-global/report-to-g20-dwg-on-the-impact-of-beps-in-low-income-countries.pdf

OECD Sources

OECD. (2014a). *Model tax convention on income and on capital: Condensed version 2014*. Paris: OECD. https://doi.org/10.1787/mtc_cond-2014-en

---

[14]For more information on location-specific advantages, see Sec. B.8.11.5., UN Practical Manual on Transfer Pricing for Developing Countries (2017); a similar example is also described on India in Sec. B.8.1.14. and Cooper et al. (2016, p. 218).

OECD. (2014b). *Standard for automatic exchange of financial account information in tax matters.* Paris: OECD. Retrieved from https://doi.org/10.1787/9789264216525-en

OECD. (2016). *Exchange of information on request—Handbook for peer reviews 2016–2020.* Retrieved from https://www.oecd.org/tax/transparency/global-forum-handbook-2016.pdf

OECD. (2017). *OECD transfer pricing guidelines for multinational enterprises and tax administrations 2017.* Paris: OECD. Retrieved from https://doi.org/10.1787/tpg-2017-en

OECD. (2019). *OECD work on tax and development—2018–2019.* Retrieved from http://www.oecd.org/tax/tax-global/brochure-oecd-work-on-tax-and-development.pdf

UN Sources

UN. (2015). *Addis Ababa Action Agenda of the third international conference on financing for development (Addis Ababa Action Agenda).* A/RES/69/313.

UN. (2017). *Practical manual on transfer pricing for developing countries.* New York: UN.

UN Report. (2013, January 28–29). *Group meetings on "Capacity building on tax treaty negotiation and administration".* Rome.

Other Sources from International Organizations

ATI. (2019). *ATI monitoring report 2017.* Retrieved from https://www.addistaxinitiative.net/sites/default/files/resources/2019-ATI-Monitoring-Report-2017.pdf

IMF. (2014). *Spillovers in international corporate taxation.* Washington, DC: International Monetary Fund. Retrieved from http://www.imf.org/external/np/pp/eng/2014/050914.pdf

Platform For Collaboration on Tax. (2019). *PCT progress report 2018–2019.* Retrieved from http://documents.worldbank.org/curated/en/702411559936259607/pdf/Platform-for-Collaboration-on-Tax-PCT-Progress-Report-2018-2019.pdf

UNCTAD. (2011). *World investment report. Non-equity modes of international production and development.* New York: United Nations.

Journals and Other Articles

Baker, P. (2012). *An analysis of double tax treaties and their effect on foreign direct investment.* Retrieved from http://www2.warwick.ac.uk/fac/soc/economics/news_events/conferences/peuk12/paul_l__baker_dtts_on_fdi_23_may_2012.pdf

Braun, J., & Zahler, M. (2017). *The true art of the tax deal: Evidence on aid flows and bilateral double tax agreements.* Discussion Paper No. 17-011, Zentrum für Europäische Wirtschaftsforschung GmbH. Retrieved from http://ftp.zew.de/pub/zew-docs/dp/dp17011.pdf

Cooper, J., Fox, R., Loeprick, J., & Mohindra, K. (2016). *Transfer pricing and developing economies—A handbook for policy makers and practitioners.* Washington, DC: World Bank Group.

Hearson, M. (2018). WHEN do developing countries negotiate away their corporate tax base? *Journal of International Development, 30,* 233–255.

Keen, M., & Mullins, P. (2017). *International corporate taxation and the extractive industries: Principles, practice, problems.* In P. Daniel, M. Keen, A. Swistak, & V. Thuronyi (Eds.), *International taxation and the extractive industries.* London: Routledge.

Knobel, A., & Meinzer, M. (2017). *Delivering a level playing field for offshore bank accounts— What the new OECD/Global Forum peer review on automatic information exchange must not miss.* Tax Justice Network. Retrieved from https://www.taxjustice.net/wp-content/uploads/2013/04/TJN_AIE_ToR_Mar-1-2017.pdf

Meyer-Nandi, S. (2018). *Swiss policy coherence in international taxation: Global trends in AEOI and BEPS in development assistance and a Swiss way forward* (p. 54). Retrieved September 28, 2019, from https://www.shareweb.ch/site/Development-Policy/Documents/formAttachments/20181005_DEZA-Final_WorkingPaper_corrected.pdf

Oguttu, W. (2017). *Tax base erosion and profit shifting in Africa—Part 2: A critique of some priority OECD actions from an African perspective.* Working Paper 65, International Centre for Tax and Development.

Rixen, T., & Schwarz, P. (2009). Bargaining over the avoidance of double taxation: Evidence from German tax treaties. *Finanzarchiv/Public Finance Analysis, 65*(4), 442–471.

Shay, S. E. (2017). An overview of transfer pricing in extractive industries. In P. Daniel, M. Keen, A. Swistak, & V. Thuronyi (Eds.), *International taxation and the extractive industries.* London: Routledge.

Tax Justice Network. (2016). *Australia passes new information sharing provision.* Retrieved from http://www.taxjustice.net/2016/02/24/15031/

Chapter 5
Medium-Term Revenue Strategies as a Coordination Tool for DRM and Tax Capacity Building

Wouter Lips and Dries Lesage

5.1 Introduction

This chapter will study the introduction of "Medium-Term Revenue Strategies" (MTRS) in developing countries. An initiative of the Platform for Collaboration on Tax (PCT), a network organization between the International Monetary Fund (IMF), World Bank, Organisation for Economic Co-operation and Development (OECD), and United Nations (UN). Low-income countries (LICs) and least-developed countries (LDCs) face a myriad of challenges when it comes to Domestic Revenue Mobilization (DRM) for achieving the Sustainable Development Goals (SDGs). One such challenge is effective taxation, both domestic and international, which encompasses policy design—also with regard to economic and gender inequality, enforcement, and anti-abuse measures. LICs and LDCs often lack the technical or administrative capacity to realize their domestic revenue potential and as such miss out on societal investments that could help drive forward the SDGs. The SDG investment gap, or the difference between current investment and the level of investment needed to achieve the SDGs, is estimated by UNCTAD to be USD2.5 trillion. According to the World Bank, between 50 and 80% of this gap will have to be bridged with domestic government resources with the rest coming from official development aid (ODA), private funding, and private capital (Niculescu 2017).

As such, it makes sense for donor governments to try and leverage some of their official development aid (ODA) into programs that help improve taxation efforts in developing countries. Taxation has always been a part of development aid efforts. The IMF, for example, has been working on tax in developing countries

W. Lips · D. Lesage (✉)
Department of Political Sciences, Ghent Institute for International Studies, Ghent University, Ghent, Belgium
e-mail: Wouter.Lips@Ugent.be; Dries.Lesage@Ugent.be

© The Author(s) 2021
I. J. Mosquera Valderrama et al. (eds.), *Taxation, International Cooperation and the 2030 Sustainable Development Agenda*, United Nations University Series on Regionalism 19, https://doi.org/10.1007/978-3-030-64857-2_5

since the 1960s. However, the issue of tax capacity building has been gaining more attention on the international agenda since the turn of the millennium. The link between taxation capacity building and development was featured prominently in all three UN Financing for Development conference outcomes[1] and was also a pillar of the G20's 2010 Multi-Year Action Plan (G20 2010).

Aid and tax capacity building for DRM are one strategy to achieve that link between tax and development. Both bilateral and multilateral donors are involved in this field. Overall commitments to DRM in 2016 amounted to about USD380 million, of which USD47 million channelled through multilateral institutions (International Tax Compact 2018a). Yet, there are several issues with the fragmentation and coordination of these tax capacity building (TCB) initiatives. Because of a lack of steering, there are issues with duplication of efforts or conflictive advice when multiple organizations are active within a developing country (IMF et al. 2017). One concrete example the authors encountered during interviews was when a number of regional tax organizations were developing guidance on tax incentives independently from each other, whereas they could have pooled their efforts.

To this end, there has been a trend toward more coordination in this specific aid regime. Bilateral donors have organized themselves, together with partner countries, in the Addis Tax Initiative (ATI), a body developed to monitor the pledge of donors to double aid for DRM efforts by 2020. It is housed in Bonn where the International Tax Compact, an offspring from the 2008 Doha FFD conference, serves as its secretariat. Since 2018, the ITC also supports the Network of Tax Organisations (NTO) which brings together the regional tax organizations. On the multilateral side, there is the Platform for Collaboration on Tax (created in 2016) whose membership comprises the International Monetary Fund (IMF), the World Bank (WB), the Organisation for Economic Co-operation and Development (OECD), and the United Nations Development Program (UNDP).

These are all examples of high-level coordination, mostly among donors. While this certainly could help with the international coordination of efforts, there is still a need for a coordination mechanism at partner country level when providing aid for DRM. Not only should there be careful attention to aligning all partners in a given country; DRM aid efforts should also respect the local context in a country and make sure that the efforts match the needs of a developing country and that its program is widely supported in its local political context. Otherwise there is a distinct risk of top-down one-size-fits-all approaches to DRM that are not in the interest of developing countries. The international community recognized this hurdle, which is why the PCT developed the concept of Medium-Term Revenue Strategies (MTRS) in 2016 (IMF et al. 2016). The concept is still in an early stage but holds potential.

In this chapter, we take a critical look at the MTRS concept. After a detailed explanation of the concept, we examine what its opportunities are and which needs it can fill. We then examine the potential pitfalls of the concept. Next, we look at the evolution of the concept, how it is currently applied, and how the partners are

---

[1]Monterey, 2002; Doha, 2008; Addis Ababa, 2015.

viewing the concept at the time of writing. Finally, we summarize our findings in a conclusion, before making some policy recommendations on how the concept could be better applied.

5.2 What Is an MTRS?

The purpose of an MTRS is supposed to be a holistic high-level roadmap for tax policy reform over 4–6 years. It should outline a country's revenue needs and gather political support from multiple actors in politics, civil society, and development partners. This can make it seem attractive for many countries that wish to improve their domestic revenue mobilization efforts and for developing partners as a coordination tool.

The first key component of the framework is setting clear *revenue goals* for a country (IMF et al. 2017). This can be expressed as a fixed amount of revenue the country wants to raise or as a desired increase of the tax to GDP ratio. It should be related to expenditure projections. Other goals can be set as well to fit the strategy. Improving the progressiveness and fairness of the tax system in a country might be one example. Reducing compliance costs and improving the perception of the tax system can be valid goals as well. These goals serve as guidelines for the other components' design and as a steering and evaluation tool for the success of the MTRS. There is a clear link here between the SDGs and the MTRS, as the set revenue goals can be tailored as a function of the public spending and investment needs in a country to reach the SDGs.

The second, and perhaps most important, component is an overview of the *taxation-related reforms* to achieve those set policy goals (De Mooij et al. 2018). These are broken down into three parts. The first is a reform of tax policies. This requires an extensive diagnosis of a country's current tax policy practices and will typically cover most forms of taxes: personal income taxes, corporate income taxes, property taxes, value-added or consumption taxes, and excises and duties. Countries can choose to alter the rates or bases of any of those taxes, remove or introduce exemptions and incentives, reduce thresholds, or introduce new forms of taxes. Although not explicitly mentioned, this could in theory also link to international taxation initiatives such as the G20/OECD Base Erosion and Profit Shifting (BEPS) Project and its four minimum standards. A second part under this component is tax administration reform. This is to ensure that the tax policy can be adequately implemented and to increase taxpayers' compliance, which is a core component of DRM efforts. The 2017 PCT update mentions that in many developing countries (especially LDCs), the revenue administration needs modernization (IMF et al. 2017). This can range from redesigned organizational structures to ICT improvements. However, reforming tax administrations has not always been a priority for countries in the past (IMF et al. 2017), and it is not the "sexiest" political reform. For this reason, widespread support of the revenue goals among civil society is a prerequisite for successfully achieving those necessary reforms. A last part here is legal framework reforms to ensure taxpayer certainty. This potentially includes an investigation of the balance between taxpayers' rights and the revenue administrations' powers.

A third component is *country commitment* to the MTRS. This component underscores the importance that the revenue goals and reforms are country-owned and tailored toward its specific needs. The highest levels of government, including the head of government and minister of finance, should ensure the necessary political support for a whole-of-government approach. The PCT recommends a reform management approach, including an accountable executive sponsor, steering committee, and management team, in order to oversee the process and sustain political support throughout the MTRS implementation method.

The last component of the MTRS is *organizing external partners* around the goals set out in the previous three components. This is the capacity building assistance component. Not only is this important to make sure all donor partners' work is coordinated, but it can also serve to ensure adequate funding for the realization of the MTRS.

The concept is still in an early phase. At the time of writing, less than 20 countries are involved in an MTRS. Only Papua New Guinea is in the early implementation phase, with all other countries still in the design or even early formulation phase:

- Early implementation: Papua New Guinea (PNG)
- Formulation support: Egypt, Indonesia, Lao PDR, Pakistan, Thailand, Uganda
- Dialogue pre-formulation: Albania, Bangladesh, Benin, Ethiopia, Georgia, Honduras, Jordan, Mongolia, Myanmar, Senegal, Uzbekistan, Vietnam (Platform for Collaboration on Tax 2019)

5.3 The Added Value of MTRS in the Multilateral Tax Capacity Building Framework

5.3.1 A Crowded Global Governance Field

Taxation is the most importance resource for state capacity. Taxation and DRM in general are also attractive concepts for donors as they promise large leverage effects of the initial aid investments, especially during a decade of increased aid fatigue due to dwindling government budgets. The relatively small amount of money flows (USD380 million) that go worldwide to aid for DRM seems puzzling in this regard. A few things help to explain this. First of all, the actual costs of technical assistance programs are relatively cheap. It mostly consists of detaching various tax experts to developing countries for training programs, policy evaluation, etc. The costs here involve flight tickets, accommodation, and so forth, but rarely entail infrastructural programs—unless IT infrastructure is part of the program, as the World Bank offers sometimes. The real costs for donor states, however, are the opportunity costs from having to miss these experts. If a country detaches one of its top transfer pricing experts through the OECD/UNDP Tax Inspectors Without Borders program for several months, for example, it might miss out on revenue itself. A second, more nefarious reason is that not all policymakers are so inclined to separate aid relationships from foreign policy goals. During interviews, one senior interviewee with the aid agency of an OECD country mentioned that, in the past, several members of parliament sitting on aid-related committees oppose reductions of traditional aid budgets because the latter functions as a tool of foreign policy (personal interview, 2017). A third reason is that aid budgets in many countries are traditionally earmarked for specific sectors, such as education or infrastructure, which represent vested interests in the sector. Funds for DRM work have to come from discretionary sources which tend to be rather small (personal interview, 2017).

Currently, the international framework for TCB and tax capacity building is a crowded field with many players. The first and money-wise largest group of actors providing aid for DRM are donor countries themselves. In 2016, France was the biggest provider of core DRM aid followed by the USA and the UK (International Tax Compact 2018a). Under the Addis Tax Initiative, donor countries, in 2015, pledged to double money for tax capacity support, following the Addis Ababa conference (Addis Tax Initiative 2015). This signals that TCB is gaining traction within national development agencies. However, following a significant increase in OECD DAC-reported commitments from USD175 million in 2015 to 330 million in 2016,[2] in 2017 the commitments were down to 192 million again (OECD 2019).

A second group of players are the multilateral institutions. In 2016, the IMF represented about 64% of the multilateral money committed to DRM efforts (International Tax Compact 2018a). Technical assistance is the biggest chunk of the IMF's Fiscal Affairs department tax work and part of its core mandate. In this context, it also manages the Revenue Mobilization Thematic Fund (RMTF) that allows donors to pool TCB resources. The IMF is also involved in the Tax Administration Diagnostic Assessment Tool (TADAT), together with the World Bank and a group of bilateral donors, and hosts its secretariat. It has also joined the International Survey on Revenue Administration (ISORA)[3] with the OECD and regional tax organizations.

Another large direct technical assistance provider is the World Bank Group. The work of the WB is more aimed at long-term development and departs from a more holistic view than the IMF which works on financial-economic issues only. The World Bank tax work can, for example, be linked to health issues through technical assistance on tobacco taxes. It is also involved in more long-term investments, such as in ICT for tax administrations through its unique loan capacity as a bank (World Bank, interview 17 November 2017).

---

[2]This is based only on OECD DAC-reported statistics. The ITC DRM database is based on the same statistics but adjusted for country projects that are not mentioned in the OECD statistics. As such, it reports more money than the OECD statistics. Unfortunately, there is no 2017 entry yet in the DRM database. As such, we refer to the OECD database here, but we can reasonably expect the trend to be the same, even with the adjustments the DRM database makes.

[3]This database collects comparable data on the capabilities of more than 150 tax administrations.

The OECD traditionally does not provide direct technical assistance and only focuses on specific issues. Its main approach is to help developing countries implement internationally agreed upon tax principles, at the moment mainly with regard to BEPS and Automatic Exchange of Information programs. The OECD offers bilateral technical assistance within the scope of specific issues, such as transfer pricing assistance. It is generally not involved in tax policy assistance, though interviewees at the OECD report demand is growing (OECD, interview 8 December 2017). The OECD also hosts Tax Inspectors Without Borders (TIWB), an initiative together with the United Nations Development Program (UNDP).

The United Nations Committee of Experts on International Cooperation in Tax Matters, which responds to the Economic and Social Council (ECOSOC), has a standard setting ambition on international taxation and publishes manuals for developing countries (sometimes financed through the International Tax Compact) on subjects such as extractive industry taxation or transfer pricing. The Department of Economic and Social Affairs (UNDESA) as part of the UN secretariat is less hands-on involved in TCB and only provides assistance on specific issues such as treaty negotiation. UN bodies generally do not have the ambition of holistic country assistance, rendering the UN the smallest player among the four most relevant multilateral organizations for TCB.

5.3.2 Coordination Mechanisms

All these different actors are involved in tax capacity building, which incites a need for at least some form of coordination. This has been recognized by those actors as well (see, e.g., IMF et al. 2017), and so we can observe two coordinative dynamics in recent years: one around bilateral donors and one for multilateral organizations.

The first centers around the Germany (Bonn)-based International Tax Compact (ITC), an organization proposed at the 2008 UN Doha Financing for Development conference whose purpose was to gather like-minded governments and multilateral organizations to find ways to strengthen tax policies in developing countries (an author's observation in Doha). In 2015, the ITC assumed the role of secretariat of the Addis Tax Initiative. The ATI is a monitoring body for the pledge of donor country to double DRM efforts by 2020. It also has a matchmaking function for convening donor and partner countries to exchange best practices and set up collaboration. The ATI currently has 44 members, i.e., 20 donor countries and 24 partner countries. There are also 16 supporting organizations (Addis Tax Initiative 2019).

Another interesting addition around the ITC is the Network of Tax Organisations (NTO), which also shares a secretariat with the ITC. It brings together nine regional tax organizations (International Tax Compact 2018b) which are increasingly getting more involved in tax capacity building as well and have a distinct advantage with regard to the local context of the countries they work for.

The second center revolves around the four multilateral organizations, namely, the Platform for Collaboration on Tax (PCT). This too was a follow-up to an organization that came out of the 2008 UN Doha Financing for Development conference: the International Tax Dialogue (ITD), involving the IMF, World Bank, OECD, and the Inter-American Center of Tax Administrations (CIAT). This was a loose network for sharing best practices, in lieu of the proposal for an international tax organization formulated by the preparatory High Level Panel led by former Mexican President Ernesto Zedillo. It never amounted to much and is currently defunct (Lesage et al. 2010).

In 2016, the OECD, IMF, World Bank, and UN organized themselves in the PCT. The PCT got political support from G20 governments, such as Japan, which had become irritated by the increasing fragmentation of the TCB regime complex (OECD senior official, interview 8 December 2017; UNDP senior official, interview 9 November 2017). Its purpose is to strengthen international standard setting with regard to DRM, TCB, and technical assistance. Its most concrete mandate, at the behest of the G20, is to create toolkits for the implementation of the OECD's BEPS minimum standards (IMF-OECD-UN-WB 2016; IMF et al. 2017). This is to help developing countries in the BEPS Inclusive Framework with the translation of those minimum standards in their domestic policies.

5.3.3   The Need for Country-Level Coordination

This increase in coordination is for the most part a good thing. All these organizations feel a real demand from developing countries for technical assistance (several interviews, Washington; New York, Bonn, Paris, 2017). What is missing from this story is a method for coordinating donors at the ground level. This is an often-overlooked aspect in designing aid strategies. If not or improperly implemented, this can do more harm than good for the developing countries, as the administrative burden of coordination and cost of incoherency then tends to fall on developing countries (Carbone 2017; Delputte and Orbie 2014). During interviews, we also got an explicit admission from one official from a multilateral institution that "they are really good at organizing high-level conceptual conferences, but less so on the ground coordination."

A framework that puts the partner country in charge, around which the partner country and donors can organize themselves, is a necessary counterweight to all the recent coordination in the field that has been largely donor- and international organization-driven. This is where the MTRS as a coordination tool fills a clear need in the international framework for TCB. It could potentially help to ensure that the implementation of technical assistance is country-driven and bottom-up and not a top-down process that follows from demanding outcomes and results from all the coordination initiatives in the last 5 years. It sets an ambition to involve all relevant stakeholders in a developing country in a holistic policy and administration reform, with the help of donors for the technical implementation. A lot of the factors where the MTRS puts emphasis on come back in the recent World Bank report on how to build trust among taxpayers and increase compliance through legitimacy (Prichard et al. 2019). These are really pertinent issues in poorer countries. The MTRS thus provides an innovation that simultaneously furthers coordination on the ground in developing countries, advocates a bottom-up approach, and aims to build trust and legitimacy.

5.4   The Pitfalls and Deficiencies of the MTRS

Despite the innovations the MTRS seems to offer, there are a few deficiencies we can observe. These are not trivial or circumstantial and could impact its effectivness in reaching its own pre-prescribed goals. While the MTRS is a framework to address tax capacity issues in a bottom-up manner, the framework itself is a top-down construct. It comes from large multilateral organizations, which do not have a flawless track record when it comes to bottom-up policymaking in developing countries even when they explicitly set out to do so.

5.4.1   Issue 1: Developing Countries Are Supposed to Do What Rich Countries Cannot

A first criticism of the MTRS as a concept is that it sets ambitious goals for developing countries that most advanced industrialized countries do not aspire to themselves. A 4–6-year country-wide consensus on tax policy and revenue administration reform, coupled with revenue goals, is a tall order. Off course, such consensus makes the implementation of external tax capacity building initiatives a whole lot easier, but all those goals are politically quite contentious in nature. Tax policy reforms in Western countries are often hard-fought policies that are seldom the product of a serene nationwide debate. Instead, they are often decided upon during short opportunity windows when governing political parties try to make as much of their preferences a reality and/or quickly need to shore up their budgets. The US Tax Cuts and Jobs Act (2017) is a good example of this. It was the product of the Republican Party having a 2-year frame where they both controlled the US Congress and held the Presidency. While building society-wide consensus with all relevant stakeholders is an aspiring goal, it is somewhat strange to expect this of developing countries, when most Western countries do not seem able to adhere to this themselves. MTRS should not be an example of "do as we say, not as we do" (Hart 2018).

5.4.2 Issue 2: The Internationally Agreed MTRS Constrains Future Governments

A second issue that can be raised is that MTRSs do not necessarily follow legislative cycles or government terms. This is problematic since an MTRS includes fiscal policy choices that determine the budgetary constraints of the whole of national policymaking. Suppose the new government has different revenue or policy positions. How well will this go with the donors who have organized around the MTRS? Can an MTRS bind the new government? It does not appear so, at least not in legal terms. It is not unthinkable, however, that donors will remind the new governments of the commitments their predecessors have made and realized already. This can put pressure on those new governments to keep their policies within the terms of the MTRS, even though they have not negotiated or agreed to it. This point does not necessarily amount to a criticism per se but underscores the importance of having a national process that is as inclusive as possible.

5.4.3 Issue 3: PCT Institutions Still Need to Prove that They Are Good at "Country Ownership"

The MTRS is a standard set by the four institutions of the PCT. This is enough to warrant scrutiny of the concept as two of those partners, the IMF and WB, have a history of damaging top-down compulsory fiscal and tax reforms in developing countries. The Structural Adjustment Programs (SAPs) of the 1980–1990s and their seemingly more benign but still contested successors, the Poverty Reduction Strategy Papers (PRSPs), remind us of a top-down approach with little country ownership and civil society participation (Lazarus 2008). The SAPs included tax programs that were based on broadening the tax base and moderating marginal tax rates (Williamson 1990) without taking into account distributive effects. This often led to regressive tax policies, following the neoliberal ideology of the Washington Consensus. Even more recent programs by the Bretton Woods institutions make little mention of the distributional effects of their proposed reforms (Damme et al. 2018). The MTRS ostensibly leaves more room for progressive tax reforms, if this is the policy goal of the country in question, but critical scrutiny of the MTRS processes and their ideological underpinnings and distributive impacts remains advisable.

5.4.4   Issue 4: Does MTRS Help to Bridge G20/OECD-Led International Tax Standards and Developing Country Needs?

Fourth, the PCT's main work program is helping developing countries to implement established international tax norms. Even though the UN is on board, observers mention that this in practice means rubberstamping the OECD-developed tax standards, mainly the BEPS work program (Montes and Rangaprasad 2018). It even holds a danger that the UN ends up endorsing policy norms that were not agreed upon in the UN Committee of Experts on International Cooperation in Tax Matters or the UN Economic and Social Council (ECOSOC). Several experts have criticized how developing countries were involved in the BEPS process and the BEPS Inclusive Framework (Mosquera Valderrama 2018). It is unclear how those norms will play a role in the MTRS, but there is a possibility that the organizations involved will push the BEPS minimum standards and the upcoming BEPS IF reforms on digital economy as part of the MTRS package. One concern with the BEPS IF is that it can pressure participating developing countries into accepting international tax reforms that end up being good for international tax governance (and the position of the OECD as the central forum), but not necessarily for them. One example is the differing implementation of the principal purpose test under BEPS Action 6, which could incite negative tax competition among developing countries (Mosquera Valderrama 2019; Mosquera Valderrama et al. 2018). Another, more pressing, example comes from the ongoing efforts to address the tax-related challenges of the digital economy. The current proposals under the pillar 1 approach[4] seem to reallocate most taxing rights to large market countries such as the USA or China. It is unclear how (smaller) developing countries would benefit from a new international tax approach that is primarily sales-based (Hearson 2019). An alternative proposal made by the Group of 24 (G24), led by India, that proposes a more formulary-based approach to taxing multinationals and puts more emphasis on labor would better serve the interests of most developing countries (Chandra Prasad 2019) but is mostly sidelined by the OECD. As a tool of the PCT, the MTRS framework could become a tool through which those reforms are technically implemented which in turn could leave developing countries worse off.

---

[4]The reform package for digital economy has two work packages. Pillar 1 investigates the reallocation of taxing rights to better comply with the reality of digital business models. Pillar 2, or the GLOBE proposal, tackles a global anti-base erosion approach.

5.4.5 Issue 5: Potential Conflict of Interest Between Donor and Partner Countries' Tax Agendas

A fifth issue is that in cases concerning DRM revenue from international taxpayers, especially corporations, there is a fundamental conflict of interest between developing countries and OECD donors which also want favorable conditions for their resident multinational companies. There is a myriad of literature on how the international tax regime is lopsided in favor of net residence countries (Cockfield 2010; International Monetary Fund 2019; Picciotto 2013), but the global tax regime is not in the scope of the MTRS.[5] What should be in its scope however are the tax treaties that developing countries conclude, especially now when many of them are part of the BEPS IF whose minimum standards will be disseminated through the network of bilateral tax treaties. Research into the tax treaties of African countries shows that they sometimes literally "negotiate away their tax base" in an effort to attract foreign direct investment through tax treaties (Hearson 2018b). The most visible ways they do so are by lowering withholding taxes on capital, compared to domestic law, or by restricting permanent establishment definitions (Hearson 2018b). Tax treaties between EU countries and developing countries, for example, are among the most residence-biased in the OECD (Hearson 2018a). There are voices that question the perceived wisdom that tax treaties are beneficial for developing countries (e.g., Dagan 2000) and even the IMF prescribes caution to developing countries when signing one (IMF 2014).

This is where the MTRS conflicts with the interests of the bilateral donors. If a developing country wants to improve its tax collection capacities, then surely its corporate tax policy toward international corporations and by extension its treaties should come into scope—especially since for developing countries corporate taxation represents a much larger share of the tax mix. This follows from the fact that they collect much less personal income tax (PIT) than high-income countries (see Fig. 5.1) while roughly collecting the same level in value-added tax (VAT). So, a reduction or increase in the amount of corporate income tax (CIT) they can collect has a much larger impact on their overall revenues.

The question here is will bilateral donors allow part of their provided aid flows for tax capacity building to strengthen a developing country's capacity in international corporate taxation through an MTRS, even though this might lead to higher source taxation for multinationals headquartered in their country? Or will they focus on domestic revenue collection in the form of consumption and personal income taxes and reduce the corporate tax discussion mainly to providing tax certainty and friendly conditions (which is supposedly one of the rationales behind signing tax treaties as well) for foreign investors? The latter could follow from an ideological position that providing a business-friendly climate is a key priority of developing countries or as a quid pro for the tax capacity aid provided. The authors do not

---

[5]Although there are also capacity issues to be addressed regarding the participation of developing countries in global tax fora. See for example: Mosquera Valderrama (2018).

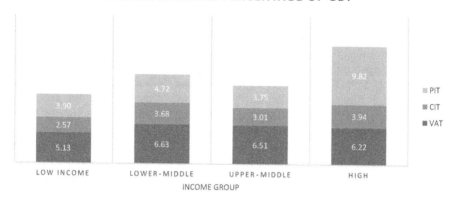

Fig. 5.1 USAID Collecting Taxes Database 2012–2013

suggest that providing medium-term tax certainty should be left out of the MTRS, as it can indeed be important to attract FDI (IMF and OECD 2019). However, focusing on tax certainty can also be a strawman that diverts attention away from anti-avoidance regulation or setting corporate tax rates at a level that is beneficial for the country. If an MTRS is truly to be a country-driven exercise, then observers should be vigilant of a priori dispositions whispered in by donor countries, especially given the divergent interests between source and residence countries. This discussion also shows how important it is for donor countries in their formulation of aid for tax capacity building and MTRS bring together the expertise of their ministries of finance and tax administrations as well as the expertise and policy objectives of their development cooperation ministry as a good practice of policy coherence for sustainable development (PCSD).

5.4.6 Issue 6: Compatibility of the MTRS with the SDGs and Sustainable Development

Lastly, the MTRS should be designed and communicated in a way that it fully supports the SDGs and (more ambitious) national sustainable development plans. This implies that the MTRS not only helps to raise aggregate tax revenues but also enables to meet objectives on, among other things, poverty and inequality reduction, gender equality, sustainable economic development (agriculture, industry, infrastructure), and ecological sustainability. On the revenue side, the MTRS should reduce regressive and promote progressive tax policies and develop environmental taxes to steer behavior. The MTRS should also be closely tied to the spending side of policymaking for sustainable development. The PCT itself stresses the importance of situating the MTRS in this wider framework (Platform for Collaboration on Tax 2019, p. 20). The only available MTRS (Papua New-Guinea), however, presents itself as a quite technocratic document providing a reform agenda in which other objectives than raising revenues or the wider agenda of the SDGs and sustainable development are ignored (Papua New Guinea 2017).

5.5 Conclusion: How to Move Forward with the Concept of Medium-Term Revenue Strategies?

The MTRS concept is still in its early stages and it is too early to really evaluate its outcomes. We would need more ongoing strategies and testimonials from participants and stakeholders at the relevant levels on the formulation and implementation process. Nonetheless it is clear that the MTRS was born out of a real need in the crowded and complex global governance landscape for tax capacity assistance. It provides a framework for on-the-ground coordination that was missing, helping to avoid duplication of efforts, coordination, and reporting costs. In that sense, we believe MTRSs are a potentially valuable addition to the tax capacity building regime, especially since it puts the recipient country in charge.

Nevertheless, we identified several actual and potential issues with regard to the ambition, partners, legitimacy, and goals of the concept that are not fully addressed by the material that exists right now on the MTRS. We do not suggest that the people or institutions involved are not aware of these or that they are not addressed at all. In addition, the perfect should not be the enemy of the good with regard to tax capacity building, and MTRS was never intended as a panacea for all the flaws that currently exist in DRM, capacity building, or international taxation. It should be evaluated as it is an additional tool in the larger toolbox of coordination in the tax capacity building regime. However, we feel it is necessary to point to the pitfalls we described and call for scrutiny of how the concept further develops.

Both the IMF and WB are heavily invested in the concept. In October 2019, they devoted a 2-day conference to it, together with senior countries' officials and the Austrian Ministry of Finance. They discussed topics such as transitioning to an MTRS, securing whole-of-government support, setting revenue and policy goals, and securing civil society support (IMF et al. 2019). It is unclear to what extent the MTRS was discussed in relation to the broader SDG agenda. IMF head of Fiscal Policy Vito Gaspar gave a rousing keynote address in which he reaffirmed the key issue of country ownership and the case for donor coordination in a "coordinated but subordinated fashion." He even added "We at the IMF are enthusiastic—even passionate!—about the MTRS" (Vito 2019).

This firm investment of the Bretton Woods institutions stands in sharp contrast with the relative silence of the OECD and UN on the MTRS approach. In the latest PCT update report, it reads "[S]o far the IMF and WBG [World Bank Group] have been most involved in supporting the design and implementation of the MTRS" and further "[T]he OECD and UN have not been involved in the design or implementation of the MTRS at the country level" and "PCT partners realize the importance of strengthening collaboration on this front" (Platform for Collaboration on Tax 2019, p. 42). There is a suggestion that the OECD and UN are not fully on board yet/anymore. This would be worrisome and reinforce our third concern that the MTRS is a concept led by two organizations that have some baggage when it comes to country-owned reforms. It also reduces the feedback loop of designing MTRS processes in a country to IMF and World Bank work. Moreover, the exclusion of the UN, arguably the most inclusive institution of the four PCT partners, means that one of the advantages of the PCT setup, learning and exchanging experiences between international institutions, is lost. The same goes for the OECD. By not helping to implement MTRSs at country level, the concept loses its direct link to the BEPS process, and the OECD loses out on the feedback from the countries that could tie back to the BEPS Inclusive Framework (Lips and Mosquera Valderrama 2020).

References

Addis Tax Initiative. (2015). *Financing for development conference the Addis Tax Initiative—Declaration*. Retrieved June 22, 2020, from https://www.addistaxinitiative.net/documents/Addis-Tax-Initiative_Declaration_EN.pdf

Addis Tax Initiative. (2019). *Addis Tax Initiative*. Retrieved November 15, 2019, from https://www.addistaxinitiative.net/about

Carbone, M. (2017). Make Europe happen on the ground? Enabling and constraining factors for European Union aid coordination in Africa. *Development Policy Review, 35*(4), 531–548.

Chandra Prasad, G. (2019). *28 developing nations back India on OECD tax proposal*. Retrieved November 15, 2019, from https://www.livemint.com/news/india/28-developing-nations-back-india-on-oecd-tax-proposal-11573577822211.html

Cockfield, A. (2010). *Globalization and its tax discontents*. Toronto: University of Toronto Press.

Dagan, T. (2000). The tax treaties myth. *Journal of International Law and Politics, 32*, 939–2000.

Damme, L., Misrahi, T., & Orel, S. (2018). *The IMF's regressive secret*. Retrieved June 22, 2020, from https://www.brettonwoodsproject.org/2008/06/art-561926/

De Mooij, R., Nazara, S., & Toro, J. (2018). In L. Bruer, J. Guajardo, & T. Kinda (Eds.), *Realizing Indonesia's economic potential*. Washington, DC: International Monetary Fund.

Delputte, S., & Orbie, J. (2014). The EU and donor coordination on the ground: Perspectives from Tanzania and Zambia. *The European Journal of Development Research, 26*(5), 676–691.

G20. (2010). *Multi-year action plan on development*.

Hart, T. (2018). *Supporting domestic revenue mobilisation: We must learn from the failures of the past*. Retrieved October 17, 2020, from https://www.odi.org/blogs/10626-supporting-domestic-revenue-mobilisation-we-must-learn-failures-past

Hearson, M. (2018a). *The European Union's tax treaties with developing countries: Leading by example?* Retrieved October 17, 2020, from https://martinhearson.net/2018/09/27/the-european-unions-tax-treaties-with-developing-countries-leading-by-example/

Hearson, M. (2018b). When do developing countries negotiate away their corporate tax base. *Journal of International Development, 30*(2), 233–255.

Hearson, M. (2019). *The OECD's digital tax proposal: Untangling the impact of 'Pillar One' on developing countries*. Retrieved November 15, 2020, from https://martinhearson.net/2019/10/14/the-oecds-digital-tax-proposal-untangling-the-impact-of-pillar-one-on-developing-countries/

IMF. (2014). *Spillovers in international corporate taxation*. IMF Policy Paper.

IMF, & OECD. (2019). *2019 progress report on tax certainty*. Retrieved November 15, 2019, from www.oecd.org/tax/tax-policy/g20-report-on-tax-certainty.htm

IMF, OECD, UN, & World Bank. (2016). *The Platform for Collaboration on Tax. Concept note.*

IMF, OECD, UN, & World Bank. (2017). *Update on activities of the Platform for Collaboration on Tax.*

IMF, World Bank, & Bundesministerium Finanzen. (2019). *Conference agenda: Medium Term Revenue Strategy (MTRS)—Building more effective tax systems.*

IMF-OECD-UN-WB. (2016, April 7–11). *The Platform for Collaboration on Tax: Concept note.*

International Monetary Fund. (2019). *Corporate taxation in the global economy.*

International Tax Compact. (2018a). *DRM database.* Retrieved July 13, 2018, from https://drm.taxcompact.net/

International Tax Compact. (2018b). *Launch of the network of tax organisations.*

Lazarus, J. (2008). Participation in poverty reduction strategy papers: Reviewing the past, assessing the present and predicting the future. *Third World Quarterly, 29*(6), 1205–1221.

Lesage, D., McNair, D., & Vermeiren, M. (2010). From Monterrey to Doha: Taxation and financing for development. *Development Policy Review, 28*(2), 155–172.

Lips, W., & Mosquera Valderrama, I. (2020). Global sustainable tax governance in the OECD-G20 transparency and BEPS initiatives. In C. Brokelind & S. Van Thiel (Eds.), *Tax sustainability in an EU and international context*. Amsterdam: IBFD.

Montes, M. F., & Rangaprasad, P. (2018). Collaboration or co-optation ? A review of the Platform for Collaboration on Tax. *South Centre Policy Brief, June* (48), 1–4.

Mosquera Valderrama, I. (2018). Output legitimacy deficits and the inclusive framework of the OECD/G20 base erosion and profit shifting initiative. *Bulletin for International Taxation, 72*(3), 1–11.

Mosquera Valderrama, I. (2019). *The principal purpose test (PPT), the BEPS inclusive framework and MLI*. Retrieved November 15, 2019, from https://www.ciat.org/the-principal-purpose-test-ppt-the-beps-inclusive-framework-and-mli/?lang=en

Mosquera Valderrama, I., Lesage, D., & Lips, W. (2018). *Tax and development: The link between international taxation, the base erosion profit shifting project and the 2030 sustainable development agenda*. UNU-CRIS Policy Paper W 2018-4.

Niculescu, M. (2017). *Impact investment to close the SDG funding gap.*

OECD. (2019). *International development statistics.*

Papua New Guinea. (2017). *Medium term revenue strategy 2018–2022.*

Picciotto, S. (2013). *Is the international tax system fit for purpose, especially for developing countries?* ICDT Working Papers, 13.

Platform for Collaboration on Tax. (2019). *PCT progress report 2018–2019.*

Prichard, W., Custers, A., Dom, R., Davenport, S., & Roscitt, M. (2019). *Innovations in tax compliance. Conceptual framework*. World Bank Group Policy Research Working Paper, 9032.

Vito, G. (2019, October 29). *Medium-Term Revenue Strategy (MTRS)—Taxation and development.* Conference of "Medium Term Revenue Strategy (MTRS)—Building More Effective Tax Systems".

Williamson, J. (1990). What Washington means by policy reform. In J. Williamson (Ed.), *Latin American adjustment: How much has happened?* Washington, DC: Institute for International Economics.

Part III
Tax Incentives and Attracting Sustainable Investment

Chapter 6
Tax Incentives in Pacific Alliance Countries, the BEPS Project (Action 5), and the 2030 Sustainable Development Agenda

Eleonora Lozano Rodríguez

6.1 Introduction

Following Ogazón and Hamzaoui (2015, p. 8), there is tension between two tax policy considerations. On the one hand, legislatures should not have trouble in designing and implementing legislative measures against base erosion. On the other hand, policymakers need to improve the attractiveness of their countries from a tax perspective. However, the existence of a "favourable" domestic tax system facilitates tax avoidance.

The Base Erosion and Profit Shifting (BEPS) Project is no stranger to this discussion. That is how, for example, Cotrut and Munyandi (2018) consider that "recent tax developments aimed at mitigating the possibilities of base erosion and profit shifting are expected to increase the importance and popularity of tax incentives (...) due to the fact that states will want to remain competitive on the international stage and multinational enterprises will look for the opportunities to minimise their tax liabilities" (p. ix).

For the above, one part of the minimum standard on BEPS Report Action 5 relates to preferential tax regimes, where a peer review was undertaken to identify features of such regimes that can facilitate base erosion and profit shifting and therefore have the potential to unfairly impact the tax base of the other jurisdictions. Very recently the Organisation for Economic Co-operation and Development (OECD) released a new publication "Harmful Tax Practices—2018 Progress Report on Preferential

Lawyer, economist, and magister in economics (Universidad de los Andes, Bogotá, Colombia). PhD in Law (Universidad de Salamanca, Salamanca, Spain). PhD in Law and LLM in Taxation, Programme Director, Universidad de los Andes.

E. Lozano Rodríguez (✉)
Universidad de los Andes, Bogotá, Colombia
e-mail: elozano@uniandes.edu.co

© The Author(s) 2021
I. J. Mosquera Valderrama et al. (eds.), *Taxation, International Cooperation and the 2030 Sustainable Development Agenda*, United Nations University Series on Regionalism 19, https://doi.org/10.1007/978-3-030-64857-2_6

Regimes" (29/01/2019), which contains results demonstrating that jurisdictions have delivered on their commitment to comply with the standard on harmful tax practices (including the Latin American and Caribbean Countries of Barbados, Curacao, Costa Rica, Uruguay and Panama).

However, Latin American countries continue to include multiple tax benefits in their legislation. The paper will explore the situation of the four countries belonging to the Pacific Alliance (Mexico, Peru, Chile and Colombia) and will make concrete recommendations as to its justice and efficiency, in order to meet the goals, set forth in the Sustainable Development Goals and in the BEPS Project.

Given the above, this document begins with a theoretical and conceptual approach to the raison d'être of tax incentives, and the consequent tax expenditure, and their desirable and problematic characteristics. It then presents the objectives that, from an international perspective, the OECD's BEPS Project and the Sustainable Development Agenda (SDA) seek to achieve with a good design and implementation of tax incentives. Following this, the paper presents the current panorama of these incentives in Latin American countries in general and in those of the Pacific Alliance in particular. Finally, we provide a number of public policy recommendations for improvement.

6.2 A Theoretical and Conceptual Approach to Tax Incentives

The first thing we need to clarify is that not all tax benefits are incentives. Some benefits are simply intended to alleviate the burden of the less privileged, as happens, for example, with the exclusion of value-added tax (VAT) from the basic family basket. As stated by Ogazón and Calderón (2018), there is no consensus on what is meant by a tax incentive. Table 6.1 lists some of the doctrine's definitions:

The above definitions allow us to conclude that a tax incentive has the following characteristics[1]:

1. *Specialty and exceptionality*: This refers to special and exceptional tax measures in relation to general rules.
2. *Favourability*: This relates to treatments that seek to favour a sector or types of investment.
3. *Effectiveness*: This seeks an objective, for example, increasing the rate of return of an investment or reducing its risks or costs.
4. *Economic instrument*: This refers to fiscal policy instruments used to attract domestic and foreign investment, depending on the type of incentive, or to alleviate the situation of existing investment.

---

[1] Some of these were also obtained by Ogazón and Calderón (2018, pp. 7 and 8).

Table 6.1 Doctrinal definitions of tax incentives

Source	Definition
Ogazón and Calderón (2018)	*Special* provisions that allow for exclusions, credits, preferential tax rates or deferral of tax liability (citing Zolt 2014, p. 5)
Ogazón and Calderón (2018)	Tax incentives can be defined in terms of their *effect* on reducing the effective tax burden for a specific project (citing also Zolt, *ibid.*)
Ogazón and Calderón (2018)	Any incentives that reduce the tax burden of enterprises to *induce them to invest* in particular projects or sectors. They are *exceptions* to the general tax regime (citing UNCTAD 2000, p. 12)
Ogazón and Calderón (2018)	All measures that provide for a more *favourable* tax treatment of certain activities or sectors compared to what is granted to the general industry (citing Klemm 2010, p. 3)
Ogazón and Calderón (2018)	In a nutshell, it can be said that, in general terms, tax incentives *depart from a general and neutral tax system*. They can be implemented in different forms, resulting in a favourable tax treatment or a reduced combined overall tax burden for the investor
Munongo et al. (2017)	*Fiscal measures* used by governments to attract investment *domestically and internationally* in certain key sectors of the economy (citing Bolnick 2004)
Munongo et al. (2017)	A statutory tax incentive is a special tax provision granted to qualifying investment projects, and this provision would not be applied to other investment projects outside the *selected qualifying investment categories*. An effective tax incentive is a special tax provision granted to qualifying investment projects with the goal of *reducing the effective tax burden* (citing Zee et al. 2002)
Tavares-Lehman (2016)	Fiscal incentives are tax provisions tailored to qualified investment projects that represent a favourable *deviation* from general tax law and regulations and aim to *increase the rate of return of a certain investment* or *reduce its risks and costs* by reducing the tax burden

Source: Authors based on the doctrine. The characteristics highlighted in bold will be discussed later

5. *Qualification*: This is a process by which it is necessary to comply with some incentive requirements in order to qualify.
6. *Period*: Usually tax incentives are guaranteed for a period of time.
7. *Coverage*: Incentives may cover one or more taxes depending on their nature.
8. *Interrelation*: Jurisdictions may implement different interrelated incentives depending on fiscal policy. Finally,
9. *Tax expense*: Every tax incentive generates an expense in public finances.

There is, however, a general tendency in the doctrine to affirm that in order to encourage investment, the tax channel is not the only one possible and that it may even become ineffective. Thus, in relation to incentives other than tax ones, Tavares-Lehman (2016, p. 22) states "there is a considerable array of types and subtypes of incentives. Very often governments offer a mix, or a package, of different types of incentives. This mix or package of measures varies greatly among countries and even subnational jurisdictions"; and he delves more deeply into those financial incentives, where he analyses, among other things, grants, subsidies, loans, wage subsidies and job training subsidies; creation of new, targeted infrastructure; and support for expatriation costs (p. 22).

Munongo, Akanbi and Robinson (2017) and James (2016, p. 173) emphasise that to attract foreign investment, it is not only the tax factor that is important but also other non-tax factors, such as macroeconomic conditions, infrastructure and adequate institutional design. Laukkaanen (2018) adds the relevance of raw material costs. Carrizosa (2008) analyses how competitiveness indicators in Latin America include, in addition to tax aspects (where he recognises that there are many exemptions in Latin America, tariffs are not neutral, and many anti-technical taxes still exist in the region), political uncertainty, macroeconomic instability, corruption, access to financing, barriers to employment, infrastructure and other transaction costs in general (e.g. licences and customs). However, some studies such as those by Zhan and Karl (2016) conclude that in order to attract foreign investment, the most commonly used vehicles are financial and regulatory taxes (p. 204).

The ineffectiveness of incentives is also widely analysed by the doctrine in both general and specific ways. Thus, for example, James (2016) states, generally speaking, "tax incentives are widely prevalent and reflect the desire of the government to support economic growth and provide value for the local economy through jobs, new skills, and technology. Governments also provide tax incentives in order to diversify their economies and support activities they hope will lead to new sources of growth that use the untapped potential of the country (...) However, this had unintended consequences, resulting in increasing opportunities for rent seeking, as discretionary power can be misused" (p. 173). Also, Redonda et al. (2018) consider that "tax incentives for investment are usually poorly designed and ineffective (...) their impact on investment is often negligible and they are likely to trigger costly windfall gains for business" (p. 5). These authors also question the environmental effects of some of the incentives, recommending that governments should not use them.

Castañeda (2018) in analysing the inefficiency and injustice of the Colombian tax system concludes that the political influence of the interest groups of the business community explains the limitations of tax policy in achieving economic growth and redistribution.[2] Van Kommer (2018) considers that tax incentives are often granted to a specific target group and specific type of income or expense; however, incentives do not come without risks of misuse or abuse. Foreseeable risk may refer to (1) increased number of applicants; (2) under-declaration of income; (3) incorrect declarations; (4) shifting to other categories of income; (5) bringing forward investments or delaying them in order to manipulate the claim of the incentive; (6) transferring income to other entities; and (7) applying the tax incentive to other taxes (p. 279).

Finally, Munongo, Ayo and Robinson (2017), in a study focusing on Southern African countries, point out the disadvantages of incentives as revenue loss, misallocation of resources, enforcement and compliance challenges and corruption

---

[2]To analyse the undue pressure of economic sectors for tax benefits, see Valdés (2019).

due to discretionality in the concession of incentives. To this end, the paper focuses on the economic impact of incentives on tax competition and regional regulatory harmonisation (pp. 159 and 165). In this regard, they state: "It was noted that the use of tax incentives to attract FDI might improve the welfare of individuals in the jurisdiction that applies the incentives, but have external cost implications for residents in other competing jurisdictions that do not adopt tax incentives. Thus, tax incentives were seen to reduce the overall welfare of residents in a region" (p. 165).

Some articles that analyse certain special tax incentives and their impact by sectors are, for example, those by Carpentier and Suret (2016), Poterba (1997), Jorgenson (1996) and Laukkaanen (2018). Despite the disparity in the number of years between these studies, the recommendations they generate for the future evaluation of tax relief policies are important. The Carpetiner and Suret document (2016) analyses how Latin American countries have included tax incentives in their jurisdictions in order to promote "Business Angels" (hereinafter, BAs). The implementation of these policies costs countries millions of dollars, where it is concluded that the economic benefits of these initiatives are obscure and unknown. So much so that programs fail to collect and provide the information needed to conduct comprehensive evaluations of these programs. Thus, the paper, also supported by previous studies, concludes "tax expenditures are generally higher than tax revenues when the additionality and displacement effects of the incentives are considered" (p. 347). However, it recognises that much remains to be analysed, since the vast majority of studies present flaws in their methodological dimension. Thus, for Carpetier and Suret, the following three questions have not been resolved by the literature, and they require measurement: (1)"even if the tax incentive programs attempt to improve investors' rate of return, little is known about whether this objective has been reached"; (2) "the programs (...) are officially dedicated to BAs, but they are generally open to all taxpayers or qualified investors"; and, finally, (3) "given that the available analyses focus on short-term effects, we know little about the performance, survival and success of firms financed by tax credits" (p. 348).

Poterba (1997) analyses the tax incentives for research and development in the United States, concluding that given their complexity, they give rise to unwanted disincentives. In this regard, he states "Tax incentives and disincentives for investment are often unintentional. The international provision of the U.S. Internal Revenue Code has become so complex that the architects who regularly patch up this structure may fail to perceive the behavioural consequences of new layers of complexity" (p. 72). Jorgenson (1996) demonstrates, through a 5-year analysis, how the new system of regulations for calculating depreciation allowances for tax purposes (the asset depreciation range system, ADR) created in 1971 in the United States generated relatively little impact during the first year and that the maximum impact on investment, gross national product and employment occurred 3 years later. It is interesting to consider that in this case there is economic information that allows us to evaluate the tax measure.

Finally, Laukkaanen (2018), in analysing the "Special Economic Zones" (hereafter SEZs), asserts that if there is an inadequate incentive design, it can result in increased evasion and competitive disadvantages. As such, for Laukkaanen, for example, multinationals can take advantage of these zones to alleviate their overall tax burden through artificial profit shifting from parent company to the entity located in a low tax SEZ, for which the analysis of economic substance is fundamental as is the inclusion in double taxation avoidance conventions of non-discrimination, mutual agreement procedure, most favoured nation clauses, limitation on benefits and principal purpose of the transaction clauses (see also Ferreira and Perdelwitz 2018[3]).

For different doctrinants incentives can take the form of tax holidays, capital investment incentives, reduced corporate tax rates, special economic zones, carry-forward loss, investment allowances, accelerated depreciation, initial allowances, investment tax credits, enhanced deductions, reduced tax rates on dividends and interest paid abroad, preferential treatment of long-term capital gains, exemptions (VAT), zero-rating (VAT) and tax havens, among others (Cotrut and Munyandi 2018; James 2016; Tavares-Lehman 2016).

6.3 International Aspirations for Tax Incentives Based on the OECD's BEPS Project and the 2030 Sustainable Development Agenda

6.3.1 BEPS Action 5 and What It Means for Tax Incentives

BEPS Action 5 seeks to combat harmful tax practices based on transparency and economic substance. The OECD has detected such practices in two areas: (1) preferential tax regimes, i.e. those that offer advantageous tax conditions for companies that carry out certain activities and therefore provide an incentive to relocate business activities, and (2) agreements with tax administrations or tax rulings and their negative tax effects at global level.

The issue of preferential tax regimes is addressed both in the 1998 report entitled "Harmful tax competition: A global issue" and in Action 5. The latter explores "geographically mobile" activities, for example, financial or service activities, which globalisation and technological advances let move at low cost from one territory to

---

[3]This chapter also delves into how limitation on benefits and principal purpose of the transaction clauses can combat treaty vulnerability to abuse of tax sparing credit clauses (p. 205). In the case of the Double Taxation Avoidance Conventions of the Pacific Alliance countries, most of which include the above clauses following the OECD Model Convention, see the following pages: https://www.mef.gob.pe/es/convenio-para-evitar-la-doble-imposicion, http://www.sii.cl/pagina/jurisprudencia/convenios.htm, https://www.sat.gob.mx/cs/Satellite?blobcol=urldata&blobkey=id&blobtable=MungoBlobs&blobwhere=1461173732131&ssbinary=true and https://www.dian.gov.co/normatividad/convenios/Paginas/ConveniosTributariosInternacionales.aspx.

another without requiring a relevant business structure, obtaining tax advantages in the host jurisdictions.

It is important to clarify that a preferential regime is potentially harmful only if it has actually created harmful economic effects according to the OECD guidelines in the BEPS Project on substantial economic activity. Thus, tax bases cannot be artificially shifted from countries where value is created to low-tax countries. In this respect, the tax advantages associated with preferential regimes should only be recognised if the entity that intends to implement them is engaged in a substantial economic activity.[4]

Action 5 of the BEPS Project expands on preferential intellectual property regimes. Thus, countries are free to establish tax incentives that encourage companies to invest in research and development, but these incentives must not generate any distortion or harmful effect on the economy, which is why the requirement for substantial activity is an essential element.

The foregoing shows that the activity performed is of sufficient substance and therefore justifies the application of a preferential tax regime, based on the nexus or relationship between income and expenses related to the development of the intangible asset. In this way, the tax benefits associated with the regime will only be applicable to income obtained from the exploitation of intellectual property on the basis of the proportion between qualified expenses and total expenses. As such, Action 5 expressly establishes a formula for calculating the benefits to be applied by this special tax regime, as well as a breakdown of its variables.[5]

BEPS Action 5 also provides that taxpayers should only be able to apply the tax benefits associated with a preferential regime if they actually substantially pursue the economic activities to which that regime refers. The schemes analysed are those that grant tax benefits to companies engaged, inter alia, in (1) headquarters regimes, (2) distribution regimes, (3) financing or leasing regimes, (4) fund management regimes and (5) banking and insurance regimes.

In conclusion, the OECD does not expect countries to eliminate their preferential regimes but accepts their application only when the entity carries out a substantial activity that justifies it. Despite the above, the role of international bodies such as the OECD and the European Union in establishing international rules and standards has been questioned in the literature. This is how it is for Van Kommer (2018): "The argument put forth by the OECD that the tax policies of preferential regimes not only harm the country whose tax base is being eroded, but those with the preferential regimes as well, has never been sufficiently demonstrated. The assertion that such policy would cause a race to the bottom and those racing will see a corresponding drop in tax revenue together with the bottoming out of tax rates has also been

---

[4]This chapter does not explore in depth the relationship between harmful tax competition and tax incentives. It is, however, an important line of research that has been addressed by others (i.e. Littlewood 2004) and will continue to be so for Latin American countries.

[5](Qualified expenses incurred in the development of the intangible asset/Total expenses incurred in the development of the intangible asset) * Total income derived from the intangible asset = Income susceptible of applying the tax benefits associated with the preferential regime.

dispelled in the past. As such, the saying of 'we're all in this together' doesn't really have much weight" (p. 305).

6.3.2   The 2030 Sustainable Development Agenda and What It Means for Tax Incentives in Latin America

The 2030 SDGs are aimed, among other things, at reducing (1) low productivity and poor infrastructure, (2) low quality in the provision of education and health services, (3) gender and territorial inequalities in relation to minorities and (4) the accelerated impact of climate change on the poorest segments of society. With an interdisciplinary understanding of sustainable development and in order to achieve the above objectives, the SDA included 17 objectives and 169 goals.

With regard to the fiscal sphere, several studies by the Economic Commission for Latin America and the Caribbean (ECLAC) have analysed tax policies that promote the mobilisation of resources within the framework of these objectives, which include the need to strengthen revenue collection. To this end, it addresses the challenges involved in taxing the digital economy as well as modifying production and consumption patterns in order to encourage the decarbonisation of the economy and achieve improvements in public health (CEPAL 2017, 2019). For the purposes of this document, however, it is very important that for ECLAC the use of fiscal incentives limits the mobilisation of resources, but it recognises that if these incentives are geared towards investment, they can contribute to sustainable and inclusive growth.

Thus, ECLAC analyses that the mobilisation of domestic resources in the region's countries is limited by the existence of substantial fiscal incentives because the cost of these tax expenditures that operate as transfers of public resources through the tax system is considerable.

Thus, it is fundamental for tax expenditures to be effectively geared towards investment in order to achieve the sustainable development goals. However, for the Commission, the use of these mechanisms should be evaluated through cost-benefit analysis, in order to analyse the interaction between tax policies and public expenditure programs. It is therefore possible to identify whether there are justifications for the establishment or maintenance of these preferential tax treatments or whether it is advisable to replace them with other more efficient and effective measures. This is because not all special tax treatments are effective in encouraging investment; it is the case of low-income countries that resort to costly temporary tax and income tax exemptions to attract investment, when investment tax credits and accelerated depreciation can generate more investment for every dollar spent.

In sum, for ECLAC, the main link between the mobilisation of domestic resources and the SDGs is the tax collection aimed at financing the public expenditure needed to achieve this broad vision of sustainable, inclusive development in harmony with the environment.

In the same line of argument, Zhan and Karl (2016) consider that in order to meet SDGs, tax incentives need to provide low-income countries the resources to improve infrastructure, health service delivery, promotion of renewable energy, research and development (R&D) and education at affordable prices (p. 207). Thus, the authors conclude, from a 2014 survey of investment promotion agencies prepared by the United Nations Conference on Trade and Development (UNCTAD),[6] incentive priorities have tended to be economic rather than environmental or social. In this regard, "the above-mentioned UNCTAD IPA survey (2014) revealed that job creation, transfer of technology, and export promotion are the top three policy objectives of existing investment incentives schemes. Thus, these schemes focus primarily on economic goals. Environmental and social SD considerations are not top priorities, although responding agencies confirmed that they have recently gained importance in investment promotion policies. About 40 per cent of IPAs consider SD to have been only somewhat or not at all important five years ago, compared to only 5 per cent today" (p. 207, SD: sustainable development).

6.4 Current Panorama of Tax Incentives in Latin America, in General, and in the Countries of the Pacific Alliance, in Particular

Since the 1950s, there have been doctrinal references to the tax situation in Latin American countries such as the paper written by Froomkin (1957). The paper analyses the policies adopted in complex sociopolitical environments such as Argentina, Brazil, Colombia, Chile and Mexico and concludes that there is an undue transfer of US regulations to these jurisdictions, which established a new approach to depreciation, leading to disparities in marginal income tax rates. The study concludes with a sentence that is shocking: "It may, perhaps, be practical to orient the reform of the tax system towards the punishment of non investors, rather than the reward of investors" (p. 10), which demonstrates the disenchantment with tax incentives.

More recent for Latin America, in general, are the studies by Atria et al. (2018), Podestá and Hanni (2019), Renzio (2019) and CEPAL (2019), the last three discussed at the recent "Regional Seminar on Tax Benefits" event held in Bogotá in September 2019 and organised by Friedrich-Ebert-Stiftung (Fescol), Dejusticia and the "International Budget Partnership (IBP)".[7] The main conclusions of these studies include the following:

---

[6]UNCTAD is the main UN body dealing with trade, investment and development issues.

[7]Some of the topics discussed in the seminar can be consulted in the article by Medina (2019). The seminar raises the interesting idea of the Centre for Economic and Social Rights, along with other Latin American organizations, to find links between fiscal policy and human rights, a document that will be published in 2020.

1. Latin American countries have increased their collection from 9.7% of the gross domestic product (GDP) in 1960 to 16.2% of the GDP in 2014. The document explains four periods of this growth and its motivations and proposes a new approach to taxation in Latin America based on relational (interaction state-society), historical (influence of history and low collection) and transnational (capital mobility caused also by tax incentives) dimensions (Atria et al. 2018).

2. "The region's countries need to achieve greater mobilisation of resources to meet the objectives of the 2030 Sustainable Development Agenda. To this end, it is essential that they generate the right conditions and policies to attract foreign direct investment and seek to strengthen tax collection, including the gradual limitation or elimination of those tax expenditures that are not cost-effective" (Podestá and Hanni 2019, p. 5).

3. "In the countries of the Americas, most of the tax incentives for companies are aimed at certain geographical areas (generally remote areas, hostile climates, border areas or regions with less relative development), as well as specific sectors or activities, such as the promotion of renewable energies; research, development and technological innovation projects; certain sectors of industry and agro-industry; tourism; the forestry sector and film projects; among others". It is concluded, however, that the use of pro-investment incentives such as accelerated depreciation or the application of tax deductions or credits related to the cost of investment is rarely used in the region (Podestá and Hanni 2019, p. 6).

4. Although there is a methodological problem in measuring fiscal expenditure in the region, it could be argued that these fiscal waivers range from 14 to 25% of effective collection. Thus, public expenditure in relation to the tax burden is of 30%. Only 1% of the GDP of Latin American countries is a pro-investment tax expenditure. It is also concluded that tax expenditure on VAT is greater than income and that that of corporate income is greater than that of individuals (Podestá and Hanni 2019, p. 6).

5. For the specific case of the Pacific Alliance countries, not including Colombia,[8] tax expenditures represent percentages of between 2.1 and 3.1% of the GDP. Mexico has the highest result with 3.1%, of which 1.7% comes from tax expenses associated with income tax and where the benefits received by natural persons are greater than those received by legal persons (0.92% and 0.77%, respectively), while tax expenses associated with VAT represent 1.4% of the GDP. In the case of Chile, its tax expenditures represent 2.9% of the GDP, 2.1% of which are associated with income tax, in equal shares between legal and natural persons; 0.8% of the GDP is associated with tax expenditures associated with VAT. Peru allocates 2.9% of its GDP to tax expenditures, with VAT accounting for the largest portion (1.6%), while expenses related to income tax represent 0.37% of the GDP, 0.2% for natural persons and 0.17% for legal

---

[8]The only data available for tax expenditures associated with income tax represent 1.3% of GDP, 0.6 for natural persons and 0.70 for legal persons (Podestá and Hanni 2019).

persons. Tax spending on pro-investment incentives is 0.9% of GDP for Peru (44% of total tax spending), 2.4% of GDP for Chile (69% of total tax spending) and 0.9% for Mexico (27% of total tax spending) (Podestá and Hanni 2019).

6. However, as discussed in the theoretical part of this paper, other non-tax factors influence investment decisions in Latin America, such as political stability, security and a stable legal environment (Podestá and Hanni 2019).

7. The majority of Latin American countries present some kind of report on their tax expenditures, but their heterogeneity is very broad, where, for example, Mexico presents an extensive and detailed report in contrast to other countries such as Paraguay. The Mexican report includes policy purposes by incentive as well as evaluations of tax expenditures by income decile, which unfortunately does not coincide with the time when budget debates take place. In the case of Colombia, in the instrument known as the "medium-term fiscal framework", there is a quantification of tax expenditures only for some national taxes (VAT and income), but not for territorial taxes, but unfortunately this information does not influence budgetary decision-making. In Chile, the budget proposal includes a chapter on tax expenditure that includes projections. Finally, in Peru, a detailed report is published that is linked to the budget proposal (De Renzio 2019, pp. 6–9).

8. Governments in Latin America often include information on estimates of lost revenue but do not publish future revenue projections, effective dates or information on the policy purposes they pursue (De Renzio 2019).

9. Some 3.7% of the GDP in Latin America corresponds to revenues not collected in recent years (2016–2019), i.e. between 10 and 20% of public revenues (De Renzio 2019).

10. An indicator called the "Open Budget Index" produced by the International Budget Partnership shows that governments are much less transparent with respect to tax expenditures than with respect to general budget information, although this situation is not as worrying in Latin America as it is in Western Europe and sub-Saharan Africa (De Renzio 2019, p. 4).

11. In Latin America in general, and in the countries of the Pacific Alliance in particular, there are no details on the process of approval, review and evaluation of tax expenditures. Nor are there accountability mechanisms that would allow for an informed debate on the role of tax expenditures as instruments of fiscal policy (De Renzio 2019, pp. 11 and 18).

12. In Latin America and the Caribbean, of 40 countries analysed, the majority implement *tax holidays* (29 equivalent to 72%), followed by 26 that use *reduced tax rates* (65%). 60% use SEZs, 47% *investment allowances/tax credits*, and 30% *R&D deductions* (Ogazón and Calderón 2018). For 24 Latin American countries analysed by James (2016), 92% use *tax holidays/tax exemption*, 50% *investment allowance/tax credit*, 33% *reduced tax rate*, 8% *R&D tax incentives* and 4% *super deductions* (Table 7.1, 2014). However, the disparity of the percentages of the two previous studies is of concern, although this may be due to the jurisdictions under analysis and to the criteria used to classify tax incentives. Also, as recognised by James (2016, p. 155), there are obstacles to

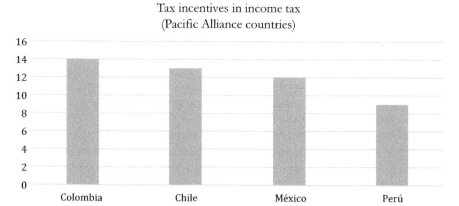

Fig. 6.1 Number of tax incentives in income tax by Pacific Alliance countries. Source: Authors based on information in Table 6.2

summarising the different types of incentives and the way in which they are administered.

Despite the previous methodological difficulties, and in order to analyse the situation of the tax incentives of the countries of the Pacific Alliance (Mexico, Peru, Chile and Colombia) in terms of income tax (direct taxation) and value-added tax (indirect taxation), I follow the categorisation by James (2016) by which the tax incentives can be classified according to the following typologies: (1) temporary tax exemptions (*tax holidays*) and a reduction of rates; (2) investment incentives (accelerated depreciation, partial deduction, tax credits and tax deferral); (3) special zones with privileged tax treatment (import duties, income tax benefits, value-added tax benefits); and (4) employment incentives (tax reductions for hiring labour). I also try not only to distinguish tax incentives from direct and indirect taxation but also to tie them to the objectives pursued by the 2030 SDA, taking into account ECLAC studies (CEPAL 2019).

From the following data, referring to income tax incentives (direct taxation), it is concluded that Colombia is the jurisdiction that most offers this type of incentive in relation to the total of the selected sample (14/24, 58%), followed by Chile (13/24, 54%), Mexico (12/24, 50%) and Peru (9/24, 37.5%) (Fig. 6.1).

As shown, Peru offers seven of the eight tax incentives in value-added tax analysed (87.5%), Colombia and Mexico, each three (37.5%), and finally Chile with 2 (25%) (Fig. 6.2).

As analysed, the objectives proposed by the 2030 SDA are aimed at consolidating economic, social and environmental sustainability. As shown in Tables 6.2 and 6.3, it is easy to find a relationship between the purposes of the incentives and the SDGs. For the economic context of the countries of the Pacific Alliance, it is essential to have cost-effective public policies to eradicate extreme poverty and inequalities and achieve an economic scenario that promotes growth, decent work, gender equality and innovation, among other purposes. In this scenario, the role of fiscal policy is

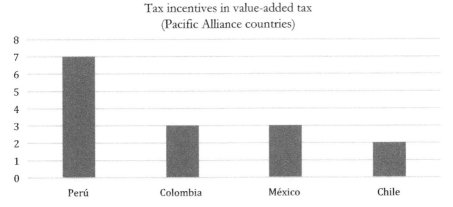

Fig. 6.2 Number of tax incentives in value-added tax by Pacific Alliance countries. Source: Authors based on information from Table 6.3

essential. Thus, the accountability of the beneficiaries as regards the incentives, in terms of the social investments undertaken, and the quantification of tax expenditure by the State is fundamental, where the amount of the latter cannot be greater than the former. In conclusion, the ideal of an equitable and progressive tax system is that tax incentives, in spite of decreasing collection, significantly increase investments to satisfy social goals.

6.5 Conclusions and Final Recommendations on Fiscal Public Policy for the Pacific Alliance Countries

Several conclusions can be drawn from the above analysis. First, not all tax benefits are incentives. But for those that are, there is no unanimity in the literature as to their definition; however, they should all meet the following characteristics: they must be special and exceptional tax measures against general rules, favourable to a sector or type of investment to attract it, they seek to increase its rate of return or reduce risks and costs, they must comply with a strict process of qualification of requirements for access, they must ideally be defined for a determined period, they include one or several taxes, they can interact with other pro-investment strategies, and they generate a negative impact on public finances if they are not cost-efficient.

The paper also concludes that, along with tax strategies, there are usually others in favour of investment and that the former are not necessarily effective, although they are the most commonly used in the global context. Faced with their undesired effects, the document analyses different general and special studies by incentives and sectors and relates the tax incentives commonly used in both direct and indirect taxation schemes.

Table 6.2 Tax incentives in income tax (direct taxation) in the countries of the Pacific Alliance and the 2030 SDA

SDGs	Type of tax incentive	Tax incentive	Chile	Colombia	Mexico	Peru
Goal 5. Gender equality	Employment incentives	1. Payroll tax credit for companies employing certain workers, including women over 40 years of age who were not legally employed in the previous year		X		
Goal 7. Affordable and non-polluting energy. Goal 12. Responsible production and consumption	Investment incentives	2. Incentives that promote the use of renewable energy	X	X	X	X
Goal 8. Decent work and economic growth	Employment incentives	3. Credits for social security contributions or additional income tax deductions for hiring certain workers such as the elderly, people with disabilities, young people or workers in certain areas or sectors, among others		X	X	
Goal 8. Decent work and economic growth.	Investment incentives	4. Credits or deductions for investment in machinery, equipment and other capital goods	X	X	X	
Goal 8. Decent work and economic growth	Investment incentives	5. Incentives for micro-, small-, and medium-sized enterprises	X	X	X	
Goal 9. Industry, innovation and infrastructure	Investment incentives	6. Income tax credits or deductions for expenditure on research and development or technological innovation	X	X	X	X
Goal 9. Industry, innovation and infrastructure	Investment incentives	7. Deductions or credits for investment in public infrastructure				X
Goal 10. Reducing inequalities		8. Revision and rationalisation of tax expenditures on personal income tax and wealth tax		X		
Goal 12. Responsible production and consumption	Investment incentives	9. Incentives for forest plantations	X	X		

Goal 13. Action for climate	Investment incentives	10. Incentives for low-carbon options such as electric vehicles, LED lighting or solar panels, among others	X		X	
Goal 9. Industry, innovation and infrastructure	Special areas with privileged tax treatment	11. Free zones—benefited from reduced income tax rates	X	X	X	X
Goal 9. Industry, innovation and infrastructure	Investment incentives	13. Legal stability contracts	X	X		X
Goal 8. Decent work and economic growth	Investment incentives	14. Exemption for publishing companies. Income obtained by publishing companies incorporated in Colombia as legal persons, whose economic activity and corporate purpose is exclusively the publication of books, magazines, pamphlets or serial collectibles of a scientific or cultural nature, are exempt from income tax and complementary for 20 years counted from the effective date of the Law		X	X	X
Goal 12. Responsible production and consumption	Investment incentives	15. Credit for solar thermal systems for the benefit of construction companies that install solar thermal systems (STS) in the homes they build. Construction companies can charge a credit against their mandatory monthly provisional payments of up to 100% of the cost of the STS installed to produce hot water in new homes whose selling price is less than a certain amount. The incentive seeks to extend the use of STS	X			

(continued)

Table 6.2 (continued)

SDGs	Type of tax incentive	Tax incentive	Chile	Colombia	Mexico	Peru
Goal 8. Decent work and economic growth	Investment incentives	16. Exemption of rents for new and remodelled hotels		X		
Goal 9. Industry, innovation and infrastructure	Special areas with privileged tax treatment	17. Centres of export, transformation, industry, commercialisation and services (CETICOS)—exempt from income tax				X
Goal 10. Reducing inequalities	Investment incentives	18. Tax expenses for personal income tax—in the form of deductions or credits. In general, they depend on the type and level of education that qualifies for preferential treatment, as well as the types of expenses covered and the age and place in the household of the person for whom the education expenses were incurred	X		X	
Goal 4. Quality education	Investment incentives	19. Tax benefits to companies in order to encourage investment in education and training of their employees. These measures in general have taken two forms: deductions or credits	X	X	X	X
Goal 9. Industry, innovation and infrastructure	Investment incentives	20. Tax benefits for companies located in a geographical area	X Tierra del Fuego		X Chiapas, Guerrero and Oaxaca	X Amazon, Andean high areas
Goal 9. Industry, innovation and infrastructure	Investment incentives	21. Tax benefits to income from foreign investment funds	X			
Goal 10. Reducing inequalities	Investment incentives	22. 165% deduction for investments or donations in cinematographic projects		X		

Goal 8. Decent work and economic growth	Investment incentives	23. Credit for investment in cinematography, theatrical production and sports infrastructure		X
Goal 12. Responsible production and consumption	Investment incentives	24. Reduced rates for the agricultural sector and agro-industry		X

Source: Authors based on the regulations of the countries analysed and ECLAC studies (CEPAL 2019)

Table 6.3 Tax incentives in value-added tax (indirect taxation) in the countries of the Pacific Alliance and the objectives of the 2030 SDA

SDGs	Type of tax incentive	Tax incentive	Chile	Colombia	Mexico	Peru
Goal 9. Industry, innovation and infrastructure	Special areas with privileged tax treatment	1. Duty-free zones (with goods and services exempt from VAT and customs duties)	X	X	X	X
Goal 9. Industry, innovation and infrastructure	Investment incentives	2. Special regime for early recovery of VAT—this regime establishes the refund of VAT on imports and/or local purchases of new capital goods, new intermediate goods, services and construction contracts, carried out in the pre-productive stage and which will be used in the execution of the projects foreseen in the investment contracts and which are destined for the execution of operations taxed with VAT or for exports				X
Goal 13. Action for climate	Investment incentives	3. Promotion of the agricultural sector—taxpayers covered by the Law for the Promotion of the Agricultural Sector may request a refund of VAT paid on the purchase of capital goods, inputs, services and construction contracts. In addition, they can depreciate hydraulic and irrigation infrastructure works at an accelerated rate of 20%. Finally, companies in the sector are affected at a reduced rate of 15%				X
Goal 8. Decent work and economic growth	Investment incentives	4. Mining incentives— refund of VAT paid in the exploration phase and deduction of investments in infrastructure constituting a public service				X
Goal 9. Industry, innovation	Special areas with privileged	5. Export, transformation, industry, commercialisation and				X

(continued)

Table 6.3 (continued)

SDGs	Type of tax incentive	Tax incentive	Chile	Colombia	Mexico	Peru
and infrastructure	tax treatment	services centres (CETICOS)—exempt from VAT				
Goal 4. Quality education	Investment incentives	6. Value-added tax exemptions for the consumption of education services, school supplies and transport. Educational services are generally defined in broad terms and include all levels, as well as their provision by public and private institutions. Few specifically mention technical and vocational education and training—Peru is the exception—but these generic definitions could be interpreted as including technical and vocational education and training provided in the formal education system, as well as that provided in non-formal institutions recognised by the corresponding government agencies	X	X	X	X
Goal 9. Industry, innovation and infrastructure	Investment incentives	7. Those responsible for VAT may deduct from the income tax payable, corresponding to the year in which it is paid, or in any of the following taxable periods, the VAT paid for the acquisition, construction or training and import of real productive fixed assets, including that associated with the services necessary to put them into use		X		
Goal 9. Industry, innovation and infrastructure		8. Hotel services for foreigners			X Zero rate	X Zero rate

Source: Authors based on the regulations for the countries analysed and ECLAC studies (CEPAL 2019)

It is also clear that the possible distortions that tax incentives may generate in the existence of preferential regimes is a concern of the OECD's BEPS Project. It is therefore essential to analyse the substantiality of economic activities, intensifying the BEPS Project into areas such as intellectual property, among others. As for its effectiveness in achieving the SDGs, it is highly pertinent to establish the connection with the pro-investment fiscal policy measures, as well as its constant monitoring and evaluation.

However, the paper explores the discouragement reported regarding tax incentives in the Latin American context by demonstrating the problems related to the quantification of the associated tax expenditure and its cost-efficiency, as well as the poor accountability of the beneficiaries of these incentives. Therefore, in the Pacific Alliance countries, there is no follow-up to such fiscal policies, let alone an adequate relationship with the budgetary processes in place in these countries, thus affecting the SDGs.

In view of the above, and following the recommendations of Redonda et al. (2018), Podestá and Hanni (2019), De Renzio (2019), Van Kommer (2018), CEPAL (2019) and James (2016) in particular, public fiscal policy on tax incentives in Latin American countries in general, and in the Pacific Alliance in particular, should take into account the following:

1. *Periodic preparation of reports on tax incentives.* Countries should provide constant, timely and detailed reports on the costs, expected benefits, expiration dates, main beneficiaries and goals of the incentives. They should also estimate, as accurately as possible, the tax expenditure that results from them.
2. *Linking tax incentive reports to budgetary decision-making.* Cost-efficiency analysis of tax incentives should be taken into account when governments prepare their annual budgets, and when they are approved by the corresponding legislature or body at the sub-national level.
3. *Constant monitoring and evaluation of the effectiveness of tax incentives and the participation of multiple actors.* Governments, along with citizen oversight and international cooperation, should follow up on fiscal policies that include tax incentives and ensure their cost-effectiveness. They should also review competition and complementarity with pro-investment mechanisms, apart from tax mechanisms.
4. *The assessment of tax incentives should include the fulfilment of the international aspirations of the OECD BEPS Project and 2030 SDA.* The international standards contained in the BEPS Project and in SDA serve to harmonise tax regimes, avoid harmful tax competition, and make them fairer and more progressive. Some tax incentives can contribute to SDGs beyond the classic social-economic objectives of jobs and growth (e.g. environment, renewable energy, gender equality).
5. *Inclusion of tax incentives only in tax rules.* It is reiterated practice in Latin American countries that non-tax regulations include tax incentives to promote sectors or activities in particular, in the best of cases, since their introduction is often motivated by particular interests and/or political pressures.

6. *Clear criteria in the law for access to tax incentives.* In order to avoid corruption in the allocation of incentives, the law must unequivocally establish the requirements for their granting and terms of validity

7. *There is a need for coordination between national and subnational governments in the monitoring and evaluation of tax incentives.* It is common in the region not to quantify the tax expenditure generated at subnational level by assigned tax incentives, where the discussion usually remains at national level. There is therefore a need for adequate coordination among the different levels of government.

The problem of tax incentives in Latin American is over-diagnosed. Thus, an effort is required from national and subnational governments to improve flat tax structures, with exceptional incentives for investment and periodic evaluations, in order to comply with international standards and achieve more equitable, progressive and efficient tax schemes.

Acknowledgement I am especially grateful for the investigative support of Alejandra Sarmiento Rojas, graduate assistant of the Master's in Taxation, and María Camila Londoño Avellaneda, the programme's academic assistant. Their rigour and dedication have meant that this work is duly supported by extensive literature on global tax incentives that allows a critical perspective of our realities in the Latin American context.

References

Action 5. *BEPS project*. Retrieved September 26, 2019, from https://www.oecd.org/tax/beps/beps-actions/action5/

Atria, J., Groll, C., & Fernanda, V. M. (Eds.). (2018). *Rethinking taxation in Latin America: Reform and challenges in times of uncertainty. Latin American political economy*. Cham: Palgrave Macmillan. https://doi.org/10.1007/978-3-319-60119-9.

Bolnick, B. (2004). *Effectiveness and economic impact of tax incentives in the SADC region*. Gaborone: SADC Tax Subcommittee, SADC Trade, Industry, Finance and Investment Directorate.

Carpentier, C., & Suret, J.-M. (2016). The effectiveness of tax incentives for business angels. In *Handbook of research on business angels*. Cheltenham: Edward Elgar. https://doi-org.ezproxy.uniandes.edu.co:8443/10.4337/9781783471720.00021.

Carrizosa, M. (2008). Tax reform: Tax policy, reform, and competitiveness in Latin America. In J. Haar & J. Price (Eds.), *Can Latin America compete?* New York: Palgrave Macmillan.

Castañeda, N. (2018). Business groups, tax efficiency, and regressivity in Colombia. In J. Atria, C. Groll, & M. Valdés (Eds.), *Rethinking taxation in Latin America. Latin American political economy*. Cham: Palgrave Macmillan.

Comisión Económica para América Latina y el Caribe (CEPAL). (2017). *Financiamiento de la Agenda 2030 para el Desarrollo Sostenible en América Latina y el Caribe: desafíos para la movilización de recursos*. LC/FDS.1/4. Santiago: CEPAL. https://repositorio.cepal.org/bitstream/handle/11362/41169/1/S1700216_es.pdf

Comisión Económica para América Latina y el Caribe (CEPAL). (2019). *Panorama fiscal en América Latina*. LC/PUB.2019/8-P. Santiago: CEPAL. https://repositorio.cepal.org/bitstream/handle/11362/44516/1/S1900075_es.pdf

Cotrut, M., & Munyandi, K. (2018). *Tax incentives in the BEPS Era* (Vol. 3). Amsterdam: IBDF Tax Research Series.

De Renzio, P. (2019). Contabilizados, pero sin rendir cuentas: La transparencia en los gastos tributarios en América Latina. *Budget Brief*. International Budget Partnership. https://www.internationalbudget.org/wp-content/uploads/tax-expenditure-transparency-in-latin-america-spanish-ibp-2019.pdf

Ferreira, V. A., & Perdelwitz, A. (2018). Chapter 6. Tax incentives and tax treaties. In *Tax incentives in the BEPS era* (Vol. 3). Amsterdam: IBDF Tax Research Series.

Froomkin, J. (1957). Some problems of tax policy in Latin America. *National Tax Journal (Pre-1986), 10*(4), 370. https://search-proquest-com.ezproxy.uniandes.edu.co:8443/docview/207270416?accountid=34489.

James, S. (2016). Tax incentives around the world. In A. T. Tavares-Lehmann, P. Toledano, L. Johnson, & L. Sachs (Eds.), *Rethinking investment incentives: Trends and policy options* (pp. 153–176). New York: Columbia University Press. http://www.jstor.org.ezproxy.uniandes.edu.co:8080/stable/10.7312/tava17298.10.

Jorgenson, D. W. (1996). *Investment: Tax policy and the cost of capital*. Cambridge, MA: MIT Press. http://search.ebscohost.com.ezproxy.uniandes.edu.co:8080/login.aspx?direct=true&db=nlebk&AN=48876&lang=es&site=ehost-live.

Klemm, A. (2010). Causes, benefits, and risks of business tax incentives. *International Tax and Public Finance, 17*(3), 315–336.

Laukkanen, A. (2018). Chapter 5. Special economic zones: The acceptance of tax incentives in the BEPS world. In *Tax incentives in the BEPS era* (Vol. 3). Amsterdam: IBDF Tax Research Series.

Littlewood, M. (2004). Tax competition: Harmful to whom? *Michigan Journal of International Law, 25*(1), 411–487.

Medina, M. A. (2019, September). Beneficios tributarios: ¿incentivos o privilegios? *El Espectador*. https://www.elespectador.com/economia/beneficios-tributarios-incentivos-o-privilegios-articulo-881597

Munongo, S., Akanbi, O. A., Robinson, Z., & College of Economic & Management Sciences, South Africa Department of Economics. (2017). Do tax incentives matter for investment? A literature review. *Business and Economic Horizons, 13*(2), 152–168. https://doi.org/10.15208/beh.2017.12.

Ogazón Juárez, L. G., & Calderón Manrique, D.. (2018). Chapter 1. Introduction to tax incentives in the BEPS era. In *Tax incentives in the BEPS era* (Vol. 3). Amsterdam: IBDF Tax Research Series.

Ogazón Juárez, L. G., & Hamzaoui, R. (2015). Chapter 1. Common strategies against tax avoidance: A global overview. In *International tax structures in the BEPS era: An analysis of anti-abuse measures* (Vol. 2). Amsterdam: IBFD Tax Research Series.

Podestá, A., & Hanni, M. (2019). *Los incentivos fiscales a las empresas en América Latina y el Caribe*. Documentos de Proyectos (LC/TS.2019/50). Santiago: Comisión Económica para América Latina y el Caribe (CEPAL)/Oxfam Internacional. https://www-cdn.oxfam.org/s3fs-public/file_attachments/incentivos_fiscales_web_1.pdf

Poterba, J. M., & National Research Council (U.S.). (1997). *Borderline case: International tax policy, corporate research and development, and investment*. U.S. Industry, Restructuring And Renewal. Washington, DC: National Academies Press. http://search.ebscohost.com.ezproxy.uniandes.edu.co:8080/login.aspx?direct=true&db=nlebk&AN=923&lang=es&site=ehost-live

Redonda, A., Díaz de Sarralde, S., Hallerberg, M., Johnson, L., Melamud, A., Rozemberg, R., Schwab, J., & von Haldenwang, C. (2018). *Tax expenditure and the treatment of tax incentives for investment*. Economics Discussion Papers No 2018-57. Kiel Institute for the World Economy. http://www.economics-ejournal.org/economics/journalarticles/2019-12

Ruiz-Vargas, M. A., Velandia-Sánchez, J. M., & Navarro-Morato, O. S. (2017). Incidencia de la política de incentivos tributarios sobre la inversión en el sector minero energético colombiano:

un análisis exploratorio de su efectividad. *Cuadernos de Contabilidad, 17*(43), 109–126. https://doi.org/10.11144/Javeriana.cc17-43.ipit.

Tavares-Lehmann, A. T. (2016). Types of investment incentives. In A. T. Tavares-Lehmann, P. Toledano, L. Johnson, & L. Sachs (Eds.), *Rethinking investment incentives: Trends and policy options* (pp. 17–44). New York: Columbia University Press. http://www.jstor.org.ezproxy.uniandes.edu.co:8080/stable/10.7312/tava17298.5.

UNCTAD. (2000). *Tax incentives and foreign direct investment: A Global Survey.* ASIT Advisory Studies No. 16.

Valdés, M. F. (2019, July). Beneficios tributarios y la ley de Murphy. *El Espectador.* https://www.elespectador.com/economia/beneficios-tributarios-y-la-ley-de-murphy-columna-872855

Van Kommer, V. (2018). Chapter 9. The effectiveness of tax incentives. In *Tax incentives in the BEPS era* (Vol. 3). Amsterdam: IBDF Tax Research Series.

Zee, H., Stosky, J., & Ley, E. (2002). Tax incentives for business investment: A primer for policy makers in developing countries. In *World development* (Vol. 30, pp. 1497–1516). Amsterdam: Elsevier Science.

Zhan, J., & Karl, J. (2016). Investment incentives for sustainable development. In A. T. Tavares-Lehmann, P. Toledano, L. Johnson, & L. Sachs (Eds.), *Rethinking investment incentives: Trends and policy options* (pp. 204–227). New York: Columbia University Press. http://www.jstor.org.ezproxy.uniandes.edu.co:8080/stable/10.7312/tava17298.12.

Zort, E. (2014). *Protecting the tax base.* Selected topics in protecting the tax base of developing countries. Draft Paper No. 3.

Chapter 7
Tax Incentives in Developing Countries: A Case Study—Singapore and Philippines

Irma Mosquera Valderrama and Mirka Balharová

List of Abbreviations

ALS	The Aircraft Leasing Scheme
ASEAN	The Association of Southeast Asian Nations
BEPS	Base Erosion and Profit Shifting
BIMP-EAGA	The Brunei Darussalam-Indonesia-Malaysia-Philippines East ASEAN Growth Area
BOI	Philippine Board of Investments
CIAT	The Inter-American Center of Tax Administrations
CIT	Corporate income tax rate
CITIRA	Corporate Income Tax Reform and Fiscal Incentives Modernization
CREATE	Corporate Recovery and Tax Incentives for Enterprises Act
CTPR	The Comprehensive Tax Reform Program

Associate Professor Tax Law, Lead Researcher GLOBTAXGOV ERC Project at Leiden University. The writing and research carried out for this chapter is the result of the ERC research in the framework of the GLOBTAXGOV Project (2018–2023). The GLOBTAXGOV Project investigates international tax law making including the adoption of OECD and EU standards by 12 countries. The GLOBTAXGOV Project has received funding from the European Research Council (ERC) under the European Union's Seventh Framework Programme (FP/2007–2013) (ERC Grant agreement n. 758671) Project (2018–2023).

Tax Assistant Blick Rothenberg. LLM International Tax Law at King's College London.

I. Mosquera Valderrama (✉)
Leiden University, Leiden, The Netherlands
e-mail: i.j.mosquera.valderrama@law.leidenuniv.nl

M. Balharová
King's College London, London, UK

© The Author(s) 2021
I. J. Mosquera Valderrama et al. (eds.), *Taxation, International Cooperation and the 2030 Sustainable Development Agenda*, United Nations University Series on Regionalism 19, https://doi.org/10.1007/978-3-030-64857-2_7

DEI	The Development and Expansion Incentive
EDB	The Economic Development Board
EEIA	The Economic Expansion Incentives Act
FDI	Foreign Direct Investment
FIRB	The Fiscal Incentives Review Board
FTC	The Finance and Treasury Centre Incentive
IBFD	The International Bureau of Fiscal Documentation
IDI	The IP Development Incentive
IMF	International Monetary Fund
IP	The Intellectual Property
IPA	Investment Promotion Agency
IPP	The Investment Priorities Plan
IRAS	The Inland Revenue Authority of Singapore
ITA	The Income Tax Act
LIA	The Land Intensification Allowance
MNE	Multinational Enterprises
OECD	The Organisation for Economic Co-operation and Development
PC	The Pioneer Certificate Incentive
PEZA	Philippine Economic Zone Authority
REG(E)	The Resource Efficiency Grant for Energy
RISC	The Research Incentive Scheme for Companies
ROHQ	Regional Operating Headquarters
R&D	Research and Development
SDGs	Sustainable Development Goals
SIPP	Strategic Investment Priorities Plan
TGC	The Training Grant for Company
TIMTA	The Tax Incentives Management and Transparency Act
UN	United Nations
UNCTAD	United Nations Conference on Trade and Development
VAT	Value-added tax

7.1 Introduction

Globalisation and increased mobility of capital allow companies to structure their business operations across various jurisdictions and to select countries that offer the most favourable investment climate. Decisive factors include, among others, lower capital costs, ability to benefit from free trade agreements and favourable tax incentives (Easson 2001). In principle, tax incentives are considered to be very useful means for attracting foreign direct investment; however, their design and implementation can have a great impact on whether they prove to be successful in a particular country. Most common types of tax incentives offered are tax holidays, reductions in tax rates and deductions for certain expenditures and free-trade zones, among others. An overview of the incentives introduced by countries to promote foreign direct investment has been developed by the United Nations Conference on Trade and Development (UNCTAD) (2000).

While tax incentives in developed countries mainly aim to promote export, research and development activities and improve the overall position of the domestic firms on global market, the primary role of tax incentives in developing countries is often the opposite. Tax incentive regimes in developing countries aim to attract foreign direct investment, often into specific regions in the country or specific market sectors.

The assessment and efficiency of tax incentive regimes in developing countries have been discussed for almost more than two decades now (Holland and Vann 1998; Raff and Srinivasan 1998; Kinda 2014; Munongo et al. 2017). Among other reasons, there are concerns whether tax incentives generate the desired economic growth and social development (Brauner 2013: 26). There are also concerns that the incentives erode the tax base without having actual effects on the level of investment in the country (Brauner 2013). Therefore, the focus is no longer only on tax incentives as the methods of attracting investment but also on the impact they have on countries' economies (IMF et al. 2015).

More recently, and in light of the Base Erosion and Profit Shifting (BEPS)[1] Action Plans, countries have been reviewed in light of BEPS Action 5. BEPS Action 5 deals with tax incentives on geographically mobile business income regarded as preferential tax regimes to assess whether these regimes can be regarded as harmful tax practices. BEPS Action 5 is one of the four minimum standards that countries participating in the BEPS Inclusive Framework have committed to implement. The assessment of BEPS Action 5 is outside the scope of this chapter (Mosquera Valderrama 2020b); however, some reference will be made to the compatibility of tax incentives in Singapore and the Philippines with BEPS Action 5.

In light of this background, the first aim of this chapter is to compare the tax incentives for developing countries with a case study of two countries: Singapore and the Philippines.[2] Singapore has been regarded in literature as one of the countries that has successfully attracted foreign direct investment; however, it is not yet clear whether this is the result of tax incentives or any other measure. The Philippines is at the time of writing in the process of introducing a comprehensive tax reform program (CTRP) that aims to redesign the tax incentives to become more

---

[1]The BEPS Project contains ten best practices and four minimum standards. The BEPS four minimum standards that should be implemented are countering of harmful tax practices and exchange of rulings (Action 5), preventing of treaty abuse (Action 6), re-examining transfer pricing documentation including country-by-country reporting (Action 13) and enhancing resolution of disputes (Action 14). At the time of writing (June 2020), 137 jurisdictions have committed to implement the BEPS 4 minimum standards. In addition, a Multilateral Convention to swiftly implement in double tax conventions some of the BEPS measures has been signed by more than 90 jurisdictions. This Convention is in force since 1 July 2018.

[2]The focus of this contribution is in corporate income tax mainly for multinationals. The main reason is the argument that tax incentives favours or not foreign direct investment (which is mainly done by multinationals). The tax incentives for small and medium enterprises and individuals are outside the scope of this analysis.

competitive in the region and to achieve social and economic growth. These countries also belong to the same region (i.e. South East Asia), and therefore, the comparison of the incentives in these countries can also contribute to best practices in the region. Following this comparison, the second aim of this chapter is to evaluate the tax incentives granted in Singapore and the Philippines considering a new proposed evaluative framework for tax incentives in light of the Sustainable Development Goals (SDGs). The economic analysis of costs and benefits is outside the scope of this contribution.[3]

This chapter is structured as follows: Sect. 7.2 introduces the framework to evaluate tax incentives developed by literature, international organisations and our own proposed framework. Section 7.3 contains a case study of Singapore and the Philippines, where their respective tax incentive regimes are analysed and other considerations for attracting investment in both countries are addressed. Due to the COVID-19 pandemic (at the time of writing June 2020), a short reference will be made to the tax incentives to provide fiscal stimuli introduced by Singapore and the Philippines. Section 7.4 provides a comparison of these two countries and the assessment of the design of tax incentives in these two countries in light of our proposed framework presented in Sect. 7.2. Section 7.5 concludes this chapter.

7.2   Framework to Evaluate Tax Incentives

This section provides an overview of the main concerns in the literature by academics and international tax organisations regarding the framework to evaluate incentives in light of the effectiveness and efficiency of tax incentives in developing countries. Thereafter, our proposed evaluative framework for tax incentives will be presented.

7.2.1   Literature

Tax incentives have been discussed extensively by academic scholars. In the analysis of literature, the findings on the relevance of tax incentives and the role they play in attracting foreign direct investment (FDI) tend to be inconclusive. For instance, van Parys and James argue that the effectiveness of tax incentives is linked to the investment climate and more specifically investor's confidence in the revenue authorities (Van Parys and James 2009). This is crucial for regions where tax

---

[3]The reason is the recent reports from the UN-CIAT and World Bank that have been published (Sects. 7.2.2.2. and 7.2.2.5, respectively). In order to contribute to the discussion of tax incentives, this contribution and the proposed assessment framework focus on the administrative considerations for the design of tax incentives which has received less attention from scholars and international organizations.

competition is high and the neighbouring countries race to the bottom to provide more favourable tax incentives. In a situation where two countries from the same region provide an identical tax incentive, it is more likely that the country with the better investment climate will attract the FDI. James estimates the chances of countries with good investment climate are eight times greater at attracting FDI as opposed to countries with less favourable investment environment (James 2010).

Bird and Zolt share this view and argue that tax policy is just a fraction of the problem and when considering the bigger picture, improving investment climate in general will prove to be more efficient in attracting more foreign direct investment (FDI) (Bird and Zolt 2008). Investment climate is influenced by a number of factors including, for example, political stability, stability of fiscal policy, adequate infrastructure and effective, transparent and accountable public administration (James 2009). Zolt also argues that tax incentives bring economic growth, which results in an increase in the spending power of local residents, and they ultimately generate greater tax revenue (Zolt 2015). Brauner, on the other hand, voices concerns that tax incentives do not bring the desired economic growth to the region and are not necessarily the decisive factor for attracting foreign investment (Brauner 2013).

7.2.2 International Organisations

7.2.2.1 2015 Toolkit on Tax Incentives for Low-Income Countries

In the 2015 Toolkit on Tax Incentives for Low-Income Countries (2015 Toolkit), the Organisation for Economic Co-operation and Development (OECD), the International Monetary Fund (IMF), the World Bank and the United Nations (UN) stated that: "Tax incentives generally rank low in investment climate surveys in low-income countries, and there are many examples in which they are reported to be redundant—that is, investment would have been undertaken even without them. Their fiscal cost can also be high, reducing opportunities for much-needed public spending on infrastructure, public services or social support, or requiring higher taxes on other activities" (IMF et al. 2015).

These organisations have therefore provided recommendations to low-income countries to improve the effectiveness and efficiency of their investment tax incentives. Some of these recommendations are: "At the national level, there is generally scope to improve the design of tax incentives (for example by placing greater emphasis on cost-based incentives rather than profit-based ones; and by targeting tax incentives better), strengthen their governance (for instance through more transparency, better tax laws and a stronger role of the Minister of Finance) and by undertaking more systematic evaluations. At the international level, countries may gain by coordinating their tax incentive policies regionally, so as to mitigate the negative spillovers from tax competition" (IMF et al. 2015: 32).

7.2.2.2 2018 UN-CIAT Design and Assessment of Tax Incentives in Developing Countries

In 2018, the United Nations and the Inter-American Center of Tax Administrations (CIAT) published a report for design and assessment of tax incentives in developing countries with a case study of the Dominican Republic (UN-CIAT 2018).[4] This report provided a cost and benefit analysis of tax incentives and also a checklist for drafting tax incentives legislation in developing countries. The checklist contained the list of things to be considered to maximise clarity and administration of tax incentives and to ensure consistency of legal drafting with the policy underlying the tax incentive.

The main elements of the cost-benefit analysis provided in the report are (1) costs—revenue costs, resource allocation costs, enforcement and compliance costs and the costs associated with corruption and lack of transparency—and (2) benefits, to attract investment and to correct market inefficiencies or general positive externalities.

In light of this analysis, one of the findings of this report is that for developed countries, it is sometimes easier to provide tax incentives than to correct deficiencies in the legal system or to improve the infrastructure of one country. However, tax incentives cannot compensate for the deficiencies in the design of the tax system or inadequate physical, financial, legal or institutional infrastructure. Therefore, this report recommends that developing countries bring the corporate tax rate regime closer to international practice and to correct the deficiencies rather than provide investors with additional tax benefits.

7.2.2.3 2018 Asian Development Bank (ADB) Tax and Development: Challenges in Asia and the Pacific

Even though there is no specific report dealing with tax incentives published by the Asian Development Bank, there has been attention to the challenges in Asia and the Pacific regarding tax incentives. For instance, the 2018 Report on Tax and Development addressed in Chap. 2 the need for tax incentives "to be controlled by the Ministry of Finance. If they are managed by the Investment Board or ministries to promoted FDI, tax incentives proliferate and can become too complex at the expense of government coffers. In such a scenario, lost revenues will have to be raised from other distortionary taxes" (Nakabayashi 2018: 12). In addition, the report stated the need to prevent a race to the bottom tax competition and the need to broaden "the tax base by rationalizing tax incentives and exemptions" (Nakabayashi 2018: 12).

The Asian Development Bank has published an overview of tax incentives which provides a comparison of the tax guidelines and regulations pertaining to direct

---

[4]The chapters were authored by three external consultants: Eric Zolt, Peter A. Harris and Duanjie Chen.

investment in South East Asia and South Asia. According to the website, "data sources include official reports and press releases from respective government were government agencies such as ministries of finance, trade and commerce; economic development boards; boards of investment; and related agencies of national governments pursuing investment creation and promotion, and to some extent, trade". However, the database does not provide the current developments, for instance, the current tax reform in the Philippines, or information related to fiscal stimulus regarding COVID-19. Therefore, for a comparison of fiscal stimuli measures, the database of international organisations (e.g. IMF) is relevant.[5]

7.2.2.4   2018 United Nations ESCAP Report on Tax Policy for Sustainable Development in Asia and the Pacific

The 2018 ESCAP report contains a chapter addressing tax incentives and tax base protection for developing countries. The focus of the chapter is on the economic effect of tax incentives. Therefore, administrative considerations regarding the complexity, arbitrariness and use of discretionary tax incentives are not addressed in this chapter (Jun 2018: 75).[6] Despite this caveat, the report addresses the choice of governments to "use a more visible and readily available tool, such as a tax holiday, to attract investors rather than resort to such time-consuming measures as enhancing macroeconomic stability and upgrading public infrastructure" (Jun 2018: 74).

The chapter contains an analysis of some Asia-Pacific countries (i.e. Singapore, Hong Kong, China and the Republic of Korea). Regarding Singapore, the author analysis is that "Singapore excels in state efficiency items compared to its neighbours. This suggest that a given incentive is likely to be more cost-effective in Singapore than, say, in the Republic of Korea because administrative costs and corruption possibilities associated with tax incentives might be much lower in Singapore" (Jun 2018: 92). The report also addresses the changes that Singapore has made to its incentive policy stating that "in fact, Singapore has adjusted its incentive policy from an aggressive, broad-based incentive scheme at earlies states of development when its competitive advantage was limited, to a more target-based one couple with lower statutory rates in the mid-1980s when it already became an attractive investment location" (Jun 2018: 93).

Finally, the report concludes based on the comparative study of countries that "effective use of tax incentives critically hinges on country-specific factors and priorities, defying 'one-size-fits-all' best practices. While investment incentives

---

[5]The COVID-19 pandemic has resulted in countries introducing, for instance, tax payment deferral, more generous loss offset provisions and tax exemptions, among others. See overview IMF website Policy Responses to COVID-19 at https://www.imf.org/en/Topics/imf-and-covid19/Policy-Responses-to-COVID-19. Accessed 16 June 2020.

[6]See also footnote 43 in Jun (2018: 75).

may work well in conjunction with strong climate investments, their roles should not be precluded in countries with weak investment climates" (Jun 2018: 94).

7.2.2.5 2020 World Bank Evaluating the Costs and Benefits of Corporate Tax Incentives

The 2020 Report by the World Bank focuses on the cost-benefit analysis of tax incentives (as it was also the case in the UN-CIAT Report). The report states that the "cost-benefit analysis can help policy makers demonstrate the direct cost (tax revenue foregone) incurred by governments against the economic benefits being pursued. Global evidence on investment location decisions suggests that while tax incentives can help attract investment, other factors, such as the wider investment climate and market opportunities, matter most. Tax incentives should therefore be conceived as part of a country's broader investment policy framework and governments should be realistic about the potential impact any measure may have. In this light, cost-benefit analysis can serve as a powerful tool to inform incentives policy reform and offer important inputs into a country's investment policy strategy" (Kronfol and Steenbergen 2020: 1).

For the authors of this report, this cost-benefit analysis can be useful to "policy reforms to improve the targeting, design, transparency, and administration of tax incentives" (Kronfol and Steenbergen 2020: 4). In order to calculate the estimate of tax expenditure related to incentive, the report addresses three approaches (i.e. calculation of the revenue foregone, or revenue gain or outlay equivalence) (Kronfol and Steenbergen 2020: 5).

The report also makes a distinction between location (attracting new firms) and behavioural (shifting firm behaviour) incentives to determine the success of the incentive (whether the business establishes in the region because of tax incentives or whether the business produce more output due to incentives) (Kronfol and Steenbergen 2020: 6). In order to measure the benefits, the report provides an overview of different tools to assess the effectiveness of locational and behavioural incentives (Kronfol and Steenbergen 2020: 6–7).

7.2.3 Proposed Evaluative Framework for Tax Incentives in Light of the SDGs

Following the analysis of tax incentives by scholars and international organisations, this chapter provides an evaluative framework of tax incentives in developing countries. This framework takes into account not only the administrative considerations and legal drafting of tax incentives but also the link of tax incentives to the sustainable development goals. This framework has been further developed by one of the authors elsewhere (Mosquera Valderrama 2020a).

Ideally, an effective and efficient tax incentive will generate social benefit, which is greater than the associated social cost of the incentive (IMF et al. 2015: 32). The resulting social benefit should improve living conditions for the people and also contribute to the country's economic growth and development. The assessment of the social cost and the resulting social benefit is crucial and also very challenging, as there are a number of factors, which need to be considered.

In order to link the analysis of tax incentives to the sustainable development goals, we argue that tax incentives in developing countries should be evaluated taking into account the "effectiveness" of tax incentives in achieving their aims (social and economic growth)—and then the cost side—and their "efficiency" in terms of revenue loss, fair taxation and equal opportunities for all citizens.

In this proposed framework, the "reference to social and economic growth and also to fair taxation and equal opportunities are linked to the sustainable development goals. These goals include achieving decent work in economic growth, eradication of poverty and building resilient infrastructure. The governments have an important role in encouraging growth and development which also contribute to SDG targets 17.1: Strengthen domestic resource mobilization and 17.16 on global partnerships for sustainable development" (Mosquera Valderrama 2020a).

This framework should be designed by each country and, if possible, take into account the practice of other countries in the region so that countries can also exchange best practices. For the purposes of the assessment of the tax incentives in Singapore and the Philippines, the following criteria can be used (Mosquera Valderrama 2020a):

- Systematic review of tax incentives. This review should focus on whether the tax incentive has achieved the specific goals in terms of effectiveness and efficiency.
- Clear target and eligibility criteria for granting the incentive, to be measured in light of the social and economic development of the region/sector/country.
- Tax incentives should be transparent, and the granting of the tax incentive should not be discretionary. To achieve greater accountability and transparency of tax incentives, it is important that the general tax expenditure of the country is periodically analysed and tax budgets are implemented (UN-CIAT 2018: 19). Efforts should be made by international organisations to train staff and use data analytics to carry out this analysis in developing countries. For instance, the OECD regional revenue statistics including the one for the Asia and Pacific Region refers to the need to include the reporting in the revenue side and the expenditure side (OECD 2019b). After providing a distinction between tax and expenditure provisions, this report also states that the focus of the report is on tax provision rather than the expenditure provision.[7] However, in our opinion, in

---

[7] Annex A of the report para. 24 states:

"Because this publication is concerned only with the revenue side of government operations, no account being taken of the expenditure side, a distinction has to be made between tax and expenditure provisions. Normally there is no difficulty in making this distinction as expenditures are made outside the tax system and the tax accounts and under legislation separate from the tax

order to increase transparency, countries should also include in their annual budgets the expenditure report as it has been done by the Philippines and Singapore (see Sect. 7.3.6).

• The tax incentive should have a fiscal budget and perhaps also a ceiling in the budget so that once reached the ceiling of revenue loss, the tax incentive will be terminated.

The institutional conditions for these incentives should be also taken into account mainly:

• Developing countries should appoint one person, typically the Ministry of Finance, to administer and monitor the tax incentives.
• Developing countries should prevent the use of several laws (investment, tax, other) to regulate tax incentives. Furthermore, to enhance transparency, legislation regulating tax incentives should be publicly available with a specific reference in English (to the incentive, the tax benefit and the criteria used to systematically evaluate the tax incentive).
• The use of one-stop-shop agencies should be encouraged, since investors may find it useful to access the information but also dealing with all permits/licenses and further questions regarding their investment. This agency should have a code of conduct to guide their activities within the agency, and in addition, a list of sanctions (administrative fine or imprisonment) should be introduced. In case that there is any corruption or bribery, the sanction for the respective agency official should be made publicly available.

For the two countries of study, Singapore and the Philippines, this framework will be further developed in Sect. 7.4.2. The following section will provide an overview of the tax incentives in Singapore and the Philippines.

7.3   Case Study: Singapore and the Philippines

At the time of writing, Singapore is ranked 2 and the Philippines 95 in the World Bank Doing Business Guide (ease of doing business worldwide), and within the East Asia-Pacific Region (25 countries), Singapore is ranked 1 and the Philippines 11 (The World Bank 2019). This shows that in terms of attractiveness to investors and ease of doing business, Singapore is a leading example in the world and the region.

---

legislation. In borderline cases, cash flow is used to distinguish between tax provisions and expenditure provisions. Insofar as a provision affects the flow of tax payments from the taxpayer to the government, it is regarded as a tax provision and is taken into account in the data shown in this publication. A provision which does not affect this flow is seen as an expenditure provision and is disregarded in the data recorded in this publication" OECD (2019), *Revenue Statistics in Asian and Pacific Economies 2019*, OECD Publishing, Paris, https://doi.org/10.1787/b614e035-en.

In order to exchange best practices, Sect. 7.2 provides a comparison of the tax incentives in Singapore and the Philippines by looking at (1) the types of incentives offered, (2) whether they are cost or profit based, (3) whether they are targeted at specific locations/sectors, (4) their overall transparency, (5) the role of the Minister of Finance, (6) systematic evaluations of incentives, (7) regional coordination and (8) other considerations including the influence of BEPS Action 5 in their tax incentives. The Philippines is currently in the process of passing a comprehensive tax reform, and only one out of four proposed packages was signed into law. The second package that dealt with tax incentives was expected to be adopted in 2019 (at the time of writing, June 2020, the adoption has not yet taken place; instead some changes have been introduced to cope with COVID-19).[8] Therefore current incentives system and the proposed changes will both be discussed in this section.

7.3.1 Type of Incentives Offered

7.3.1.1 Singapore

Corporate tax in Singapore is levied at 17%, which makes it the country with the lowest corporate income tax rate in the Association of Southeast Asian Nations (ASEAN) region. On top of this, Singapore provides generous tax incentives including concessionary tax rates for selected industries and free-trade zones.[9] Due to the COVID-19 pandemic, Singapore has introduced several measures to support business. For companies, the fiscal stimulus measure aims to ease the cash flow of companies; therefore, two measures have been introduced a deferral of payment (3 months) of corporate income tax and the extension of tax filing deadlines.[10]

The main legislative sources of incentives are the Economic Expansion Incentives (relief from income tax) Act (EEIA) and the Income Tax Act (ITA). The administration of incentives is vested in government statutory boards, based on industry segmentation,[11] and in the Inland Revenue Authority of Singapore (IRAS).

The Economic Development Board (EDB), forming part of the Ministry of Trade and Industry, administers a number of the incentives offered. The objective of Singapore's tax incentives is to attract companies that will contribute to the wider benefit in Singapore. EDB expects the companies to accomplish this via local spending, creation of skilled employment, financing research and development or

---

[8]See Sect. 7.3.1.2.

[9]For example, the Jurong Port and the Changi Airport Group.

[10]See for an overview of the measures the website of the IRAS at https://www.iras.gov.sg/irashome/ COVID-19-Support-Measures-and-Tax-Guidance/COVID-19-Support-Measures-and-Tax-Guid ance/. Accessed 16 June 2020.

[11]Including Enterprise Singapore, Maritime Port Authority of Singapore for the shipping sector and Monetary Authority of Singapore for the financial sector and Singapore Economic Development Board.

anchoring cutting-edge technology. EDB defines its goal as "to develop high-value and substantive economic activities in Singapore" (EDB Singapore 2018).

Some tax incentives aim to encourage companies to grow certain treasury management and strategic finance capabilities[12] or grow aircraft leasing industry in Singapore.[13] Other tax incentives focus on development of research in the areas of science and technology,[14] on providing the employees with various training programmes[15] and on encouraging the use and commercialisation of intellectual property rights from research and development (R&D) activities.[16] These incentives are tied to certain activities ascertained as beneficial to Singapore's development and aim to enable long-term economic growth. There are also incentives that support facilities to be more energy efficient and improve competitiveness.[17]

The incentives administered by the EDB can be split into three main categories: (1) growing industries; (2) innovation, R&D and capability development; and (3) productivity. These incentives include the Pioneer Certificate Incentive (PC) and Development and Expansion Incentive (DEI), Finance and Treasury Centre (FTC) Incentive, Aircraft Leasing Scheme (ALS), Research Incentive Scheme for Companies (RISC), Training Grant for Company (TGC), Intellectual Property Development Incentive (IDI), Resource Efficiency Grant for Energy (REG(E)) and Land Intensification Allowance (LIA). For example, under the PC and DEI, companies enjoy exemption from corporate tax or a concessionary rate of 5 or 10%. Companies benefit from 8% concessionary tax rate on income from qualifying FTC activities under the FTC incentive and 5 or 10% on qualifying IP income under the IDI. In 2019, the Ministry of Finance published the Income Tax (Amendment) Bill, which extends and refines tax incentive schemes for funds managed by Singapore-based fund managers (IBFD 2019).

7.3.1.2 Philippines

The corporate income tax rate in the Philippines is 30% for both domestic and non-resident corporations, the highest corporate income tax rate in all of ASEAN

---

[12]Finance and Treasury Centre (FTC) Incentive.

[13]Aircraft Leasing Scheme (ALS).

[14]Research Incentive Scheme for Companies (RISC).

[15]Training Grant for Company (TGC).

[16]IP Development Incentive.

[17]Resource Efficiency Grant for Energy (REG(E)), as part of the Enhanced Industry Energy Efficiency package, with the Energy Market Authority (EMA), Singapore Economic Development Board (EDB) and the National Environment Agency (NEA), each rolling out initiatives to extend stronger support to companies in their drive to become more energy efficient and reduce carbon emissions. In addition to this, the Land Intensification Allowance (LIA) aims to promote the intensification of industrial land use towards more land-efficient and higher value-added activities.

countries.[18] Despite the corporate income tax (CIT) revenue increasing each year, the tax incentive regime lacks efficiency.[19] Even though the Philippines provide the most generous tax incentive system[20] in the region, when compared to neighbouring countries, Philippine's inward FDI does not reach the desired amounts (Philippines Department of Finance 2018c). Philippines' incentives under the current regime include tax holidays, regional operating headquarters incentives and concessionary tax rates under the Regional Operating Headquarters (ROHQ) and gross income earned tax regimes.

Incentives are legislated under the Omnibus Investments Code of 1987 and the Special Economic Zone Act of 1995, which include both fiscal and non-fiscal incentives. At the heart of Philippines incentives system are income tax holidays offered to Board of Investment (BOI)/Philippine Economic Zone Authority (PEZA)-registered activities with pioneer status (6 years income tax holidays) and non-pioneer status (4 years income tax holidays). After the lapse of income tax holidays, PEZA-registered activities can then benefit from 5% gross income earned (GIE) tax regime. The GIE is given for an indefinite period of time and applies to all income, value-added tax (VAT) and local taxes. As of 2015, the Tax Incentives Management and Transparency Act (TIMTA) requires that tax incentives granted to registered investments are reported (Philippines Department of Finance 2018c).

Multinational enterprises (MNEs) that establish ROHQ in the Philippines benefit from a preferential CIT rate of 10% and are exempt from numerous local taxes, charges and fees. ROHQs are set up to render R&D services and product development to its affiliates, branches and subsidiaries. This ROHQ regime has been listed on OECD BEPS 5 Preferential Tax Regimes List and is currently marked as in the process of being eliminated (see Sect. 7.3.8.2).

The Comprehensive Tax Reform Program (CTRP) The aim of the reform is to correct the country's deficient tax system caused by special treatment and exemptions for some taxpayers. According to Philippines Department of Finance, this special treatment coupled with lack of transparency leads to unequal, complex and inefficient tax system (Philippines Department of Finance 2018c). The proposed reform will likely impact all of these incentives. The aim of the CTRP is to "accelerate poverty reduction" and to "sustainably address inequality" (Philippines Department of Finance 2018c). The CTRP introduced four packages, with the first package enacted in 2017 and the second to be adopted in 2019. A reform of tax incentives is covered in Package 2: "Corporate Income Tax Reform and Fiscal

---

[18]Philippines 30%; Indonesia 25%; Malaysia and Lao DPR both 24%; Vietnam, Thailand and Cambodia all 20%; and Singapore 17%.

[19]According to OECD's individual country statistics office and DOF staff calculations, revenue productivity was 12.3%, second lowest in the region right behind Indonesia.

[20]Compared to tax holidays in other ASEAN countries, where Brunei officially provides the longest tax holiday (20 year), the Philippines offer 4 years + 8 years tax holidays and after that indefinite benefit of just 5% gross income tax (GIT).

Incentives Modernization (CITIRA)".[21] This package has been recalibrated in light of the COVID-19 pandemic. The new Package 2 is referred as the Corporate Recovery and Tax Incentives for Enterprises Act (CREATE). According to the Philippines Department of Finance website, the recalibration was necessary "to make it more relevant and responsive to the needs of businesses, especially those facing financial difficulties, and increase the ability of the Philippines to attract investments that will benefit the public interest" (Philippines Department of Finance 2018f).[22]

The goal of CTRP Package 2 in its CITIRA form is to (1) lower the CIT rate gradually from 30 to 20% over the next 10 years; (2) reorient fiscal incentives towards strategic growth industries; and (3) make incentives available to investors who make net positive contributions to society (Department of Finance 2018f). In addition, corporations registered for corporate incentives will receive further deductions for labour costs, training costs, purchases from local suppliers, infrastructure development, research and development, accelerated depreciation allowance and enhanced net-operating loss carryover.

The new measures proposed by the CTRP Package in its CREATE form are mainly the introduction of fiscal stimuli for business.[23] These measures include an immediate 5% corporate income tax reduction starting July 2020, extension of the applicability of carryover for losses incurred in 2020 from 3 to 5 years for non-large taxpayers, companies benefiting from the 5% gross income earned (GIE) incentives will benefit from a sunset clause from 4 to 9 years (in CITIRA form was 2–7 years); and more flexibility for the President in granting fiscal and non-fiscal incentives, which according to the Department of Finance, it "will be critical as the country competes internationally for high-value investments".[24]

The CTRP recognises the need for tax incentives in order to attract investment, which supports achieving Philippines' objectives, including job creation, stimulation of domestic industries and encouraging innovation. However, the Philippines also

---

[21]See for a short overview package 2 https://taxreform.dof.gov.ph/wp-content/uploads/2019/08/CTRP-Package-2-Corporate-Income-Tax-and-Incentives-Reform-1-page-briefer.pdf.   Accessed 16 June 2020.

[22]See also https://taxreform.dof.gov.ph/news_and_updates/pcci-head-says-create-to-give-phl-fighting-chance-in-attracting-more-investments/. Accessed 16 June 2020.

[23]CREATE is one of instruments under the Philippine Program for Recovery with Equity and Solidarity or PH-PROGRESO. PP-PROGRESO is currently being discussed at the Senate. Report to the Joint Congressional Oversight Committee dated 8 June 2020. https://www.officialgazette.gov.ph/downloads/2020/06jun/20200608-Report-to-the-Joint-Congressional-Oversight-Committee.pdf. Accessed 16 June 2020.

See for a short overview http://www.neda.gov.ph/wp-content/uploads/2020/05/Economic-recovery-program-v9-short-for-Sulong_1589436221.pdf. Accessed 16 June 2020.

[24]Website Department of Finance https://taxreform.dof.gov.ph/tax-reform-packages/p2-corporate-recovery-and-tax-incentives-for-enterprises-act/. Accessed 16 June 2020. See Report to the Joint Congressional Oversight Committee dated 8 June 2020. https://www.officialgazette.gov.ph/downloads/2020/06jun/20200608-Report-to-the-Joint-Congressional-Oversight-Committee.pdf at 15. Accessed 16 June 2020.

acknowledge the need for fair and accountable incentives systems. The rationale is that the money supporting the incentives comes from the government's budget and would otherwise be part of public spending that benefits the society. To ensure fair and accountable tax incentives regime is in place, incentives need to be (1) performance based, (2) targeted, (3) time bound and (4) transparent. However, the discretionary power to the President to grant fiscal and non-fiscal tax incentives in CREATE may reduce the effectiveness of the transparency goal of the CTRP reform.

The new tax incentives will also include sunset provisions, putting a time limit on the benefits the companies can enjoy. As a result, tax incentives will no longer be granted for indefinite periods of time as, e.g. tax holidays, which could be prolonged but will rather be time restricted. This can result in greater accountability and improved performance of the MNEs.

7.3.2   Cost-Based Incentives vs. Profit-Based Incentives

Profit-based incentives are linked to the profits of the company and include, e.g. reduced tax rates or tax holidays that exempt the profits in their entirety. Cost-based tax incentives reduce costs for the company and can include, e.g. tax credits and accelerated depreciation. Profit-based incentives, although easier to administer when introduced, require continuous monitoring[25] to ensure the taxpayers qualify for the incentives, which is not always easy (Abramovsky et al. 2018). This can prove to be particularly difficult for tax administrations in developing countries, where resources are limited. Therefore, scholars and international organisations recommended for developing countries to introduce cost-based tax incentive even though it is more complex to administer (Abramovsky et al. 2018; IMF Toolkit).

Singapore and the Philippines have a mix of profit-based and cost-based incentives, and while there is a prevalence of profit-based incentives in both countries at the moment, this will likely change for the Philippines following the introduction of the second package in the CTRP which is expected to be adopted in 2019.

7.3.2.1   Singapore

In Singapore, profit-based incentives prevail. This is mainly due to the concessionary tax rates and exemptions offered to a wide range of activities. While incentives

---

[25]Both profit-based and cost-based incentives require monitoring, but profit-based incentives are usually subject to stricter qualifying conditions as well as targets that need to be reached with the investments. Therefore, a higher level of monitoring is required to ensure the companies continuously meet the conditions to qualify for the incentive and also that they deliver the wanted results— e.g. creation of desired number of jobs, meeting their investment targets, etc. This monitoring has to be done on a regular basis and requires more financial and human resources.

offered under the EEIA are mainly profit based, incentives offered under the ITA are a mixture of exemptions, deductions and rate reductions.

7.3.2.2 Philippines

In the Philippines, tax incentives under the current regime are prevalently profit based and focus on reducing the tax rates for companies. The reason for this could be the high corporate tax rate to begin with and the need to lower this to attract investment. The proposed CTRP aims to lower the corporate income tax rate so the focus of the new incentive regime will shift to cost-based incentives instead. The proposed deductions for companies registered for incentives further prove that the new incentive system will look to introduce more cost-based incentives with the objective of achieving social benefits.

7.3.3 Targeted Incentives

7.3.3.1 Singapore

The issue with targeted tax incentives is that they can put non-targeted firms at disadvantage. They may however be justified in cases where it reduces the cost of the policy or when targeting certain mobile investments is more cost-effective (Abramovsky et al. 2018). Singapore offers a number of incentives that target specific industries, such as exemptions and concessionary rates for angel investors, fund management companies, businesses engaged in various shipping and maritime activities and companies setting up global or regional headquarters in Singapore. When looking at the activities, it mainly targets areas of manufacturing and services, trading, investment and financial services, shipping and research and development activities.[26] To benefit from the incentives, investors must meet qualitative and quantitative criteria. As a result, only selected investors benefit from the incentive, and the associated costs are therefore kept to minimum.

---

[26]Headquarter and internationalisation activities, manufacturing and services activities, trading activities, finance and treasury activities, R&D and IP management and human capital and capability development.

7.3.3.2 Philippines

At the time of writing (June 2020), tax incentives target companies in different sectors, and the resulting effective CIT rates are unequal.[27] The investment activities that are targeted are included in the Investment Priorities Plan (IPP). The 2017 IPP listed the following investment priorities areas for 2017–2019: export activities, agriculture, basic industries, infrastructure, industrial service facilities, engineering, logistics, BIMP-EAGA investments, tourism, health and education, halal, banking and energy investments (IPP 2017).

Under the new tax reform CTRP, incentives are to be targeted at a specific group of companies or an industry, thereby limiting the number of companies benefiting from them. This should eliminate the unfair grant of benefits to big MNEs whose effective tax rate is then well below what local micro and small enterprises pay. Incentives will be targeted at activities, which bring significant benefits to the country (Philippines Department of Trade and Industry-Board of Investments 2018).

7.3.4 Granting of Tax Incentives: Transparency

7.3.4.1 Singapore

The EDB publishes brochures and circulars on its website. They provide an overview of each incentive including the assessment criteria as well as detailed administration of the incentive. However, since Singapore's tax incentives are not all covered through income tax law, their extent is not as straightforward and clear as it could be. The IRAS attempts to make them transparent by having a consolidated list published on their website along with instructions how and where to apply. Each incentive also describes detailed administration of the incentives and mentions the provision of either the Income Tax Act (ITA) or Economic Expansion Incentives Act (EEIA), where the incentive was implemented.

The design and administration of Singapore's incentives by numerous bodies results in more complex coordination of incentive measures. This could lead to inconsistencies and an overlap of incentives (OECD 2015). While tax authorities worry about forgone revenue, agencies and bodies are primarily focused on attracting investment. It can also render the tax incentives inefficient, as investors can potentially benefit from incentives offered by various bodies and thereby erode their tax base.

---

[27] According to the Philippines Department of Finance, effective tax rates for agriculture and fishery businesses can be as little as 6.9% and, e.g. manufacturing and energy businesses are taxed at around 10%.

7.3.4.2 Philippines

According to a survey conducted by the World Economic Forum, inefficient government bureaucracy, corruption, tax regulations and tax rates were identified as some of the biggest problems when it comes to conducting business in the Philippines (World Economic Forum 2018). This need for transparency and simplicity was also highlighted by Yasuyuki Sawada, Chief Economist and Director General of Asian Development Bank.

At the moment, incentives are provided through 123 investment laws and 192 non-investment laws. Having incentives in a number of legislations creates a complex incentive regime, which leads to lack of transparency (OECD 2016). With the CTRP, these 123 special laws will be replaced by one single law.

As of June 2020, incentives can be granted by 1 of 19 Investment Promotion Agencies (IPAs), and in order to benefit from them, registration with Philippine Economic Zone Authority (PEZA) or Board of Investments (BOI) is necessary for most of them (Philippines Department of Finance 2018a, b, c, d, e, f). To be able to register with BOI, the business activity must be listed in the 2017 Investment Priorities Plan.[28] The fact that incentives are granted through numerous agencies results in less transparency and increased complexity when it comes to monitoring decisions to whom and under what circumstances the incentives were granted. This leaves room for undesired discretion and can result in tax base erosion by investors who would normally not qualify for the incentive.

Following the current tax reform CTRP, the Fiscal Incentives Review Board (FIRB) is to serve as the overall administration of IPAs and incentives. FIRB will have an oversight over 13[29] existing IPAs and will be responsible for monitoring that the benefiting taxpayers are continuously meeting the qualifying conditions and are reaching the desired targets. This should simplify the incentive regime and aid the overall transparency, as all incentives will be administered and monitored by one central body.

---

[28]In 2017 IPP, these were, namely, (1) all qualified manufacturing activities, (2) export activities, (3) activities based on special laws granting incentives and (4) priority activities for projects located in the Autonomous Region in Muslim Mindanao (ARMM).

[29]While the Philippines have 19 investment promotion agencies, 13 of them "are largely autonomous, each with its own mandate, menu of tax incentives and authority to grant them largely without the approval or knowledge of the DOF", and these will now come under oversight of DOF. See more at: https://www.dof.gov.ph/dof-says-firb-to-promote-good-governance-enhance-grant-of-tax-incentives-to-firms/. Accessed 16 June 2020.

7.3.5   Role of the Ministry of Finance

7.3.5.1   Singapore

Under the Income Tax Act, the Minister of Finance appoints a Comptroller of Income Tax, who is responsible for the assessment and collection of tax in Singapore (ITA 2014). The Ministry of Finance therefore has primary responsibility for the assessment and development of tax incentive proposals. The proposals for new tax incentives can only be accepted if the incentives further the country's economic objectives and are then, if adopted, included in the annual budget submitted to Parliament.

Due to the nature of Singapore's political system, the government effectively controls much of the legislature, and the Ministry of Finance has the government's support for its proposals. After Parliament approves the proposals, the tax incentives become effective, but the main push comes straight from the Minister of Finance. Each year a budget report is published, detailing which incentives are accounted for in the budget. The budget provides an end date for some of the tax incentives, thereby ensuring that they are budgeted only for a specific number of years.[30]

7.3.5.2   Philippines

The Department of Finance participates in talks elaborating on the IPP as opposed to Philippines Bureau of Internal Revenue, which has very minor involvement. It can prioritise different activities based on national and budgetary needs through the IPP.

7.3.6   Assessing the Cost of the Incentive (Revenue Foregone)

Since one of the concerns about incentives is the direct cost (revenue foregone) incurred by governments, it is of great importance that incentives are transparent regarding the revenue foregone. More recently, the World Bank report evaluating the costs and benefits of tax incentives has stated the need to foster greater transparency of public finances. According to the 2020 World Bank Report, "systematically estimating the revenue foregone from incentives can result in greater transparency of public finances. Especially since the costs associated with tax incentives can face less scrutiny than direct government spending, estimating and incorporating such analysis as part of the budgetary process can lead to more informed budgetary and fiscal policy decision-making" (Kronfol and Steenbergen 2020: 9).

Furthermore, the World Bank report states that it is important in the calculation of the direct costs (revenue foregone) to consider "not only corporate income tax

---

[30]For example, the Land Intensification Allowance and the IP Development Incentive.

incentives, but should also extend to the wider combination of tax concessions offered to firms, including customs duties, capital gains tax, pay-as-you-earn, and value added tax" (Kronfol and Steenbergen 2020: 5).

7.3.6.1 Singapore

In order to ensure consistency and accountability, the Ministry of Finance provides guidelines for administering tax incentives and requires agencies to monitor the companies that receive tax incentives for their compliance with the obligations and commitments. Furthermore, the EDB lays down the assessment process for each of the incentives it administers.

All of the incentives are subject to the provisions of the Economic Expansion Incentives Act, and in addition to this, companies need to submit regular reports to the EDB so their performance can be evaluated. The analysis of revenue and expenditure is also provided in Singapore and submitted to the Parliament for evaluation in the Budget Day.[31]

7.3.6.2 Philippines

In the Philippines, the Department of Budget and Management provides for a Budget of Expenditures and Sources of Financing Report.[32] In December 2015, the Tax Incentives Management and Transparency Act (TIMTA) was passed. Its aim is to promote transparency and accountability in the area of granting and administration of tax incentives. TIMTA was tasked with creating a single database system to record and evaluate the impact of Philippines' tax incentives. Furthermore, TIMTA is responsible for monitoring and tracking the tax incentives granted by IPAs. TIMTA is regarded as a positive development towards transparency. According to Sawada, Chief Economist and Director General Asian Development Bank, due to TIMTA "it is now possible to evaluate whether tax incentives have delivered employment, income and export growth" (Sawada 2018).

In light of the CTRP, Philippines Department of Finance carried out an initial cost-benefit analysis of the tax incentives under the old regime and concluded that: "on average, there is no difference between the performance of firms receiving incentives and firms not receiving incentives in terms of employment, exports,

---

[31]The most recent of 2019 is available at https://www.singaporebudget.gov.sg/docs/default-source/budget_2019/download/pdf/FY2019_Analysis_of_Revenue_and_Expenditure.pdf.   Accessed 16 June 2020.

[32]For instance, the 2019 report is available at https://www.dbm.gov.ph/index.php/budget-documents/2019/budget-of-expenditures-and-sources-of-financing-fy-2019. Accessed 16 June 2020. See also 2015 Report Fiscal Transparency Evaluation https://www.imf.org/en/Publications/CR/Issues/2016/12/31/Philippines-Fiscal-Transparency-Evaluation-43014.   Accessed 16 June 2020.

investments, and productivity. This means many incentives are redundant" (Philippines Department of Finance 2018c).

According to the proposed CTRP Package 2 (pending adoption; see Sect. 7.3.1.2), incentives will be granted to investors who encourage upskilling, create more and better jobs, promote research and development, encourage innovation, stimulate domestic industries, invest in agribusiness, diversify their product base to higher value exports, reinvest their capital, invest in less developed areas and invest in areas recovering from calamities or armed conflict (Department of Finance 2018a). There is a clear aim for the incentives to aid economic and social growth of the country.

The CTRP Package 2 also plans to introduce performance-based incentives. Performance-based incentives will as their name suggests set performance targets/ requirements that the company needs to meet in order to be able to benefit from the tax incentive. These targets will aim to benefit the society and will result in positive development. The main difference compared to the incentives under the old regime is that they will no longer be granted to "everyone" and "for free". Incentives will instead be given to firms that actually need them and if they also meet the performance requirements. The introduction of these types of incentives will require more evaluations on how these objectives and performance requirements are being met.

7.3.7 Regional Cooperation

7.3.7.1 Singapore

Singapore is a member of ASEAN and has a number of free trade agreements in place.[33] Singapore has also signed the Convention on Mutual Administrative Assistance in Tax Matters and is member of the OECD Global Forum on Transparency and Exchange of Information for Tax Purposes. Regional cooperation, especially in regions with developing countries, which compete to attract the investments, is crucial in minimising or avoiding harmful tax competition. OECD acknowledges the need for regional cooperation and also links it to enhanced transparency (OECD n.d.). Singapore has the lowest CIT rate in the region, and this can encourage other countries to provide favourable incentives and compensate for their higher tax rates. While it encourages positive change, e.g. creation of tax incentives and revision of existing tax rules, the negative spillovers can cause neighbouring countries to race to the bottom (Nugroho 2012).

---

[33]Singapore is a member of the Asia Regional Integration Center.

7.3.7.2 Philippines

The Philippines is a member of ASEAN and has signed the Convention on Mutual Administrative Assistance in Tax Matters. Furthermore, the Philippines is a member of the OECD Global Forum on Transparency and Exchange of Information for Tax Purposes.

7.3.8 BEPS Action 5 Review

From the two countries of study, Singapore as a member of the BEPS Inclusive Framework has committed to the implementation of BEPS 4 Minimum Standards including BEPS Action 5. At the time of writing (June 2020), the Philippines is not a member of the Inclusive Framework. Even though the assessment of BEPS Action 5 is outside the scope of this chapter (Mosquera Valderrama 2020b), it is important to take into account that despite the fact that the Philippines is not a member of this framework, both countries have been reviewed for their preferential tax regimes. As a result, Singapore and the Philippines have amended or abolished some of these incentives to comply with the recommendations of the BEPS Action 5 peer review report.

7.3.8.1 Singapore

Singapore as one of the members of Inclusive Framework on BEPS was initially included on the 2015 list of harmful tax practices (OECD 2017). The 2015 report reviewed some of Singapore's tax incentives, all of which proved to be not harmful or they were subsequently amended or abolished.[34] No regimes are subject to review on the 2018 report.

7.3.8.2 Philippines

Even though the Philippines has not committed to the BEPS Inclusive Framework, the Philippines has been reviewed in their tax incentives in light of BEPS Action 5. The 2018 report reported that the Regional Area Headquarters was out of scope since it did not apply to mobile activities, while the Regional Operating

---

[34]Development and Expansion Incentive—services, Pioneer Service Company, Aircraft Leasing Scheme, the Finance and Treasury Centre, the Insurance Business Development and Financial Sector Incentive, the Global Trade Programme, Maritime Sector Incentive and DEI legal services incentive, International Growth Scheme, IP Development Incentive.

Headquarters has some potential harmful features, and it was in the process of being eliminated (OECD 2019a: 24).

7.4 Comparison and Framework for Assessment of Tax Incentives

7.4.1 Comparative Analysis Tax Incentives in Singapore and the Philippines

In the description in Sect. 7.3, some differences can be highlighted between Singapore and the Philippines. The first notorious difference is the corporate tax rate which in Singapore is 17% while in the Philippines is 30%. In addition, there are differences in the way that tax incentives are being granted in both countries mainly regarding legislative sources and agencies granting the tax incentives. While Singapore has a more centralised decision-making with 2 main legislative sources, the Philippines has incentives in 123 investment law and 192 non-investment laws. In addition, the granting of tax incentives is organised in Singapore by industry segmentation, whereas in the Philippines, there are 13 Investment Promotion Agencies granting the incentives.

The Philippines is since 2017 in the process of introducing a CTRP to reduce the tax rate and to correct the country's complexity of the tax systems including the different type of tax incentives. However, it remains to be seen how many of the proposals will pass, since from the four packages only one (at the time of writing June 2020) has been adopted. However, the government of the Philippines is aware of the need to change their tax incentive regime and also the need to provide more transparency in the granting of tax incentives.

While Singapore is successful in attracting foreign investment, it is hard to tell whether it was achieved through its tax incentives. It could be argued that opposed to other developing countries or countries in transition, Singapore did not have investment deterrents (e.g. bad economic or political climate). This supports the argument that tax incentives on their own cannot correct the tax regime and investment climate in the country and thereby make it more attractive for investors. Even the government stresses that without these non-tax factors, tax incentives would likely not be effective in attracting foreign investment (Zolt 2015). The well-educated and highly skilled workers, extensive network of infrastructure, efficient public transport, clean environment, high quality of life and overall political and economic stability all contribute to Singapore's position among the most attractive business destinations.

However, this is not the case for the Philippines, since the high tax rate and the unstable political climate make difficult to attract foreign investment. The changes introduced by the new CTRP including the reduction of the tax rate can partially solve this issue. But the tax incentive should not be the only motivation for countries to introduce changes. Attention should be given to infrastructure, economic and political climate so that foreign investors will decide to invest in the country regardless of the tax incentives.

Furthermore, other elements that need to be kept in mind for a stable investment system are transparency in tax incentives including a systematic assessment before and after the tax incentives have been granted. The elements of the evaluative framework of tax incentives will be provided in the following section.

7.4.2 Evaluative Framework for Tax Incentives in Light of the SDGs

Tax incentives need to be assessed on a case-by-case basis; however, there are certain elements in an evaluative framework of tax incentives that should be considered in all instances. This framework has been developed elsewhere (Mosquera Valderrama 2020a), and it will be used to analyse the tax incentives of Singapore and the Philippines so that countries can also exchange best practices.

- Systematic review of tax incentives: The review takes place in both countries; however, it is more focused on the granting of tax incentives. There is no clarity whether the review takes place before or after the tax incentive is granted. The assessment in the Philippines of the tax incentives before introducing the CTRP showed that many incentives were redundant. However, this assessment should not only take place at the time that there is a new tax reform but on a regular basis.

  The comparison in Sect. 7.3 shows that such assessment is very limited in the two countries. For the assessment, it is important that the government carefully plans the amount of revenue foregone to give the tax incentive and, also if necessary, to have a ceiling of the amount of revenue foregone. After the incentive is being granted, this incentive should be evaluated systematically by the government taking into account the requirements to give the incentive and whether the incentive is still necessary. Therefore, the two countries can benefit from establishing a specific time for the review of the tax incentive before and after the tax incentive is granted and on a regular basis (every 2 years) and also include in the review the specific budget evaluations that can limit the amount of revenue foregone in the tax incentive.

- The incentive should have a clear target and eligibility criteria for granting the incentive; this target should be measurable to achieve the social and economic development of the region/sector/country. This is not the case in the two countries of study. The current Philippine tax reform aims to attract investment that makes positive contributions to society, but it is not clear as to the criteria to achieve this objective. In Singapore, the Economic Development Board could have a role in designing clear targets and eligibility criteria for granting the incentive which can be also measured in the light of the social and economic development.

  Due to the COVID-19 pandemic, tax incentives are being introduced to ease cash flow from business. However, it is also important that even in COVID-19, the introduction of these tax incentives have a clear target and eligibility criteria. The description shows that while Singapore decided to grant deferral of tax payments and tax filing, the Philippines decided to immediately reduce the tax rate from 30 to 25%, to introduce favourable rules for carry forward of losses, to extend sunset clauses for certain type of incentives (see Sect. 7.3.1.2) and to give to the President the discretionary power to grant tax incentives.

- Transparency and discretionary power. There should be no room for administrative discretion on the granting of tax incentives; one person/body should be in charge of granting tax incentives, and the incentive should be transparent (publicly available on the website of the tax administration or administrative agency). In both countries, the role of the Ministry of Finance is very important in the granting of tax incentives. However, one problem in both countries is the design and administration of incentives by several bodies resulting in complex coordination and lack of transparency. For instance, the Philippines has 19 Investment Promotion Agencies in charge of granting incentives. This is already being targeted in the new CTRP by introducing a Fiscal Incentives Review Board to serve as overall administration and to have an oversight over 13 of the 19 IPAs granting incentives.[35] However, the COVID-19 measure granting discretionary power to the President may affect the path taken by the Philippines to increase the transparency and reduce the discretionary power in granting tax incentives.

The monitoring by one central body is desirable. However, it is also important that this body has a code of conduct to guide their activities including also a list of sanctions (administrative fine, dismissal or imprisonment) in case that there is any corruption or bribery. The Philippines has already such a Code of Conduct with several sanctions (Rule XI)[36]; nevertheless, one of the problems identified in the Philippines by the World Economic Forum Global Competitiveness Index is corruption (see Sect. 7.3.4.2). Therefore, one possible way to enhance more transparency is to make the sanction for the respective agency official publicly available.

Singapore provides a consolidated list of tax incentives which is published where the Philippines does not. This should change in order to achieve more transparency. In addition, both Singapore and the Philippines could benefit from drafting for each incentive a fiscal budget and perhaps also a ceiling in the budget so that once reached the ceiling of revenue loss, the tax incentive will be terminated. The amount of allocated budget used can be made available on a year basis to investors so that they are not surprised when the ceiling has been reached.

To achieve greater accountability of tax incentives, it is important that the general tax expenditure of Singapore and the Philippines is periodically analysed

---

[35]See supra n. 32.

[36]"Code of Conduct and Ethical Standards for Public Officials and Employees", approved on February 20, 1989 and which took effect on March 25, 1989. https://www.bir.gov.ph/index.php/anti-corruption-law.html

and tax budgets are implemented. From the comparison in Sect. 7.3.6, there is a budget published each year in Singapore and the Philippines specifying which incentives are accounted for in the budget. However, this budget also requires monitoring and systematic evaluation, and efforts should be made by international organisations to train staff and use data analytics in developing countries to conduct cross-sectoral policy-oriented research on how tax incentives influence investments. The main objective should be to find out how incentives are being used, including in which sector, and their impact in terms of investment and/or foregone revenues.

- Both Singapore and the Philippines introduced their incentives in the Income Tax Law and Investment Law, but in the Philippines, the number of investment laws (i.e. 123) and non-investment laws (i.e. 192) providing incentives creates more complexity in the tax regime. Both countries provide the information in English in the respective government websites. However, this information should have not only the incentive but also the criteria to be used to systematically evaluate the tax incentive.

7.5 Conclusions and Recommendations

Following the analysis of tax incentive regimes in Singapore and the Philippines, this chapter concludes that when properly drafted and implemented, tax incentives can be very effective in attracting foreign direct investment; however, they do not seem to be sufficiently attractive for the investors on their own.

The case studies show two very different experiences of countries in the same region. Singapore succeeded in attracting foreign investment and is often seen as a role model for other developing countries and countries in transition. However, Singapore did not create tax incentives with the aim to correct market imperfections (Lipsey and Lancaster 2016). It complemented its already attractive investment environment instead. On the other hand, the Philippines tax incentives under the old regime compensated for its high CIT. The proposed reform corrects this by setting out clear objectives to be achieved and how to monitor the efficiency and effectiveness of the incentives. To properly analyse the new regime and how successful it will prove, ex-post analysis and systematic evaluations will need to be carried out to check if the initial cost-benefit analysis will be confirmed.

When designed and implemented correctly, tax incentives can also contribute to social and economic development of the country. It is important to keep in mind the primary objectives of the tax incentive when it is being drafted and in addition to design considerations. Already existing studies that attempted to assess the extent to which tax incentives attract foreign direct investment provide different framework references and use different methodologies to carry out their assessment (see Sect. 7.2). That is the main reason why their findings are inconclusive and there are dividing views on this topic.

General consensus is that an overall attractive investment climate will have a greater impact on investors' decision than beneficial tax incentives on their own. The persuasiveness of the tax incentive will depend on its design and implementation, coupled with the general tax system in the country and other factors including political and fiscal stability and developed infrastructure.

References

Abramovsky, L., Bird, N., Harris, T., & Tyskerud, Y. (2018). *Review of corporate tax incentives for investment in low- and middle-income countries*. London: Institute for Fiscal Studies.

Bird, R. M., & Zolt, E. M. (2008). Tax policy in emerging countries. *Environment and Planning C: Government and Policy, 26*, 73–86. Retrieved June 16, 2020, from https://doi.org/10.1068/cav3

Brauner, Y. (2013). The future of tax incentives for developing countries. In Y. Brauner & M. Stewart (Eds.), *Tax law and development*. Cheltenham: Edward Elgar.

Easson, A. J. (2001). Tax incentives for foreign investment, part I: Recent trends and countertrends. *Bulletin for International Fiscal Documentation, 55*(7), 266–274.

EDB. (2018). *Incentive and schemes*. Retrieved June 16, 2020, from https://www.edb.gov.sg/en/how-we-help/incentives-and-schemes.html

Holland, D., & Vann, R. J. (1998). Income tax incentives for investment. In V. Thuronyi (Ed.), *Tax law design and drafting* (Vol. 2). Washington, DC: IMF.

IMF, OECD, UN, et al. (2015). *Options for low income countries' effective and efficient use of tax incentives for investment*. A report to the G-20 Development Working Group by the IMF, OECD, UN and World Bank. Retrieved 16 June 2020, from https://doi.org/10.1596/22923

James, S. S. (2009). *Incentives and investments: Evidence and policy implications*. Washington, DC: World Bank Group. Retrieved June 16, 2020, from http://documents.worldbank.org/curated/en/945061468326374478/pdf/588160WP0Incen10BOX353820B01PUBLIC1.pdf

James, S. S. (2010). *Providing incentives for investment: Advice for policy-makers in developing countries*. Investment Climate in Practice, No. 7 Investment Policy and Promotion Note. Washington, DC: World Bank Group.

Jun, J. (2018). Tax incentives and tax base protection in developing countries. In T. Subhanij, T. Banerjee, & Z. Jian (Eds.), *Tax policy for sustainable development in Asia and the Pacific*. United Nations Publication ST/ESCAP/2806. Bangkok: United Nations Economic and Social Commission for Asia and the Pacific (ESCAP). Retrieved June 16, 2020, from https://www.unescap.org/publications/tax-policy-sustainable-development-asia-and-pacific

Kinda, T. (2014). *The quest for non-resource-based FDI: Do taxes matter?* IMF working paper WP14/15.

Kronfol, H., & Steenbergen, V. (2020). *Evaluating the costs and benefits of corporate tax incentives: Methodological approaches and policy considerations* (English). FCI in focus. Washington, DC: World Bank Group. Retrieved June 16, 2020, from http://documents.worldbank.org/curated/en/180341583476704729/Evaluating-the-Costs-and-Benefits-of-Corporate-Tax-Incentives-Methodological-Approaches-and-Policy-Considerations

Lim, K. (2019). *Report, budget for 2019—Public consultation on draft income tax (amendment) bill 2019: Responses*. IBFD.

Lipsey, R. G., & Lancaster, K. (2016). The general theory of second best. *Review of Economic Studies, 24*(1), 11–32.

Mosquera Valderrama, I. J. (2020a). Tax incentives: From an investment, tax and sustainable development perspective. In J. Chaisse, L. Choukroune, & S. Jusoh (Eds.), *Handbook of international investment law and policy*. Singapore: Springer.

Mosquera Valderrama, I. J. (2020b). Regulatory framework for tax incentives in developing countries after BEPS action 5. *Intertax, 48*(4). Kluwer Law International BV.

Munongo, S., Akanbi, O. A., & Robinson, Z. (2017). Do tax incentives matter for investment? A literature review. *Business and Economic Horizons, 13*(2), 152–168. Retrieved June 16, 2020, from https://doi.org/10.15208/beh.2017.12

Nakabayashi, S. (2018). Tax challenges in Asia and the Pacific. In S. Araki & S. Nakabayashi (Eds.), *Tax and development—Challenges in Asia and Pacific* (p. 12). China: ADBI. Retrieved June 16, 2020, from https://www.adb.org/publications/tax-and-development-challenges-in-asia-pacific

Nugroho, A. D. (2012). Tickets to ride: The race for preferable CIT regimes towards ASEAN economic community. *Intertax, 40*(10). Kluwer Law International BV.

OECD. (2015). *Tax and development—Principles to enhance the transparency and governance of tax incentives for investment in developing countries.*

OECD. (2016). *Investment policy reviews: Philippines* (p. 171). Retrieved June 16, 2020 https://doi.org/10.1787/9789264254510-en

OECD. (2017). *Harmful tax practices—2017 progress report on preferential regimes: Inclusive framework on BEPS: Action 5.* OECD/G20 Base Erosion and Profit Shifting Project. Retrieved June 16, 2020, from https://doi.org/10.1787/9789264283954-en

OECD. (2019a). *Harmful tax practices—2018 progress report on preferential regimes: Inclusive framework on BEPS: Action 5.* OECD/G20 Base Erosion and Profit Shifting Project. Retrieved June 16, 2020, from https://doi.org/10.1787/9789264311480-en

OECD. (2019b). *Revenue statistics in Asian and Pacific economies 2019.* Paris: OECD Publishing. Retrieved June 16, 2020, from https://doi.org/10.1787/b614e035-en

OECD. (n.d.). *Principles to enhance the transparency and governance of tax incentives for investment in developing countries.* Retrieved June 16, 2020, from http://www.oecd.org/ctp/tax-global/transparency-and-governance-principles.pdf

Philippines Department of Finance. (2018a). *CTRP package 2: Corporate income tax and incentives reform.* Retrieved June 16, 2020, from http://taxreform.dof.gov.ph/presentations-and-references/ctrp-package-2-corporate-income-tax-and-incentives-reform-act-1-page-briefer/

Philippines Department of Finance. (2018b). *Package 1: TRAIN.* Retrieved June 16, 2020, from http://taxreform.dof.gov.ph/tax-reform-packages/p1-train/

Philippines Department of Finance. (2018c, July 23). *Presentation: Comprehensive tax reform program, proposed package 2: Corporate income tax reform and fiscal incentives modernization.* Retrieved June 16, 2020, from https://taxreform.dof.gov.ph/wp-content/uploads/2019/06/TRABAHO-CTRP-Package-2.pdf

Philippines Department of Finance. (2018d). *About tax reform.* Retrieved June 16, 2020, from http://taxreform.dof.gov.ph/about-tax-reform/

Philippines Department of Finance. (2018e). *Corporate income tax and incentives rationalization.* Retrieved June 16, 2020, from http://taxreform.dof.gov.ph/tax-reform-packages/p2-corporate-income-tax-and-incentives-rationalization/

Philippines Department of Finance. (2018f). *Package 2: Corporate recovery and tax incentives for enterprises act (CREATE).* Retrieved June 16, 2020, from https://taxreform.dof.gov.ph/tax-reform-packages/p2-corporate-recovery-and-tax-incentives-for-enterprises-act/

Philippines Department of Trade and Industry-Board of Investments. (2018, November 22). *Strategic investment priorities plan—Tax reform for attracting better and high-quality opportunities.* Retrieved June 16, 2020, from http://industry.gov.ph/wp-content/uploads/2018/11/Strategic-Investment-Priorities-Plan-SIPP-Supporting-the-Growth-and-Development-of-Industries.pdf

Philippines Investment Priorities Plan. (2017). Retrieved June 16, 2020, from http://www.philexport.ph/c/document_library/get_file?uuid=82d463c3-75df-4431-b089-f9930d682175&groupId=127524

Raff, H., & Srinivasan, K. (1998). Tax incentives for import-substituting foreign investment: Does signaling play a role? *Journal of Public Economics, 67*(2), 167–193.

Sawada, Y. (2018). *TRAIN 2 and the features of a good tax system.* Retrieved June 16, 2020, from https://www.adb.org/news/op-ed/train-2-and-features-good-tax-system-yasuyuki-sawada

Singapore Income Tax Act. (2014). *Chapter 134. Original enactment: Ordinance 39 of 1947.*

The World Bank. (2019). *Ease of doing business rankings.* Retrieved June 16, 2020, from https://www.doingbusiness.org/en/rankings

UN-CIAT. (2018). *Design and assessment of tax incentives in developing countries: Selected issues and a country experience* (p. iii). Retrieved June 16, 2020, from https://www.ciat.org/Biblioteca/Estudios/2018_design_assessment_tax_incentives_UN_CIAT.pdf

UNCTAD. (2000). *Tax incentives and foreign direct investment. A global survey.* ASIT Advisory Studies No. 16 UNCTAD/ITE/IPC/Misch.3. Retrieved June, 16, 2020, from https://unctad.org/en/docs/iteipcmisc3_en.pdf

Van Parys, S., & James, S. S. (2009). *Why tax incentives may be an ineffective tool to encouraging investment? The role of investment climate.* Washington, DC: IMF, World Bank Group. Retrieved June 16, 2020, from http://ssrn.com/abstract=1568296

World Economic Forum. (2018). *The global competitiveness index 2017–2018 edition.* Retrieved June 16, 2020, from http://www3.weforum.org/docs/GCR2017-2018/03CountryProfiles/Standalone2-pagerprofiles/WEF_GCI_2017_2018_Profile_Philippines.pdf

Zolt, E. M. (2015, April 23–24). *Tax incentives: Protecting the tax base.* Paper for Workshop on Tax Incentives and Base Protection. New York: United Nations.

Chapter 8
Foreign Investors vs. National Tax Measures: Assessing the Role of International Investment Agreements

Julien Chaisse and Jamieson Kirkwood

8.1 Introduction

The 2030 Agenda for Sustainable Development is an agreed blueprint for sustainable development, and its 17 Sustainable Development Goals (SDGs) are the means to facilitate this. The SDGs neither conflict with nor hinder taxation or investment policies. At the same time, the globalization of trade and investment has profoundly affected the practices and policies of international taxation. Indeed, tax professionals now require cross-disciplinary expertise to adequately understand the challenges faced by investors making investments across borders.

Moreover, in recent decades there has been a significant removal of many of the non-tax barriers to cross-border trade and investment. Firstly, international organizations, such as the World Trade Organization (WTO), the International Monetary Fund (IMF), the World Bank, and the Organization for Economic Cooperation and Development (OECD), have been pushing trade liberalization policies and the removal of exchange controls and controls on inward and outward investments (See Ring 2010). Additionally, the rapid proliferation of free trade agreements, which have removed or reduced the customs duties and tariffs on inward and outward transactions, reduced non-tax barriers and put in place trade facilitation mechanisms which has also had an enormous impact.

Indeed, most countries have entered into IIAs, and where the IIAs operate, investment-related activity such as Foreign Direct Investment (FDI) or NTMs will

J. Chaisse (✉)
School of Law, City University of Hong Kong, Hong Kong, China
e-mail: julien.chaisse@cityu.edu.hk

J. Kirkwood
Faculty of Law, Chinese University of Hong Kong, Hong Kong, China
e-mail: Jamieson.Kirkwood@link.cuhk.edu.hk

© The Author(s) 2021

I. J. Mosquera Valderrama et al. (eds.), *Taxation, International Cooperation and the 2030 Sustainable Development Agenda*, United Nations University Series on Regionalism 19, https://doi.org/10.1007/978-3-030-64857-2_8

become subject to the regulations provided in the IIA. This means that NTMs can therefore become breaches of IIAs, where the NTMs are deemed to conflict with the specific IIA. According to UNCTAD, there are currently 2659 active IIAs.

Additionally, the investment disputes which have dealt with tax issues will be identified, and it will also be demonstrated that both international investment law and investment arbitration, albeit unintentionally, significantly contribute to the regulatory framework applicable to tax policies. This chapter both identifies the theoretical convergence between tax and investment regimes and also identifies the actual provisions of IIAs that national policy-makers should observe and comply with in order to avoid investment arbitration (see Swenson et al. 2011).

8.2   When Foreign Investment Meets Tax

To determine whether an IIA is applicable to tax matters, the basic question is whether a given investment subject to NTMs constitutes a "foreign investment" within the meaning of that IIA. If yes, the investment will trigger the application of the IIA, which provides the framework for assessing the foreign treatment in the host state, including the treatment in terms of taxation (see Vieira 2014).

It is important to remember that IIAs are very different from Double Taxation Avoidance Agreements (DTAAs). While DTAAs allocate the taxing jurisdiction between the source and residence countries, in contrast, IIAs are not intended to provide specific taxation measures.

8.2.1   The Broad Notion of Investment in IIAs

The concept of "investment" does not have a generally accepted definition but will rather be specific to each treaty. Often, IIAs adopt a broad definition of "investment" that refers to "every kind of asset," "both tangible and intangible," of a foreign investor in a host country, suggesting that any economic activity is covered by that IIA. (Note also some IIAs have also focused on foreign investment in an "enterprise" rather than in a variety of assets.) The effect is the great scope of application of the related norms. Correspondingly, "foreign investment" is protected, with respect to all types of treatment adopted by the host state, and therefore tax is brought under the umbrella of IIAs.

8.2.2   The Diversity of Tax Exceptions in IIAs

As control over taxation matters is generally seen as a fundamental aspect of sovereignty, states' fiscal policies are generally excluded from IIAs' scope of

Table 8.1 Typology of tax exceptions in IIAs

Type of exclusion	Examples	Legal effect
General exclusion	"The provisions of this Agreement shall not apply to matters of taxation in the area of either Contracting Party. Such matters shall be governed by the domestic laws of each Contracting Party and the terms of any agreement relating to taxation concluded between the Contracting Parties." Agreement between the Government of Hong Kong and the Government of New Zealand for the Promotion and Protection of Investments, H.K.-N.Z., art. 8.2, July 6, 1995, 1889 U.N.T.S. 333	Such a provision excludes tax matters from the treaty scope of application without any reservation. It is impossible to bring a tax-related dispute before an investment tribunal on the ground of such a treaty
General exclusion (but with reservations for EXP and compensation)	"Nothing in this Agreement shall apply to taxation measures except as expressly provided for in paragraphs 3, 4 and 5." Article 21, China-Japan-Korea, Republic of Trilateral Investment Agreement 2012	Such a provision excludes tax matters from the treaty scope of application but with a reservation. The caveat is that disputes relating to EXP and compensation can be brought to ISDS, and therefore it is crucial to determine if a tax measure is expropriatory or not

Source: Compiled by the authors

application. However, this does not mean that investment arbitrators do not decide upon tax measures. IIAs might contain tax exceptions, but these are rather complex and often misunderstood.

Exclusions for tax measures are provided as follows:

1. Some IIAs differentiate between direct and indirect tax measures and often only subject the latter to the IIA regime.
2. Other IIAs rely on different exceptions, such as limiting the scope to national treatment (NT), most favored nation (MFN) treatment, fair and equitable treatment (FET), or a combination of all of these (see Stephan 2010).

Examples as regards the typology of tax exceptions are provided in the Table 8.1. Differing exceptions (or no exceptions) are provided by the specific treaty. Consequently, those IIAs that do not provide adequate tax exceptions may generate tax disputes under the treaty.

8.2.3 Interpretation by Investment Tribunals

The complexity has been added to by investment tribunals that have also developed specific, although inconsistent, approaches to the interpretation of taxation exclusions. For instance, the *Occidental Exploration v. Ecuador* Final Award interprets a taxation provision to permit claims based on the bilateral investment treaty's (BIT) FET standard. However, the *Pan American Energy LLC and BP Argentina Exploration Company v. The Argentine Republic* case disagrees with the approach taken in *Occidental Exploration v. Ecuador*. Significantly, the *Burlington Resources Inc. v. Republic of Ecuador* case holds that under Article X of the BIT, "matters of taxation" are as a rule excluded from the scope of the treaty and examines the claims advanced by the claimant individually in order to ascertain whether the taxation law is challenged or not with respect to each claim. Also, the *Nations Energy Corporation v. Panama* case interprets the BIT to exclude claims stemming from taxation matters based on the FET standard. Finally, in a very straightforward manner, the *Quasar de Valors v. Russia* Award on Preliminary Objections notes that a taxation exclusion cannot provide a loophole to escape the central undertakings of investor protection.

8.2.4 The Multitude of Tax Disputes Before Investment Tribunals

Nevertheless, despite this enormous complexity, there is a multitude of tax disputes before international investment tribunals, which represents a significant change in the landscape of international investment. This can partly be explained because, as described below, the standard dispute resolution mechanism of international tax treaties is generally unsatisfactory to the investor.

8.2.4.1 Tax Treaty Dispute Resolution Mechanisms

Either:

1. The Mutual Agreement Procedures (MAPs) but investors have to go through a lengthy process and are not guaranteed to have a case heard by an arbitration tribunal (Arts. 25 (1) and (2) of the OECD Model Convention provide the regulations on how investors should proceed during tax disputes). Also other drawbacks include a lack of transparency (i.e., how the tax authority makes the decision to accept or reject the case is not disclosed); procedural inefficiencies (e.g., the MAPs impose a relaxed responsibility on the competent authority, who just needs to "endeavor" to settle the controversy but is not "obliged" to settle the

dispute); no right for taxpayers/investors to be treated fairly; and an inherent inability to resolve issues of double taxation, transfer pricing, etc. (This is because the MAPs fail to determine the allocation of taxes each contracting country should receive.)

2. The OECD Model Tax Convention, if applicable, does provide the possibility of arbitration (see Christians 2009). However, similarly, an investor also cannot directly access arbitration and must go through a difficult process (the investor must first qualify under Arts. 25(1) and (2) of the OECD Model Tax Convention). Although this might expand, the arbitration clause serves only as an extension of the MAPs (and only for the issues which cannot be solved in the MAPs process but not for the whole dispute as stated in Art. 25(5) of OECD Model Tax Convention). The arbitration clause is a supplement to the MAPs and cannot replace them. The OECD has commented that the arbitration clause is an "additional dispute resolution technique which can help to ensure that international tax disputes will, to the greatest extent possible, be resolved in a final, principled, fair and objective manner for both the countries and the taxpayers concerned." In fact this OECD sees this as a bar on applying for arbitration if the local court has already resolved the tax dispute. For this reason, the Art. 25(5) of the OECD Model Tax Convention avoids bestowing parallel authority (i.e., to a domestic court and an international tribunal) to deal with the matter. Another interpretation of the arbitration clause is that the investor has to waive the right to access the domestic courts in order to request that tax disputes be submitted to arbitration under the OECD Model Convention or international tax treaties (to avoid parallel authority), a 2-year waiting period (the waiting period stated in Art. 25(2) of the OECD Model Tax Convention), representation only at the state level (The investor is excluded from being a claimant in arbitration and standing is given to the contacting state's competent authority, i.e. the tax authority) and an inadequate enforcement regime. In this case, the decision only binds the two contracting states, and if the losing contracting state does not comply with the arbitral decision, the winning contracting state or the taxpayer/investor can do nothing. Remarkably, there is no enforcement mechanism under the international tax treaties, and no sanction or confiscating measures can be imposed upon the losing contracting state for any non-compliance of the arbitral decision.

These unsatisfactory processes are an exogenous factor explaining the multitude of tax disputes before investment tribunals.

8.2.5   Other Endogenous Factors

The two main additional factors explaining the multitude of tax disputes before investment tribunals are as follows:

1. One of the key features of investment protection consists of allowing foreign investors to challenge the host government's actions before an international arbitral court.
2. The expansion of foreign investment into an ever-increasing number of types of investments inevitably generates tension with host states that may result in innovative and complicated disputes that an arbitral tribunal is asked to resolve.

8.3 The Judicial Review of Tax Regulations by Investment Tribunals

Unsurprisingly, therefore, since 1999, at least 32 tax-related cases have been brought to international arbitration. However, this number is likely to be only the tip of the iceberg as many arbitration cases remain unknown to the public, are not disclosed, or are still being negotiated.

8.3.1 Tax Disputes Not Won by the Investor

Not all investment claims result in an award that the host state will have to pay. In fact, the data shows that slightly more than 50% of the investment claims dealing with tax matters resulted in a tribunal decision in favor of the state. This article has identified 17 disputes that resulted in a decision denying a breach of the relevant IIA. This first category of decisions indicates that foreign investors considered using IIAs to submit claims against a number of countries and tax measures. Such a trend shows that IIAs are a potential recourse against some domestic tax measures. Table 8.2 provides the details of each of these 17 disputes.

In these 17 disputes, there is a great diversity of tax measures that were at the origin of the dispute, namely, windfall profits tax, tax investigations, value-added tax, taxation of income trusts, import taxes, corporate income tax, tax stamps on cigarettes, duty-free regime, etc. Unsurprisingly, the broad scope of application of IIAs allows tribunals to look at a wide variety of tax measures.

There is also diversity in the countries involved in these disputes since the countries do not belong to the same economic category. That being said, it is hard to expand the analysis further because, in most of these disputes, the states have proven that they use tax laws or regulations in a manner compatible with the relevant IIA. Alternatively, if the tribunal rejected the claim for lack of jurisdiction, nothing can be concluded as to the potential breach of investment law by a domestic tax measure. The scenario is radically different when one looks at the disputes lost by various host states.

Table 8.2 Investment disputes not won by the investor

Case name	Tax area	Treaty	Year of claim	Award date	Outcome
Corn Products International Inc. v. Mexican States	Imposition of a new tax on soft drinks and syrups sweetened by artificial sweeteners	NAFTA	2003	August 18, 2009	Not public
Paushok v. Mongolia	Resource management (oil and gas), tax (windfall profits tax), employment (performance requirements)	Russia-Mongolia BIT	2007	April 28, 2011	Tribunal accepted jurisdiction over claims, denied claims except the taking of the gold. The claimants had 60 days to claim damages
Burlington Resources v. Ecuador	Windfall profits tax, enforcement of that tax, physical takeover of the oil fields	USA—ECUADOR	2008	December 14, 2012	Tribunal rejected jurisdiction over umbrella clause but accepted jurisdiction over *caucidad* decrees. Tribunal decided Ecuador expropriated claimant's investment unlawfully. Other claims are dismissed
Phoenix Action v. Czech Republic	Administration of justice (court decisions), tax (investigations), border control (customs)	Croatia-Czech Rep BIT	2004	April 15, 2009	Tribunal rejected jurisdiction over claim. The claimant had to pay all arbitration costs
Noble Energy v. Ecuador	Utilities (electricity), privatization (energy), tax (value-added tax), public order (enforcement of electricity rates), energy (subsidies)	USA Ecuador BIT	2005	Settled	Tribunal accepted jurisdiction. Case subsequently settled by agreement between claimant and respondent state
Gottlieb v. Canada	Tax (taxation of income trusts), resource management (oil and gas)	NAFTA	2007		Claim rejected following agreement of respondent state and claimant's state

(continued)

Table 8.2 (continued)

Case name	Tax area	Treaty	Year of claim	Award date	Outcome
					of nationality that taxation measure did not constitute an expropriation
TCW v Dominican Republic	Utilities (electricity), privatization (energy), public order (theft of electricity), tax (investigations)	CAFTA	2007	Consent Award/ July 16, 2009	Case settled by agreement of claimant and respondent state before any decision on jurisdiction
Lacich v Canada	Tax (taxation of income trusts), resource management (oil and gas)	NAFTA	2009	Withdrawn	Claim withdrawn before tribunal established
Link-Trading v Moldova	Tax (import taxes), border control (customs), industrial policy (free economic zones)	USA Moldova BIT	1999	April 18, 2002	Tribunal accepted jurisdiction over claim but decided that respondent state did not violate treaty. The claimant was required to pay toward legal costs of respondent
Tokios Tokeles v. Ukraine	Culture (print publishing), tax (investigations)	Lithuania-Ukraine BIT	2002	July 26, 2007	Tribunal accepted jurisdiction over claim but decided that respondent state did not violate treaty. Tribunal split arbitration costs between claimant and respondent state
EnCana v. Ecuador	Tax (value-added tax), public contracting (oil production), resource management (oil)	Canada-Ecuador BIT	2003	February 3, 2006	Tribunal rejected jurisdiction over claim except expropriation, decided that respondent state did not violate treaty. The respondent state

(continued)

Table 8.2 (continued)

Case name	Tax area	Treaty	Year of claim	Award date	Outcome
					had to pay all arbitration costs
Plama Consortium Limited v. Bulgaria	Environmental protection (environmental liability), administration of justice (bankruptcy administration), public order (occupations of oil refinery), tax (corporate income tax), privatization (oil refinery)	ECT and Bulgaria-Cyprus BIT	2003	August 27, 2008	Tribunal accepted jurisdiction over claims arising from ECT but decided that the claimant is not entitled to any of the substantive protections provided by the ECT and respondent state did not violate treaty. Tribunal required claimant to pay all arbitration costs as well as legal costs of respondent state
Grand River v. USA	Public health (anti-smoking), administration of justice (settlement with cigarette manufacturers), tax (tax stamps on cigarettes)	NAFTA	2004	January 12, 2011	Tribunal rejected jurisdiction over claims of Grand River, accepted jurisdiction over claims of Arthur Montour but decided that the respondent state did not violate the treaty and split the arbitration costs
Amto LLC. v. Ukraine	Tax procedure (energy, industrial policy, privatization)	ECT	2005	March 26, 2008	Tribunal accepted jurisdiction over claim, but decided that respondent state did not violate treaty. The arbitration costs were split between the parties and each party bore its own legal costs

(continued)

Table 8.2 (continued)

Case name	Tax area	Treaty	Year of claim	Award date	Outcome
EDF v. Romania	Public order (corruption investigations), border control (customs), tax (duty-free regime), international relations (European Union accession)	UK-Romania BIT	2005	October 8, 2009	Tribunal accepted jurisdiction over claim but decided that respondent state did not violate treaty. Tribunal split arbitration costs between claimant and respondent state but required claimant to pay $6 million toward legal costs of respondent state
The Rompetrol Group N.V. v. Romania	Irregularities during the privatization, tax fraud, corruption, abuse of power, money laundering	Netherlands-Romania BIT	2005	May 6, 2013	The tribunal accepted jurisdiction over claims, decided that there was no breach of the treaty
Jan Oostergetel and Theodora Laurentius v. The Slovak Republic	Bankruptcy, tax arrears	Netherlands-Slovak Republic BIT	2006	April 23, 2012	Tribunal decided that respondent state did not breach treaty, ordered the claimants to bear the arbitration costs and to pay the respondent 2 million euros as contribution to legal and other costs

Source: International Investment Arbitration and Public Policy (IIAPP) Database (available at http://www.iiapp.org) and relevant awards. Table compiled by authors

8.3.2 Tax Disputes Lost by the Host States

Out of the 32 disputes dealing with tax matters, 15 have been lost by the host states. These disputes are the most interesting because they show what can go wrong in terms of designing tax policy in accordance with IIAs. Table 8.3 produces the details of each of these 15 disputes.

Table 8.3 Investment disputes lost by host states

Case name	Tax area	Treaty	Year of claim	Award date	Outcome
Feldman v. Mexico	Tax (excise tax on cigarettes), border control (customs, gray market exports of cigarettes)	NAFTA	1999	December 16, 2002	Tribunal accepted jurisdiction over claim, decided that respondent state violated treaty (NT). The court awarded specifically "$16,961,056 Mexican pesos (principal amount of $9,464,627.50 plus interest of $7,496,428.47). Tribunal split arbitration costs between claimant and respondent state
Goetz v. Burundi	Cancellation of license to operate in a free economic zone	Belgium-Luxemburg-Burundi BIT	1999	February 10, 1999	Indirect expropriation subject to compensation amounted to roughly $3 million
Enron Corporation & Ponderosa Assets LP v. The Argentine Republic	Stamp tax	Argentine-USA BIT	2001	May 22, 2007	Tribunal decided that Argentina breached FET and umbrella clauses and awarded a compensation of $106.2 million
Occidental Exploration and Production Company v. Ecuador Case No. UN 3467	Tax (value-added tax), public contracting (oil production)	USA-Ecuador BIT	2002	July 1, 2004	Tribunal accepted jurisdiction over claim, decided that respondent state violated treaty (NT and FET), and awarded approximately $75.0 million (plus interest) against respondent state.

(continued)

Table 8.3 (continued)

Case name	Tax area	Treaty	Year of claim	Award date	Outcome
					Tribunal required respondent state to pay 55% of arbitration costs
Archer Daniels Midland Co. & Tate Lyle Ingredients Americas, Inc. v. United Mexican States	Imposition of a new tax on soft drinks and syrups sweetened by sweeteners other than sugar	NAFTA	2003	November 21, 2007	Tribunal decided that Mexico breached articles on NT and performance requirement and that the tax imposed does not amount to a valid countermeasure. Tribunal awarded US$33.0 million
El Paso Energy International Company v. Argentine Republic	Resource management (oil and gas), utilities (electricity), privatization (energy), monetary system (financial crisis, currency reform)	Argentina-USA BIT	2003	October 31, 2011	Tribunal decided that the Argentine Republic breached FET, awarded a compensation of $43.0 million plus interest, split the arbitration costs. Parties bear their own legal costs and expenses
Duke Energy v. Ecuador	Utilities (electricity), public contracting (electric power procurement), border control (customs), tax (import taxes)	USA-Ecuador BIT	2004	August 18, 2008	Tribunal accepted jurisdiction over claim except custom duties, decided that respondent state violated treaty (NT and umbrella clause), and awarded approximately $5.6 million (plus interest) against respondent state. Tribunal split arbitration costs between claimant

(continued)

Table 8.3 (continued)

Case name	Tax area	Treaty	Year of claim	Award date	Outcome
					and respondent state
Hulley v. Russia	Tax (tax evasion investigations), public order (seizures of facilities), administration of justice (court decisions), privatization (oil industry)	ECT	2005	July 18, 2014	Tribunal accepted jurisdiction, decided that Russia breached expropriation article, awarded damages of $40 billion
RosInvestCo v. Russia	Tax (tax evasion investigations), public order (seizures of facilities), administration of justice (court decisions), privatization (oil industry)	UK-USSR BIT	2005	December 22, 2010	Tribunal accepted jurisdiction, decided that Russia breached expropriation article, awarded damages of $3.5 million, split the arbitration costs
Yukos Universal v. Russia	Tax (tax evasion investigations), public order (seizures of facilities), administration of justice (court decisions), privatization (oil industry)	ECT	2005	July 18, 2014	Tribunal accepted jurisdiction, decided that Russia breached expropriation article, awarded damages of $1.8 billion
Mobil v. Venezuela	Resource management (oil), public contracting (oil production), tax (corporate income tax)	Netherlands-Venezuela BIT	2007	October 9, 2014	The tribunal accepted jurisdiction over claims except the claim arising out of increase in the income tax rate. It awarded compensation of about $1411 million plus interest for expropriation and $9.0 million plus interest for the production and export curtailments. It split

(continued)

Table 8.3 (continued)

Case name	Tax area	Treaty	Year of claim	Award date	Outcome
					the arbitration costs
Quasar de Valores Sicav SA v. The Russian Federation	Tax (tax evasion investigations), public order (seizures of facilities), administration of justice (court decisions)	Spain-USSR BIT	2007	July 20, 2012	Tribunal accepted jurisdiction, decided that Russia breached expropriation article, awarded damages of around $2.0 million in total
Renta 4 v. Russia	Tax assessment, public order (seizures of facilities), administration of justice (court decisions), privatization (oil industry)	Spain-USSR BIT	2007	March 30, 2009	Quasar case was formerly known as Renta 4 case. In the jurisdictional award, the tribunal accepted jurisdiction over claims of only four of the seven claimants of the Renta 4 case. Therefore, the case is renamed as Quasar
Tza Yap Shum v. Republic of Peru	Tax assessment	China-Peru BIT	2005	July 7, 2011	Expropriation case is not available in English
Veteran Petroleum v. Russia	Tax (tax evasion investigations), public order (seizures of facilities), administration of justice (court decisions), privatization (oil industry)	ECT	2005	July 18, 2014	Tribunal accepted jurisdiction, decided that Russia breached expropriation article, awarded damages of $50,020,867,798

Source: International Investment Arbitration and Public Policy (IIAPP) Database (available at http://www.iiapp.org) and relevant awards. Table compiled by authors

These 15 disputes have been lost by only 7 countries, all of which are developing countries or transition economies.

The majority of cases (nine awards) concluded with a finding of expropriation. However, two claims were consolidated into a single case for *Renta 4* and *Quasar de Valores v. Russia*. Also, as part of the *Yukos* case, three separate claims by former

Yukos shareholders were filed by Hulley Enterprises Limited (Cyprus), Yukos Universal Limited (Isle of Man), and Veteran Petroleum Limited (Cyprus). As a result, there are only six truly different tax disputes that resulted in a finding of expropriation.

The *Señor Tza Yap Shum v. Peru* dispute offers a comprehensive illustration of the type of problematic interactions between a taxpayer and an administration that may result in an investment dispute. In 2002, Mr. Tza Yap Shum established a $400,000 investment and began operating a fish product export business (TSG). However, in 2004, the Peruvian tax authority, after conducting a routine audit, decided that the amounts and values of the raw materials purchased had not been properly declared and might mean that sales had been under-declared. The authority issued a new tax assessment based on a "presumed basis" of $4 million and also took so-called interim measures to enforce the tax assessment that had been imposed to secure money for the Treasury. All banks in Peru were directed to retain any funds related to TSG passing to them and to redirect such funds to the tax authority. Almost immediately, TSG's business became inoperable because the company was unable to pay suppliers or receive payments from its customers.

The arbitral tribunal determined that the interim measures amounted to expropriation. The tribunal concluded that the interim measures significantly interfered with the operation of TSG, were imposed in an arbitrary manner, and did not respect the internal rules and guidelines for its own interim measures and that the local regulators did not make any effort to verify whether these rules were followed. Indeed, the actual tax claim might have been justified, but the temporary enforcement measures taken were so damaging to the operations of the company that the tax claim itself was rendered irrelevant because the company could not survive the measures.

The case illustrates that the recovery measures a state takes to collect tax debts are sensitive from the perspective of the protection foreign investors have under IIAs as well as under general international law. Such measures may easily have an expropriatory effect, even when the amount of tax that is recovered is in itself not confiscatory. A tax debt that is not enormous, but that is disputed and hence not finally determined, may be collected by the state with the use of measures that are so drastic and disproportionate that they result in the discontinuation of the investment. A temporary closure of business facilities, the seizure of business assets or bank accounts, or even the temporary imprisonment of executives of the local company on allegations of tax fraud may all result in the investment losing all value and prospects. In this case, the amount of tax due is secondary to the effect of the recovery measures themselves.

In terms of substance, one can observe that four key substantive provisions have been important to conclude a breach of the relevant IIA has occurred, namely, the expropriation clause, the FET clause, the full protection and security (FPS) standard, and the NT provision.

8.4   Tax as the Last Barrier to Investment

Finally, there is a real risk that tax could become "the last trade and investment barrier," either by design or default. This is because tax systems remain national and are likely to remain so for the foreseeable future (even in regional groupings like the EU), but these national tax systems have to operate in an increasingly global environment where cross-border activities are growing in importance, financial markets are highly integrated, large companies increasingly see themselves as truly global corporations, and technology enables firms and individuals to exploit to the maximum in this increasingly borderless world. Consequently, national tax barriers to investment flows remain (see Christians 2012). Some examples are highlighted below.

8.4.1   National Tax Barriers to Investment Flows

First, a major problem is the unrelieved double taxation on cross-border income and capital that occurs if the same income is taxed both in the residence state and the source state. This may influence decisions by multinational enterprises (MNEs) as to where to invest (the OECD's BEPS Project addresses this but will increase this risk, at least in the short term, because it will trigger a number of domestic tax reforms across the world).

Second, there remain inconsistencies in the way in which customs, value-added tax (VAT), and direct tax authorities apply transfer pricing rules to cross-border transactions between related parties within multinational groups, and this may lead to significant compliance costs for companies.

Third, there is a risk of creating a climate of tax uncertainty. The emergence of new players, the rapid development of new technologies, the more aggressive approach to tax planning on the part of some MNEs, and the lack of a global consensus on what should be the international tax rules will lead to more tax uncertainty (it now appears unlikely that BEPS will lead to any fundamental review of the core features of the current international tax framework, with the positions of the OECD countries, Brazil, Russia, China, and South Africa (BRICS); other emerging economies; and developing countries diverging. This lack of agreement will, at least in the short term, lead to a period of uncertainty, a lack of coherence, and disputes between countries).

Fourth, some countries are putting in "exit" taxes under both personal and corporate income taxes, and these taxes may decrease the mobility of capital and labor.

Finally, under the leadership of the WTO and the World Customs Organization (WCO), many tariffs and specific excise barriers to cross-border trade in goods and services have been removed, but friction continues, owing to the inconsistent way in which these rules are sometimes applied.

8.4.2 The New Horizon: Promoting Cooperation Between Tax Authorities

The OECD has concluded that the appropriate response to the pressures of globalization is better cooperation between governments. This is the approach the OECD has followed for many years in the direct tax area and with some success. The OECD Model Tax Convention forms the basis for the 3,600 bilateral tax treaties around the world, which minimize frictions between national tax systems (see also Rosenzweig 2012).

The OECD has many other success stories regarding taxation, e.g.

1. It has been at the forefront of promoting cooperation between tax authorities to counter both double taxation and double non-taxation of cross-border income.
2. Its transfer pricing guidelines are now used as the basis for national legislation both in OECD countries and many non-OECD countries.
3. In close cooperation with the EU, it has also done pioneering work on VAT; this started just over a decade ago, and in the long term, it should lead to more effective cooperation between the 160 countries that currently operate VAT/goods and services tax (GST) systems.
4. The Forum on Tax Administration provides a platform for commissioners from more than 40 countries to come together on a regular basis, and this grouping has now become a powerful voice both in shaping the debate on tax administrations across the world and in helping the commissioners to work together to cope with the challenges of globalization.
5. Removing bank secrecy as a barrier to the effective exchange of information between tax administrations.
6. The Base Erosion and Profit Shifting (BEPS) Project in 2013. The main purpose of the BEPS project is to effectively prevent double non-taxation and no or low taxation cases associated with artificially segregated taxable income from its revenue-generating activities.

Nevertheless, the question remains as to whether these forms of non-binding cooperation will be sufficient to avoid tax being used to protect domestic markets, to discriminate in favor of, or against, non-residents, or to give a competitive advantage to a country's enterprises.

8.5 Conclusion

This article evidenced an important reality: there are a growing number of international arbitration cases that involve a tax issue. This is not totally surprising. After all, foreign investment decisions and tax regulations are deeply intertwined. However, each was historically regulated by different authorities and agreements and used to belong to different spheres; however, today the spheres overlap.

In the coming years, such a trend will continue to increase, and because of the shortcomings of the tax dispute resolution mechanisms, many disputes might end up before investment tribunals.

The early jurisprudence of the International Centre for the Settlement of Investment Disputes (ICSID) has already given a strong indication that tax disputes related to foreign investment are also legal disputes that arise directly out of the investment for which the ICSID tribunal may have jurisdiction. Although none of these early cases are directly related to tax matters, tribunals felt it is important to warn the parties that it may one day be appropriate to link investment protection to tax law. In *AMCO v. Indonesia*, the tribunal observed that tax matters may well be covered by ICSID's jurisdiction. In *Kaiser Bauxite v. Jamaica*, the government had agreed to a tax stabilization clause, and the tribunal asserted that a dispute over increased taxes would fall under the scope of Article 25 paragraph 1 of the ICSID Convention, because "the dispute concerning the alleged legal rights and obligations stemming from particular provisions in Kaiser's agreements with the Government is a legal dispute." A similar situation and decision was found in *Alcoa Minerals v. Jamaica*. In this chapter, more recent cases have been reviewed. For example, in *Feldman v. Mexico*, the issue was the failure of the tax authorities to refund excise taxes for exported cigarettes, which was held by the international arbitration tribunal to be a violation of the NT provision of the IIA. In *Occidental v. Ecuador*, a case in which the investor was victorious, the dispute sprang from the refusal of the Ecuadorian tax authority to refund input VAT to a foreign investor.

It is important to note that an arbitration tribunal in an international investment case does not sit as a court of appeal to the local tax court or administrative body that decides tax cases in that state. Whether a certain tax is applicable under the laws of a state is a matter for the courts and administrative bodies of that state, not for the arbitration tribunal. The arbitration tribunal decides whether the state breached any international obligations as set out in the IIA, in general international law or, perhaps, in the contract between the state and the investor. In other words, it is not the role of the arbitration tribunal to interpret and apply the tax laws of a state to an investor. But the way a state applies its tax laws, even if applied correctly under that state's law, may very well constitute a breach of the obligations of that state under international law. As such, the matter can be both a question for a local tax court (to be decided solely on the tax laws of that state) and for an arbitration tribunal (to be decided on international investment law).

The last decade has witnessed a dramatic surge in investment disputes between foreign investors and host country governments. Arbitral panels have been charged with the task of applying the rules of IIAs in specific cases, a task which is not often straightforward given the broad and sometimes ambiguous terms of these arrangements. The new phenomenon of investment arbitration has brought about a number of decisions from different arbitral fora in the tax sector, contributing to the formation of a jurisprudence that is elucidating the meaning of key provisions and contributing to the emergence of global economic regulation of tax matters. Importantly, 15 disputes have resulted in significant compensation being paid by host states for breaching IIA commitments by imposing tax measures. The details of these

15 disputes show that there a number of provisions which have proven decisive to justify the claims of the taxpayers, namely, protection against expropriation, FET, FPS, non-discrimination, the umbrella clause, and procedure. These six investment provisions indirectly constitute part of the international regime of tax matters, which is increasingly being shaped by investment tribunals' awards and international investment agreements.

Acknowledgment We would especially like to thank Irma Mosquera, Shintaro Hamanaka, Xu Yan, Noam Noked, and Karl P. Sauvant for indispensable feedback and comments.

References

Christians, A. (2009). Your own personal tax law: Dispute resolution under the OECD Model Tax Convention. *Willamette Journal of International Law and Dispute Resolution, 17*(2), 172–185.

Christians, A. (2012). How nations share. *Indiana Law Journal, 87*(4), 1407–1453.

OECD Model Tax Convention on Income and on Capital: Condensed Version 2017. Retrieved June 19, 2020, from https://doi.org/10.1787/mtc_cond-2017-en

Ring, D. (2010). Who is making international tax policy: International organizations as power players in a high stakes world. *Fordham International Law Journal, 33*(3), 649–722.

Rosenzweig, A. H. (2012). Thinking outside the (tax) treaty. *Wisconsin Law Review, 2012*(3), 717–786.

Stephan, P. B. (2010). *Comparative taxation procedure and tax enforcement.* Oxford: Oxford University Press.

Swenson, C. D., Beaumont, S. J., Bennett, M., & Conway, K. (2011). Managing cross-border tax disputes. *Taxes: The Tax Magazine, 89*(6), 57–68.

UNCTAD. *International investment agreements navigator.* Retrieved June 19, 2020, from https://investmentpolicy.unctad.org/international-investment-agreements

Vieira, M. (2014). The regulation of tax matters in bilateral investment treaties: A dispute resolution perspective. *Dispute Resolution International, 8*(1), 63–84.

Cases

Alcoa Minerals of Jamaica Inc. v. Jamaica, ICSID Case No. ARB/74/2Antoine Goetz et consorts v. République du Burundi, ICSID Case No. ARB/95/3.

Amco Asia Corporation and others v. Republic of Indonesia, ICSID Case No. ARB/81/1.

Archer Daniels Midland Company and Tate & Lyle Ingredients Americas, Inc. v. The United Mexican States, ICSID Case No. ARB (AF)/04/5.

Burlington Resources Inc. v. Republic of Ecuador, ICSID Case No. ARB/08/5 (formerly *Burlington Resources Inc. and others v. Republic of Ecuador and Empresa Estatal Petróleos del Ecuador (PetroEcuador)*).

Corn Products International, Inc. v. United Mexican States, ICSID Case No. ARB (AF)/04/1.

Christopher and Nancy Lacich v. Government of Canada, NAFTA.

Duke Energy Electroquil Partners & Electroquil S.A. v. Republic of Ecuador, ICSID Case No. ARB/04/19.

EDF (Services) Limited v. Romania, ICSID Case No. ARB/05/13.

El Paso Energy International Company v. The Argentine Republic, ICSID Case No. ARB/03/15.

EnCana Corporation v. Republic of Ecuador, LCIA Case No. UN3481, *UNCITRAL (formerly EnCana Corporation v. Government of the Republic of Ecuador)*.

Enron Corporation and Ponderosa Assets, L.P. v. Argentine Republic, ICSID Case No. ARB/01/3 (also known as: Enron Creditors Recovery Corp. and Ponderosa Assets, L.P. v. The Argentine Republic).

Gottlieb Investors Group v. Government of Canada, NAFTA.

Grand River Enterprises Six Nations, Ltd., et al. v. United States of America, UNCITRAL.

Hulley Enterprises Limited (Cyprus) v. The Russian Federation, UNCITRAL, PCA Case No. AA 226.

Jan Oostergetel and Theodora Laurentius v. The Slovak Republic, UNCITRAL.

Kaiser Bauxite Company v. Jamaica, ICSID Case No. ARB/74/3.

Limited Liability Company Amto v. Ukraine, SCC Case No. 080/2005.

Link-Trading Joint Stock Company v. Department for Customs Control of the Republic of Moldova, UNCITRAL.

Marvin Roy Feldman Karpa v. United Mexican States, ICSID Case No. ARB(AF)/99/1 (also known as Marvin Feldman v. Mexico).

Mobil Corporation, Venezuela Holdings, B.V., Mobil Cerro Negro Holding, Ltd., Mobil Venezolana de Petróleos Holdings, Inc., Mobil Cerro Negro, Ltd., and Mobil Venezolana de Petróleos, Inc. v. Bolivarian Republic of Venezuela, Decision on Jurisdiction.

Nations Energy Corporation, Electric Machinery Enterprises Inc., and Jamie Jurado v. The Republic of Panama, ICSID Case No. ARB/06/19.

Noble Energy, Inc. and Machalapower Cia. Ltda. v. The Republic of Ecuador and Consejo Nacional de Electricidad, ICSID Case No. ARB/05/12.

Occidental Exploration v. Ecuador LCIA Case No. UN3467.

Pan American Energy LLC and BP Argentina Exploration Company v. The Argentine Republic, ICSID Case No. ARB/03/13.

Phoenix Action, Ltd. v. The Czech Republic, ICSID Case No. ARB/06/5.

Plama Consortium Limited v. Republic of Bulgaria, ICSID Case No. ARB/03/24.

Quasar de Valores SICAV S.A., Orgor de Valores SICAV S.A., GBI 9000 SICAV S.A. and ALOS 34 S.L. v. The Russian Federation SCC Case No. 24/2007.

Sergei Paushok, CJSC Golden East Company and CJSC Vostokneftegaz Company v. The Government of Mongolia, UNCITRAL.

Renta 4 S.V.S.A, Ahorro Corporación Emergentes F.I., Ahorro Corporación Eurofondo F.I., Rovime Inversiones SICAV S.A., Quasar de Valors SICAV S.A., Orgor de Valores SICAV S. A., GBI 9000 SICAV S.A. v. The Russian Federation, SCC No. 24/2007.

RosInvestCo UK Ltd. v. The Russian Federation, SCC Case No. V079/2005.

Señor Tza Yap Shum v. The Republic of Peru, ICSID Case No. ARB/07/6.

TCW Group, Inc and Dominican Energy Holdings, L.P. v. The Dominican Republic, UNCITRAL.

Tokios Tokelés v. Ukraine, ICSID Case No. ARB/02/18.

The Rompetrol Group N.V. v. Romania, ICSID Case No. ARB/06/3.

Veteran Petroleum Limited (Cyprus) v. The Russian Federation, UNCITRAL, PCA Case No. AA 228.

Yukos Universal Limited (Isle of Man) v. The Russian Federation, UNCITRAL, PCA Case No. AA 227.

Part IV
Harmful and Helpful Tax Practices for Sustainable Development

Chapter 9
Tax Expenditure Reporting and Domestic Revenue Mobilization in Africa

Agustin Redonda, Christian von Haldenwang, and Flurim Aliu

9.1 Tax Expenditure and Tax Expenditure Reporting

Governments pursue public policy objectives through revenue collection and public spending. However, they also rely on tax expenditures (TEs). The term refers to benefits granted to specific sectors or groups through preferential tax treatments such as exemptions, deductions, credits, deferrals and lower tax rates. Governments use TEs to promote economic growth and attract investments but also for the pursuit of social welfare objectives and to incentivise specific patterns of behaviour, such as energy consumption from renewable sources.

TEs are hence used widely as public policy instruments, and they are costly. In the United States, the federal government is estimated to forego more than USD1.5 trillion in 2019, an amount equal to 44% of tax revenue collection and slightly more than 7% of gross domestic product (GDP) (US Treasury 2020). Existing estimates, though limited in scope, show that TEs range from 0.7 to 6.6% of GDP in Latin America and from 3.3 to 7.5% of GDP in Africa (World Bank 2015).

Yet, despite their significant fiscal cost, TEs are often very opaque. Transparency on the range and magnitude of existing TEs is limited, and new provisions are being introduced regularly without adequate scrutiny. This lack of scrutiny may sometimes be justified by the urgency of the situation. For instance, all over the world governments have introduced tax reliefs as a short-term response to the coronavirus disease

A. Redonda (✉) · F. Aliu
Council on Economic Policies, Zürich, Switzerland
e-mail: ar@cepweb.org

C. von Haldenwang
German Development Institute, Deutsches Institut für Entwicklungspolitik (DIE), Bonn, Germany
e-mail: christian.vonhaldenwang@die-gdi.de

© The Author(s) 2021
I. J. Mosquera Valderrama et al. (eds.), *Taxation, International Cooperation and the 2030 Sustainable Development Agenda*, United Nations University Series on Regionalism 19, https://doi.org/10.1007/978-3-030-64857-2_9

2019 (COVID-19) pandemic.[1] However, in a majority of cases, TEs are used to pursue more strategic goals, and they tend to persist over time. This makes the issue of TE reporting and transparency a very relevant issue, particularly for low-income countries with limited capacities for domestic revenue mobilization (DRM).

Official reports on TEs are based on very heterogeneous standards both with respect to the quality and the scope of the data they provide. In France, for instance, the budget appendix dedicated to TEs explicitly acknowledges that 254 TEs out of 474 cannot be quantified, or only a rough order of magnitude can be given (Direction du Budget 2019). Switzerland published its last report on federal TEs in 2011 (Département Fédéral des Finances 2011). Australia, despite being at the forefront in terms of TE reporting, does not provide estimates for 49% of all TEs (143/289) in its Tax Expenditures Statement 2017 (Australian Treasury 2018). The picture is significantly worse when it comes to developing economies. In regions such as the Middle East and North Africa, less than 10% of the countries report on TEs on a regular basis (World Bank 2015).

As a result, TEs are hardly ever subject to sound cost-benefit analyses. Indeed, empirical studies assessing the effectiveness and efficiency of TEs are rare, and, when available, results are often not the expected ones.[2] At the same time, identifying and phasing out costly and ineffective provisions are crucial in order to improve the equity and fairness of the tax system, to increase the mobilization of domestic resources and to raise the quality of public expenditure systems. TE reform has become even more crucial in the current situation, when governments will have to cope with the medium- and long-term effects of the COVID-19 crisis.

In South Africa, for instance, the government grants pension-related TEs to promote the growth of pension savings and to provide the elderly with a stable income upon retirement. According to the latest TE report, in 2016 these provisions were the largest TE in South Africa, amounting to 72,991 million Rand (ca. 5.1 billion euros), i.e. 35% of total TEs. Pension-related TEs have been at the heart of an intense debate. The South African government has been trying to deal with a policy design trade-off between providing generous benefits to boost individual savings and the risk of compromising the equity of the tax system due to the excessive use of these provisions, particularly by those at the top end of the income distribution. As acknowledged in a Technical Discussion Paper published by the South African Treasury in 2012, "the barriers to a more effective tax incentive regime are the

---

[1] An overview over tax measures taken to confront the pandemic can be found at https://www.oecd.org/tax/tax-policy/, accessed on 27.05.2020.

[2] For instance, many tax incentives implemented to attract investment have been proven to perform poorly. This is the case of several tax incentives granted by low-income economies such as tax holidays and special economic zones (WB 2017) as well as patent boxes (Alstadsæter et al. 2018; Klemens 2017) and other tax incentives to boost R&D. Yet, the lack of effectiveness of TEs goes beyond tax benefits for businesses. The mortgage interest deduction (Hilber and Turner 2014) and the myriad of tax benefits to boost pension savings (Duflo et al. 2006) have also been proven to be ineffective. For a more detailed overview on the lack of effectiveness and efficiency of TEs, see Redonda (2016).

complexity of the current regime [. . .] as well as the fact that the regime is open to abuse through excessive contributions by employers and high-income earning individuals. [. . .] The tax exemption has no nominal monetary cap in the case of higher-income employees, allowing them to make tax-exempt contributions way in excess of the amount required to maintain a reasonable standard of living in retirement" (South African National Treasury 2012). A comprehensive reform was implemented in 2016 to simplify and harmonise the pension system in the hope that this would improve the fairness of the whole system. Yet, as shown by Axelson et al. (2020), pension-related TEs are still highly regressive in the country.

The goal of this chapter is twofold: first, to discuss the role of TE reporting as a key component of a more effective and fairer tax system as well as a determinant for DRM and, second, to provide an overview of TE reporting in Africa.

9.2   The Fiscal Cost and (in)Effectiveness of Tax Expenditures

Revenue mobilisation is vital for many low- and middle-income economies. The financing gap for achieving the Sustainable Development Goals (SDGs) for developing countries alone has been estimated at roughly USD2.5 trillion (UNCTAD 2014). External financing—including official development assistance and foreign direct investment (FDI)—is certainly an important source of revenue. Yet, the mobilisation of domestic resources should be considered the most important revenue source to support inclusive and sustained economic growth (Brys et al. 2016). Tax revenues amounted to USD4.3 trillion in 2016 for low- and middle-income countries alone, which is more than double the amount of international public and private capital these countries received in the same year (von Haldenwang and Laudage 2019).

Indeed, the mobilisation of domestic resources through taxation is particularly relevant for many reasons. Revenues collected through the tax system are generally more stable and predictable than those coming from foreign aid or domestic non-tax sources, e.g. royalties from the minerals sector. Moreover, the contribution of taxes can strengthen the social contract between citizens and their government and thus have a positive effect on governance. Unfortunately, though, tax-to-GDP ratios in many low- and middle-income economies are strikingly low. Whereas the average tax-to-GDP ratio for advanced economies is 26%, about half of developing countries collect less than 15% of GDP in taxes—a threshold that has recently been identified as the minimum required to allow developing economies to take off economically (IMF 2017a).

Increasing tax revenues is an ambitious and complex task. It entails working on issues such as designing efficient tax systems, improving institutional capacity, increasing tax compliance, cooperating with other revenue bodies at an international scale and empowering tax administrations at various government levels, among others. Beyond these technical issues, however, fiscal contract and fiscal sociology debates show that improving tax systems is above all a systemic task that involves addressing the quality of public policies, the strengthening of governmental checks and balances and the legitimacy of government in general (Bird and Zolt 2015; Prichard 2019).

It is against this background that the frequent and sustained use of TEs should be analysed. While ideological positions may play a role, for instance, with regard to the private or public provision of social security or health insurance, it can be assumed that in most developing countries, TEs are employed for two main reasons: tax competition and political convenience. Tax competition refers to the fact that capital-hungry countries are under pressure to grant incentives for investments to the degree that this is an established practice among its competitors. Convenience means that these instruments are readily available to reward specific clientele groups or to obtain rents. This makes them an important pillar of the politics of taxation and the political economy of tax bargaining.

Phasing out ineffective TEs—which appears a low-hanging fruit for developing countries at first glance—is in fact a difficult, at times even risky undertaking. Institutional and power lock-ins evolve around specific TEs, making it politically costly to dismantle them. Public protests are widely documented in the literature, particularly with regard to fossil fuel subsidies, which often have a large impact on the costs of living of poorer urban households (for instance, see Chelminski 2018). Protests are often fuelled by a general lack of trust in government, as citizens refuse to trade present benefits for a promise of uncertain future compensations. In addition, powerful economic groups or large individual companies lobby for the extension of sector- or firm-specific tax breaks, and politicians lobby for keeping certain territorial TE schemes, such as special economic zones (SEZs), that favour their electoral districts or local constituencies (for instance, see Daude et al. 2017).

The Inter-American Center of Tax Administrations (CIAT) Tax Expenditure Database (TEDLAC) shows that, on average, TE as percentage of GDP amounted to 3.5% in the region, ranging from 0.7% in Colombia to 6.6% in Dominican Republic (Pelàez Longinotti 2018). Kassim and Mansour (2018) review TE reporting in 26 low- and middle-income economies and show that the revenue foregone through these provisions is in most of the cases significant. In their sample, TE as a share of GDP ranges from 1.38% in Burkina Faso to 4.69% in Poland and 6.13% in Ghana. Likewise, TE as a share of total tax revenue is as high as 27.8% in Poland, 41.67% in Ghana and a staggering 58% in Mauritania.

It has been argued that, despite their fiscal cost, TEs can be a valid policy instrument for governments worldwide. Indeed, under certain conditions (e.g. when eligibility conditions are directly linked to tax return data, when it is more important to maximise the number of beneficiaries than to minimize excess claims or when the policy objective is to incentivize a clear and broadly defined activity by reducing its net price), TEs could be more cost-effective than direct spending and may hence be the best option to pursue a specific public policy goal (Toder 2000).

Yet, TE provisions are generally ineffective in reaching their stated goals. The use of tax incentives to attract investments is a case in point. Low- and middle-income economies often grant far-reaching tax holidays and tax exemptions that have little impact on investment or growth and, in addition, significantly reduce the availability of public funds (IMF et al. 2015).

To sum up, scaling back ineffective TEs would broaden tax bases and, at the same time, allow countries to reduce marginal tax rates and/or save resources that, in turn, could be allocated to more productive or more effectively targeted purposes. However, a necessary condition for a sound evaluation of the cost and impact of these provisions is data (in particular, revenue foregone estimates), which—when existent—are generally published in governmental TE reports or statements. While it is certainly true that public reporting alone is not sufficient to achieve more rationality in TE, it is hard to engage in meaningful discussion on individual TE provisions without access to reliable, detailed and timely data.

9.3 Tax Expenditure Reporting

Systematically identifying, estimating and reporting the fiscal cost of TEs can be a time- and resource-intensive task. As discussed by Heady and Mansour (2019), countries could adopt a gradual approach that takes their institutional and data capacities into account. The returns to such a process are potentially high, since it is critical to assess the effectiveness and efficiency of these provisions and, hence, to ensure the alignment of public policies with their stated goals. In addition, publishing comprehensive and detailed TE reports is crucial not only as a policy tool for policymakers but also as a means for increasing government transparency and accountability.

Yet, despite their significant impact on government budgets, TEs are generally much less an object of public scrutiny than direct spending. As acknowledged by the Australian Treasury, "Tax Expenditures, like direct expenditures, affect the government's budget. However, unlike direct expenditures, tax expenditures once legislated become part of the tax law with a recurring fiscal impact and do not receive regular scrutiny through the budget process" (Australian Treasury 2004). Indeed, TE reporting lags way behind best practice in most countries, and several countries that issue reports do not even estimate the revenue foregone through these provisions. An assessment of TE reporting in the 43 Group of 20 (G20) and OECD economies, based on 9 key dimensions that reflect good practice in TE reporting, shows that 8 countries have not reported on TEs in the last 10 years, 26 have published a basic report (e.g. by providing estimates for a reduced subset of TEs or estimates based on aggregate figures only) during the same period and only 9 governments have published a detailed and comprehensive TE report on a regular basis (Redonda and Neubig 2018).

Furthermore, the same assessment shows that among the 43 G20 and OECD economies, TE under-reporting (i.e. difference between the number of effectively estimated TEs and the number of those provisions that are listed without an estimate of their fiscal cost) is highly prevalent. For instance, the share of estimated TEs with respect to listed provisions is as low as 17% in Greece and 20% in New Zealand (Redonda and Neubig 2018). Yet, a larger ratio of estimated/listed provisions does not necessarily indicate that the report is more comprehensive. As will be illustrated with the South African example later in the chapter, the number of TEs included in the reports (estimated and/or listed) is very often far from reflecting the number of TEs effectively implemented by the government.

Moreover, while there is significant room for improving the estimation and reporting of TEs in advanced economies, the situation is even more worrisome in middle- and low-income countries. Indeed, in most of these countries, TE reporting is rudimentary at best, due to data constraints, insufficient human and financial resources as well as weak institutions, among other factors. According to figures provided by the World Bank in 2015, the percentage of countries that periodically estimates the revenue forgone through TEs amounts to 33% in Latin America and the Caribbean, 21% in sub-Saharan Africa, 14% in South Asia and 10% or less in the Middle East and North Africa, Europe and Central Asia as well as East Asia and the Pacific. Likewise, Kassim and Mansour (2018) show that TE reporting quality remains considerably weak in several areas in most of the 26 low- and middle-income countries covered by their study. For instance, only about half of the reviewed countries have a legal requirement to report on TEs, only three reports provide forecast estimates for future years and roughly half of the countries provide a discussion of the benchmark system in their reports.[3]

9.4   Tax Expenditure Reporting in Africa

As shown in Fig. 9.1, out of 54 African countries reviewed by the Global Tax Expenditures Database (GTED) team, 20 (about 37% of the countries) reported their TE to the public at least once between the years 2000 and 2019.[4] The remaining 63% of the countries did not publish any TE reports during this period. We start our

---

[3]This information is crucial since TEs are defined as deviations from a benchmark, which represents the standard taxation treatment and, at the same time, could include certain elements of the tax system which depart from a uniform treatment of taxpayers, i.e. fundamental structural elements of the tax system such as the progressive income tax rate scale for individual taxpayers (Australian Treasury 2011).

[4]The GTED is a joint effort of think tanks and research institutions from Europe, Asia, Africa and Latin America, led by the Council on Economic Policies (CEP) and the German Development Institute (DIE) and financed by the German Federal Ministry for Economic Cooperation and Development (BMZ). The main goal of the project is to build the first online Global Tax Expenditures Database to increase transparency, generate trustworthy information and expand research in the field of TEs. The GTED is set up with official data on TEs published by governments worldwide, in a consistent format to increase the level of international comparability. The GTED will be made publicly available and free of charge through an online platform that will also include a

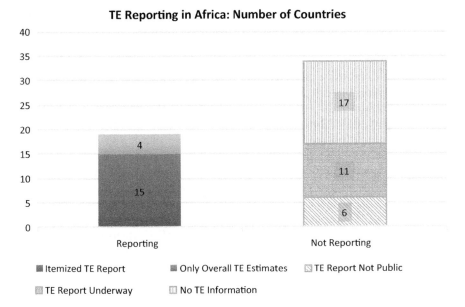

Fig. 9.1 Overview of TE reporting in Africa ("Itemized TE report" refers to TE reports that provide subcategorization beyond tax base information. The most advanced version of an itemized TE report is one that provides revenue foregone and accompanying information at the TE provision level.). Source: Global Tax Expenditures Database, www.GTED.net

discussion by taking a more detailed look at this second group before zooming in on the 20 countries that provided at least some information.

9.4.1   African Countries Without Publicly Available TE Reports

For the purposes of transparency and political debate, TE reports have to be public. Ideally, they should be found on open and easily accessible governmental websites or repositories. References to such reports in official government statements should include information on where to find them. For 6 out of the 34 countries classified as not having a public TE report, we found references to internal TE reports, but no further information was given. One such example is Ghana. In the FY 2019 Budget Speech, the Ghanaian Finance Minister states that "[between 2010 and 2018], about six different studies have been conducted into Ghana's tax exemptions regime by the Revenue Policy Division of the Ministry of Finance, International Monetary Fund

---

repository for blogs, working papers and further publications as well as events on TEs organized by the partners. For more details, see Redonda and von Haldenwang (2021).

(IMF), Organisation for Economic Cooperation & Development (OECD), GIZ and the World Bank" (Ministry of Finance, Republic of Ghana 2018). However, we were not able to find any of these reports. Similarly, the Eswatini (formerly known as Swaziland) Revenue Authority claims that it carries out a TE analysis biennially. "[Exemptions] under Income Taxes are reported every 2 years after carrying out a Tax Expenditure Analysis. The last report done was for 2013/14 and the next report will be undertaken in the new financial year, 2016/17" (Eswatini Revenue Authority Annual Report 2016). However, these reports are also not available.

Furthermore, 11 countries claim to be in the process of carrying out a TE analysis or are considering the possibility of doing so. Chad, for example, is reported to have started a TE analysis in 2016 but has since not published any information regarding that particular analysis or TE in general. "Since September 2016, with the support of the World Bank EFSO [Emergency Fiscal Stabilization Development Policy Operation], the [Chad] Government put a freeze on any new tax exemptions, except those under the Vienna convention or those related to PTF [Partnership Transparency Fund] until an ongoing study on tax expenditure would be completed and new measures adopted" (World Bank 2018). Similarly, Ethiopia is also reported to have a TE analysis "near completion," but additional information about the analysis is not available (IMF 2018). Table 9.1 provides information on the TE reporting state of the art in each of the assessed countries.

Lastly, the remaining 17 countries do not have any information regarding TEs on any online platform. In the case of the Central African Republic, for example, the IMF reports, "[tax] exemptions and tax expenditures are rarely detailed and assessed in the budget documentation or are maintained for several years without clear legal basis and economic justification" (IMF 2019a). Similarly, in Kenya, "[there] is no reporting of tax expenditures. Despite a constitutional requirement for a public record of tax waivers to be published, and the PFM Act's requirement for an annual report, no such reports are available" (IMF 2017b). This shows that some governments even ignore legal or constitutional norms on TE analysis and reporting.

9.4.2 African Countries with Publicly Available TE Reports

A total of 20 African countries reported on their TEs at least once in the last 20 years. However, the information reported during this period varies substantially across countries. Countries like the Democratic Republic of the (DR) Congo, Lesotho, Seychelles, Sierra Leone and South Sudan only provide very rudimentary estimates of TEs in budget-related documentation, without any further details. For example, in the FY 2019 Budget Speech, the South Sudan Finance Minister claimed that "exemptions have reached recorded level of sixty-nine billion South Sudanese Pounds, which deprived the government of the most resources for capital investment and development" (Ministry of Finance and Planning, Republic of South Sudan 2018). However, the ministry did not provide any information on how it calculated those estimates. This is a case that could also qualify as non-reporting. Similarly, the

Table 9.1 Overview of TE reporting in Africa, by country

TE report available			TE report not available	
Itemized TE report	Only overall TE estimates	TE report not public	TE report underway	No TE information
Benin	DR Congo	Cameroon	Algeria	Angola
Burkina Faso	Lesotho	Ghana	Botswana	Burundi
Ivory Coast	Seychelles	Mozambique	Chad	Cape Verde
Gabon	Sierra Leone	Swaziland	Egypt	Central African Republic
Guinea	South Sudan	Uganda	Ethiopia	Comoros
Liberia		Equatorial Guinea	Gambia	Congo
Madagascar			Guinea-Bissau	Djibouti
Mali			Niger	Eritrea
Mauritania			Nigeria	Kenya
Mauritius			Togo	Libya
Morocco			Zambia	Malawi
Rwanda				Namibia
Senegal				Sao Tome and Principe
South Africa				Somalia
Tanzania				Sudan
				Tunisia
				Zimbabwe

Source: Global Tax Expenditures Database, www.GTED.net

Lesotho Revenue Authority Annual report includes a small section with an overall estimate on "Revenue Foregone on Tax Relief Measures," or similarly titled (Lesotho Revenue Authority Annual Report 2016). However, the report does not break down the overall TE estimate or provide a clear description on how this estimate was calculated. The General Directorate for Imports of DR Congo also publishes overall TE estimates in several of its annual reports with little accompanying information (Ministère des Finances et du Budget, Republique du Congo 2017).

In fact, only 15 African countries have ever published itemized reports. Nonetheless, as shown in Fig. 9.2, this number is steadily rising. The first TE report in Africa was published in Morocco in 2005. Two years later, Mauritius also started reporting on TEs. South Africa started reporting only in 2011. In 2018, the number of reports published in Africa reached a record of seven reports. Nonetheless, the numbers also highlight the inconsistency of TE reporting among African countries. As shown in Fig. 9.2, 10 out of the 15 African countries classified as having reported on TEs had only ever published one or two reports. Two countries (Mali and Senegal) published between three and five reports, and only three governments—Mauritius, Morocco and South Africa—publish TE reports regularly. Tanzania is a special case since it has covered 12 years of TE estimates in one single TE report.

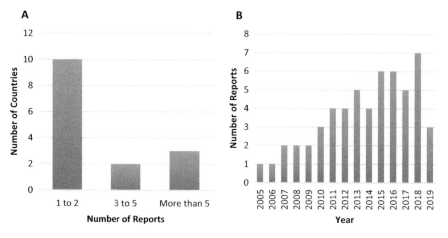

Fig. 9.2 Number of reports per country and per year. Source: Global Tax Expenditures Database, www.GTED.net

However, even for these reporting countries, much progress is needed in terms of coverage.

The quality and the scope of most TE reports do not match the standards developed, for instance, by the IMF (2019b). Morocco and Ivory Coast are notable exceptions due to the broad scope of information provided in their reports. Morocco publishes in-depth information—detailed description, legal reference, tax base, incentive mechanism, budgetary category, targeted beneficiaries, policy objective and revenue foregone—for each of its TE provisions. Ivory Coast publishes the same kind of detailed information but does only include aggregate estimates of revenue foregone. Both countries provide much of the information that can be found in the most advanced and in-depth reports of countries such as Australia and Canada. Only information regarding the number of beneficiaries of each TE provision is missing from the TE reports of these two countries.

Apart from these two cases, most of the countries with TE reports provided revenue foregone estimates that were aggregated either at the tax base or at the budgetary category level, without supplying specific information at the TE provision level. Such information would be required, however, to perform cost-benefit evaluations and hence assess the effectiveness and efficiency of these provisions. Moreover, no country presents consistent data on the number of beneficiaries per provision.[5] Less than half of the countries specified the budgetary category, revealed a policy objective, specified the targeted beneficiaries or included a detailed description for each TE provision. This kind of information is not only crucial for policymakers, but it is also important to increase transparency and accountability

---

[5]Rwanda provides information on the number of beneficiaries for some provisions, but not for most. Hence, it received a negative score in the evaluation.

towards the society. On the other hand, most countries did present information on methodology, the legal reference and the tax base of specific TE provisions.[6]

Following Kassim and Manosur (2018) and Redonda and Neubig (2018), we evaluate the TE reports of the 15 reporting countries. As shown in Table 9.2, Morocco, Burkina Faso and Ivory Coast provide the most detailed TE information at the provision level. On the other hand, Mauritius and South Africa are the countries providing the least detailed information at the provision level. However, the difference between the South African report and the Mauritian report is that the former publishes some information at the TE provision level and describes its methodology, whereas the latter only publishes an itemized table regarding TE in its budget-related documentation without any accompanying information.

Table 9.2 highlights the heterogeneity and, at the same time, the overall need for improvement in African TE reporting. For example, countries such as Mauritius, South Africa, Gabon and Liberia did not provide any information at the provision level. The Gabon report barely fits the definition of an "itemized report" as it only lists nine TE subcategories and only reports on TE from value-added tax (VAT). Moreover, countries such as Benin, Guinea, Madagascar and Senegal provide revenue foregone estimations at the provision level but do not provide any other companion information such as a policy objective. These two pieces of information are the most important when conducting cost/benefit analyses yet rarely reported together by African countries. Indeed, only 3 out of 15 African TE reports present both revenue foregone estimates and policy objectives at the TE level.

Finally, even though we observe an increase in the number of countries reporting on TEs, the overall quality of the reports has not improved across years. Reports published prior to 2018 and those published in 2018 or 2019 received roughly the same score in the evaluation. Mauritius, Morocco and South Africa are the only countries for which an individual evaluation across time is possible. The three countries show barely any change in the quality and scope of their reporting, i.e. their first and last TE reports followed the same format. While this may be an indicator of consistency, it is also obvious that a large amount of relevant information is still missing in most reports.

9.4.3 What the Current Reports Reveal About TE in Africa

Some key messages can be drawn from the current TE reports from Africa. Table 9.3 shows each reporting country's total TE as a percentage of the total amount of taxes collected and as a percentage of each country's GDP during the same year. On average, the revenue foregone on TE among African countries amounted to 17.8% of

---

[6]Most countries did not provide methodology information at the provision level. However, most governments that do report use only one methodology to calculate the revenue foregone for all TE provisions, which is then described in one section of the report.

Table 9.2 Evaluation of TE reporting, latest available year

Country	Revenue foregone	Methodology	Detailed description	Legal reference	Tax base info	Incentive mechanism	Budgetary category	Targeted beneficiaries	Number of beneficiaries	Policy objective
Benin (2019)	✓	✓			✓	✓	✓	✓		
Burkina Faso (2016)	✓	✓		✓	✓	✓	✓	✓		✓
Ivory Coast (2017)		✓	✓	✓	✓	✓	✓	✓		✓
Gabon (2018)		✓								
Guinea (2017)	✓	✓		✓	✓		✓			
Liberia (2016)										
Madagascar (2015)	✓	✓		✓	✓					
Mali (2019)		✓								
Mauritania (2013)		✓	✓	✓	✓					
Mauritius (2016)										
Morocco (2019)	✓	✓	✓	✓	✓	✓	✓	✓		✓
Rwanda (2018)	✓	✓	✓	✓	✓	✓				✓
Senegal (2014)	✓	✓	✓	✓	✓	✓		✓		
South Africa (2018)		✓								

| Tanzania (2018) | ✓ | ✓ | ✓ | ✓ | ✓ | | | | |

Source: Global Tax Expenditures Database, www.GTED.net

The evaluation is based on the most recent report of each country—year in parenthesis

Table 9.3 TE as a percentage of total tax collected and GDP

Country	Year	% of tax collected	% of GDP
Benin	2017	18.20	2.40
Burkina Faso	2016	8.61	1.38
DR Congo	2016	10.21	0.65
Ivory Coast	2017	9.80	1.32
Gabon	2017	12.10	1.24
Guinea	2017	21.70	2.63
Lesotho	2016	17.60	3.96
Liberia	2016	18.89	4.70
Madagascar	2015	17.00	1.79
Mali	2017	17.32	2.64
Mauritania	2013	58.41	
Mauritius	2017	9.22	1.76
Morocco	2018	13.01	2.78
Rwanda	2018	14.30	4.60
Senegal	2014	39.60	7.80
Seychelles	2019	1.04	0.34
Sierra Leone	2017	8.76	1.20
South Africa	2017	14.90	3.90
Tanzania	2012	27.00	4.40
Average		17.77	2.75

Source: Global Tax Expenditures Database, www.GTED.net
Includes the countries which provided only overall estimates
South Sudan only provided an overall estimate of total "exemptions" in local currency. However, due to a drop of GDP by 80% during the same reporting year, it is hard to calculate a meaningful TE/GDP ratio. Similarly, due to a steep currency devaluation in Mauritania between 2010 and 2017, it is hard to calculate a meaningful TE/GDP ratio for that country as well

total tax collected. However, the TE share of total tax collected varied substantially across countries. In countries like Mauritania and Senegal, for example, this share was as high as 58.4% or 39.6%, respectively. Meanwhile, in Burkina Faso, Seychelles and Sierra Leone, TE was less than 9% of total tax collected. Similarly, TE as a share of GDP also varied across African countries. On average, TE accounted for 2.7% of GDP across African countries. However, this share was as low as 0.3% in the Seychelles and as high as 7.8% in Senegal. Furthermore, it is important to note that some countries such as Gabon, Liberia and Sierra Leone only reported their TE for one specific tax base (VAT in the case of Gabon and customs for the rest). Hence, the share of TE in total tax collected or in total GDP for these countries is likely higher.

As shown in Table 9.4, TE across African countries came from similar tax bases. VAT expenditure comprised the largest share of TE in most African countries. On average, almost half (49%) of TE across African countries originated from VAT-related exemptions and rate reductions. Customs duties were also a big source for TE across Africa. More than one-fifth (20% on average) of TE stemmed from

Table 9.4 Share of total revenue foregone by tax base

Country	Year	VAT (%)	PIT (%)	CIT (%)	Customs (%)	Stamp duty (%)	Excise (%)	Others (%)
Benin	2017	62.7	0.1	1.5	10.3	25.0	0.1	0.3
Burkina Faso	2016	40.7		21.0	26.1	8.5	0.0	3.8
DR Congo	2016	66.7						33.3
Ivory Coast	2017	69.6		9.2			0.7	20.5
Gabon	2017	100.0						0.0
Guinea	2017	40.0			34.0		11.0	15.0
Lesotho	2016	38.2	61.8					0.0
Liberia	2016				100.0			0.0
Madagascar	2015	24.2	0.5	2.5	42.0		8.0	22.7
Mali	2017	60.3		11.7	24.2	2.7		1.1
Mauritania	2013	49.1	9.6	4.4	27.1	0.7		9.1
Mauritius	2017	33.5	8.0	46.0	2.3		10.2	0.0
Morocco	2018	52.9	15.9	15.6	2.7	2.4	0.9	9.5
Rwanda	2018	60.7			27.5			11.8
Senegal	2014	45.8	22.5	11.4	9.7	2.8		7.8
Seychelles	2019	4.6	71.2	18.5	5.7			0.0
Sierra Leone	2017				100.0			0.0
South Africa	2017	35.4	36.6	4.7	23.3			0.0
Tanzania	2012	44.0						56.0

Source: Global Tax Expenditures Database, www.GTED.net

customs-related taxes.[7] Income tax-related expenditure was also important, even though its significance varied by country. For example, personal income tax (PIT) expenditure was less than 1% of TE in Benin and Madagascar, while it was more than 35% in South Africa and as high as 71.2% in the Seychelles. Similarly, corporate income tax (CIT) expenditure was lower than 3% in Benin and Madagascar but higher than 45% in Mauritius. However, the presentation of income TE varied by country. While 11 countries reported CIT and PIT separately, other countries did not differentiate between CIT and PIT. In these cases, income tax TE was included in the "other" category. Moreover, revenue foregone from excise taxes and especially stamp duties usually comprised a small portion of TE (except for stamp duty TE in the case of Benin). Lastly, taxes such as apprenticeship taxes, export taxes and other country-specific taxes also comprised a small portion of TE and were included in the "other" category.

In addition, while beneficiary information was absent from a lot of African TE reports, some insight can nonetheless be drawn from the available information. As shown in Table 9.5, businesses benefited the most from African TE. On average, a

---

[7]The numbers from Gabon, Liberia and Sierra Leone were removed when calculating those averages since these countries only reported their TE for one singular tax base.

Table 9.5 Share of revenue foregone by beneficiary type

Country	Year	Public sector (%)	Businesses (%)	Households (%)	NGOs (%)	IGOs (%)	Others (%)
Benin	2017	23.1	39.6	34.0		1.6	1.7
Burkina Faso	2016	10.1	75.5	11.3	0.0		3.1
Ivory Coast	2017	28.6	63.5		0.8	4.3	2.8
Gabon	2017						
Guinea	2017		64.8	2.6			32.6
Liberia	2016						
Madagascar	2015		79.6	0.6			19.9
Mali	2017						
Mauritania	2013		61.4				38.6
Mauritius	2017						
Morocco	2018	2.7	47.4	48.4			1.5
Rwanda	2018						
Senegal	2014	5.2	20.5	61.7		7.2	5.4
South Africa	2017						
Tanzania	2012	17.1	7.8		0.4		74.7

Source: Global Tax Expenditures Database, www.GTED.net

little over 50% of TE across African countries stemmed from exemptions and other incentives given to businesses. Households were also important beneficiaries of TE. They received a little over 25% of the TE. However, the TE share of businesses and households in some countries is even higher since they reported the TE given to those two beneficiaries jointly, on top of reporting their individual shares (in such cases, the joint share is added to the "other" category in Table 9.5). Moreover, while the government was often an important beneficiary of TE, intergovernmental organizations (IGOs) and non-governmental organizations (NGOs) were usually not. Lastly, country-specific beneficiaries such as the mining sector or TE provisions with missing beneficiary information were categorized as "other."

Yet, it is important to note that the numbers reported in Tables 9.3, 9.4 and 9.5 must be interpreted with caution. As shown in Fig. 9.3, countries do not estimate the revenue foregone for all TE provisions they report. Hence, the numbers reported above either understate or overstate the significance of some categories and the total magnitude of TE. For example, while two-fifths of the sample countries do not specify the share of TE provisions evaluated, some countries such as Benin and Madagascar report that they evaluated less than 50% of their TE provisions. Burkina Faso and Mauritania report that they evaluated around 60% of their TE provisions. Lastly, Ivory Coast, Guinea, Morocco and Senegal report having evaluated 70% or more of the TE provisions identified in their tax codes. However, even if the countries claim to have evaluated the revenue foregone from a majority of their provisions and their TE/GDP ratio may seem realistic, often, a portion of their TE provisions is not included in their reports.

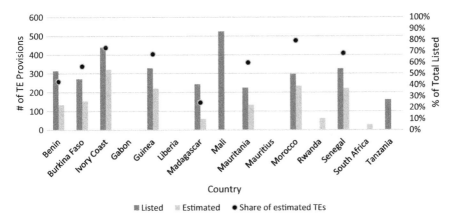

Fig. 9.3 Percentage of TE provisions evaluated. Source: Global Tax Expenditures Database, www. GTED.net

South Africa is a case in point. The latest TE statement published by the treasury reports estimates for 34 provisions, 13 TEs granted through PIT, 9 through CIT, 7 through VAT and 5 through customs and excise taxes. Total TEs in 2016, the latest available year, were estimated at Rands 209,007 accounting for 18.3% of total gross tax revenue and 4.7% of GDP.

Yet, these figures should be interpreted cautiously since the statement does not include several TEs. For instance, individuals working overseas for a 183-day term can claim back tax deductions on income earned for the period they were outside the country. In addition, as PTEs, tax-free savings accounts (TFSAs) aim at boosting individuals' savings by fully exempting the money invested into a TFSA from any tax on interests, dividends, capital gains and withdrawals. Moreover, individuals can deduct various work-related expenses. For example, individuals using their vehicle for work purposes can also claim a deduction. The depreciation on devices (e.g. laptops, smart phones) bought and maintained in one's personal capacity for work may also be claimed as a tax deduction. Finally, employers that work from home on a regular basis and in a specifically dedicated space are also allowed to claim certain running costs associated to that space, including rent, electricity and maintenance expenses.

When it comes to businesses, income from international shipping of a resident company that holds a share in a South African-flagged ship is exempt from CIT. Moreover, the Headquarter Company (HQC) Regime eliminates multiple fiscal and regulatory barriers to encourage foreign investors to use South Africa as a holding company/HQC jurisdiction. Among other benefits, this regime exempts eligible businesses from dividends tax and capital gains taxes. Finally, as in several low- and middle-income economies, South Africa created several SEZs, i.e. designed areas for targeted economic activities where a myriad of tax benefits are in place. These benefits include a reduced 15% CIT rate (compared to the standard 28% rate), a 10% building allowance, an employment tax incentive as well as additional VAT and duties reliefs for firms operating within a customs-controlled area of an SEZ.[8]

The list of existing TEs that are not covered by the TE statement is likely to be much broader for other countries as well. A first step towards a more transparent reporting on TEs would be to include all existing provisions even when, for some of them, revenue foregone estimates are not provided. Ideally, the report will progressively increase the number of estimated provisions in order to increase transparency and accountability.

9.5   Conclusion

This chapter has discussed the role of TE reporting as a key component of a more effective and fairer tax system. In addition, it has given an overview of TE reporting in Africa, based on data provided by the GTED. With few exceptions, TE reporting is at a very initial stage in most countries of the region. As a result, citizens and political decision-makers in a majority of African countries do not have access to timely and detailed information on a set of highly relevant policy instruments that cause major drains to the public budget and, consequently, cannot assess the costs and benefits that these provisions generate for society. With anecdotal evidence dominating the public debate, under-reporting of existing TE regimes tends to further undermine the legitimacy and perceived fairness of taxation.

While Africa is the only region fully covered by the GTED at this moment, it is not at all clear that the other world regions perform significantly better. On the one hand, TE reporting is much more widespread in Latin America, as data presented by CIAT shows.[9] On the other hand, other regions—Asia in particular—are rather uncharted territory in terms of TE reporting as well. Even among the OECD and G20 countries, the frequency and quality of reports are highly heterogeneous, as Redonda and Neubig (2018) observe.

It should be noted, however, that the TE topic has recently attracted more attention by scholars, international organisations and civil society. Efforts such as the Latin America Tax Expenditure Research, Advocacy, and Learning (LATERAL) project led by the International Budget Partnership (IBP)[10] aim at covering existing knowledge gaps and raising public awareness of the issue. Several international organisations have produced reports and guidelines that aim at improving TE reporting (for instance, see IMF 2019b). Yet, much more remains to be done. What is still missing at this stage is decisive action to agree on joint international standards for the robust, public, exhaustive and timely assessment of the costs and

---

[8]Although the total fiscal cost of SEZs is difficult to be estimated, some of these provisions such as the Employment Tax Incentive (ETI) may be included in the TE Statement.

[9]See https://www.ciat.org/tax-expenditures/?lang=en, accessed 13.09.2019.

[10]See https://www.internationalbudget.org/analysis-insights/lateral-project/, accessed 18.09.2019.

benefits of TEs. We believe that the GTED will make a substantial contribution towards this end.

References

Alstadsæter, A., Barrios, S., Nicodeme, G., Skonieczna, A., & Vezzani, A. (2018). Patent boxes design, patents location, and local R&D. *Economic Policy, 33*(93), 131–177.

Australian Treasury. (2004). *Tax expenditures statement 2003.* https://treasury.gov.au/publication/tax-expenditures-statement-2003

Australian Treasury. (2011). *Tax expenditures statement 2010.* https://treasury.gov.au/publication/tax-expenditures-statement-2010/tax-expenditures-statement-2010

Australian Treasury. (2018). *Tax expenditures statement 2017.* https://treasury.gov.au/sites/default/files/2019-03/2017-TES.pdf

Axelson, C., Pomeranz, D., & Redonda, A. (2020). The distributive impact of pension-related tax expenditures in South Africa. *mimeo.*

Bird, R. M., & Zolt, E. M. (2015). Fiscal contracting in Latin America. *World Development, 67,* 323–335.

Brys, B., Perret, S., Thomas, A., & O'Reilly, P. (2016). *Tax design for inclusive economic growth.* OECD Taxation Working Paper 26. OECD Publishing.

Chelminski, K. (2018). Fossil fuel subsidy reform in Indonesia. In J. Skovgaard & H. van Asselt (Eds.), *The politics of fossil fuel subsidies and their reform* (pp. 193–211). Cambridge: Cambridge University Press.

Daude, C., Gutierrez, H., & Melguizo, A. (2017). Doctoring the ball: The political economy of tax incentives for investment in the Dominican Republic. *Journal of Economic Studies, 44*(1), 2–23. https://doi.org/10.1108/JES-05-2015-0090.

Département Fédéral des Finances. (2011). *Quels Sont les Allégements Fiscaux Accordés par la Confédération? Département Fédéral des Finances (DFF) de la Confédération Suisse* (in French). https://www.estv.admin.ch/dam/estv/fr/dokumente/allgemein/Dokumentation/Zahlen_fakten/berichte/2011/Welche%20Steuerverg%C3%BCnstigungen%20gibt%20es%20beim%20Bund%20Bericht.pdf.download.pdf/2011_Steuerverguenstigung_f.pdf

Direction du Budget. (2019). *Évaluations des Voies et Moyens. Tomme II. Dépenses Fiscales. Annexe au Projet de Loi des Finances pour 2019* (in French). https://www.performance-publique.budget.gouv.fr/sites/performance_publique/files/farandole/ressources/2019/pap/pdf/VMT2-2019.pdf

Duflo, E., Gale, W., Liebman, J., Orszag, P., & Saez, E. (2006). Saving incentives for low- and middle-income families: Evidence from a field experiment with H&R block. *The Quarterly Journal of Economics, 121*(4), 1311–1346.

Eswatini Revenue Authority. (2017). *Eswatini revenue authority annual report, 2016.* http://www.sra.org.sz/documents/ANNUAL%20REPORT%202016.pdf

Heady, C., & Mansour, M. (2019). *Tax expenditures and their use in fiscal management: A guide to developing countries.* How to Note 19/01, International Monetary Fund (IMF). https://www.imf.org/~/media/Files/Publications/HowToNotes/HTNEA2019002.ashx

Hilber, C., & Turner, T. (2014). The mortgage interest deduction and its impact on homeownership decisions. *Review of Economics and Statistics, 96*(4), 618–637.

IMF. (2017a, April). *Fiscal monitor. Achieving more with less.* IMF. http://www.imf.org/en/Publications/FM/Issues/2017/04/06/fiscal-monitor-april-2017

IMF. (2017b). *Kenya fiscal transparency evaluation.* International Monetary Fund. https://www.imf.org/external/pubs/ft/scr/2016/cr16221.pdf

IMF. (2018). *The federal Democratic Republic of Ethiopia staff report for the 2017 article IV consultation*. International Monetary Fund. https://www.imf.org/~/media/Files/Publications/CR/2018/cr1818.ashx

IMF. (2019a). *Central African Economic and Monetary Community (CEMAC): Selected issues. A regional approach to enhancing governance and reducing the potential for corruption*. International Monetary Fund. https://www.elibrary.imf.org/view/IMF002/25705-9781484392843/25705-9781484392843/25705-9781484392843_A001.xml?redirect=true

IMF. (2019b). *Tax expenditure reporting and its use in fiscal management*. A Guide for Developing Economies How To Notes 19/01. Washington, DC: International Monetary Fund.

IMF, OECD, UN, & World Bank. (2015). *Options for low income countries' effective and efficient use of tax incentives for investment*. A Report to the G-20 Development Working Group. https://www.imf.org/external/np/g20/pdf/101515.pdf

Kassim, L., & Mansour, M. (2018). Les Rapports sur les Dépenses Fiscales des Pays en Développement : Une Evaluation. *Revue d'économie du développement, 26*(2), 113–167. (in French).

Klemens, B. (2017). *Intellectual property boxes and the paradox of price discrimination*. CEP Working Papers 1703, Council on Economic Policies (CEP).

Lesotho Revenue Authority. (2017). *Lesotho revenue authority annual report 2016*. http://passthrough.fw-notify.net/download/860771/http://www.lra.org.ls/sites/default/files/2018-02/LRA%20Annual%20Report%20-%202016.pdf

Ministère des Finances et du Budget, Republique du Congo. (2017). *Loi de Finances 2018* (French). https://www.finances.gouv.cg/fr/loi-de-finances-2018

Ministry of Finance and Planning, Republic of South Sudan. (2018). *Budget speech FY 2018/19*. http://grss-mof.org/wp-content/uploads/2018/09/Budget-Speech-Final-July-12-_-12-05-pm.pdf

Ministry of Finance, Republic of Ghana. (2018). *The budget statement and economic policy of the government of Ghana for the 2019 financial year*. http://www.mofep.gov.gh/sites/default/files/budget-statements/2019-Budget-Statement-and-Economic-Policy_.pdf

Pelàez Longinotti, F. (2018). *Overview of tax expenditures in Latin America: Main statistics of the CIAT database*. Working Paper, Inter-American Center of Tax Administrations (CIAT).

Prichard, W. (2019). *Tax, politics, and the social contract in Africa*. Oxford: Oxford University Press.

Redonda, A. (2016). *Tax expenditures and sustainability. An overview*. CEP Discussion Note 16/03, Council on Economic Policies (CEP).

Redonda, A., & von Haldenwang, C. (2021). *CEP/DIE Companion to the Global Tax Expenditures Database, GTED WP 2021/1*. mimeo.

Redonda, A., & Neubig, T. (2018). *Assessing tax expenditure reporting in G20 and OECD economies*. CEP Discussion Note 2018/3, https://www.cepweb.org/assessing-tax-expenditure-reporting-in-g20-and-oecd-economies/

South African National Treasury. (2012). *Improving tax incentives for retirement savings*. Technical Discussion Paper E for Public Comment. http://www.treasury.gov.za/comm_media/press/2012/Improving%20tax%20incentives%20for%20retirement%20savings.pdf

Toder, E. (2000). Tax cuts or spending—Does it make a difference? *National Tax Journal, 53*, 361–371.

UNCTAD. (2014). *World investment report 2014. Investing in the SDGs: An action plan*. United Nation Conference on Trade and Development (UNCTAD). https://unctad.org/en/PublicationsLibrary/wir2014_en.pdf

US Treasury. (2020). *Tax expenditures*. https://home.treasury.gov/policy-issues/tax-policy/tax-expenditures

von Haldenwang, C. , & Laudage, S. (2019). *Financing for development and domestic revenue mobilisation: More international reforms are needed*. Briefing Paper 13/2019. Bonn: DIE.

World Bank. (2015). *World Bank East Asia and Pacific Economic Update. Staying the course*. World Bank (WB). http://pubdocs.worldbank.org/en/414911444005973491/pdf/EAP-Economic-Update-2015-10.pdf

World Bank. (2017). *Special economic zones in the Dominican Republic: Policy considerations for a more competitive and inclusive sector: Special economic zones, global value chains, and the degree of domestic linkages in the Dominican Republic* (Spanish), http://documents.worldbank. org/curated/en/734421487332577036/Special-economic-zones-global-value-chains-and-the-degree-of-domestic-linkages-in-the-Dominican-Republic

World Bank. (2018). *Republic of chad, first economic recovery and resilience development policy operation.* World Bank. http://documents.worldbank.org/curated/en/416901537280719716/pdf/116242-PGD-OUO-9-Chad-1st-Economic-Recovery-Resilience-DPO-PD-August-14.pdf

Chapter 10
Negative Spillovers in International Corporate Taxation and the European Union

Leyla Ates, Moran Harari, and Markus Meinzer

10.1 Introduction[1]

Since 2011, the detrimental effects of spillovers on domestic as well as global stability have led the International Monetary Fund (IMF) to conduct extensive analysis of their widespread impact. The resulting reports have aimed to encourage discussion at multilateral forums in order to foster policy attention and multilateral dialogue. To begin with, these reports focused on the external effect of the world's five largest economies, namely, China, the Euro Area, Japan, the United Kingdom and the United States (IMF 2019a). Later on, the reports shifted focus towards a thematic approach and have brought key spillover issues to the forefront of the international agenda (IMF 2019b).

There are two principal reasons why international corporate taxation has featured so prominently in the IMF spillover reports. First, cross-border taxation has significance for macroeconomic stability at both the national and international levels (IMF 2013). Second, tax avoidance by multinationals has gained prominence in public

---

[1]Some passages of this article, predominantly in Sects. 10.2 and 10.3, have been taken from a previously published report: Tax Justice Network (2019). The authors and the publisher of the original report kindly gave their permission for reuse of the text in this article.

L. Ates (✉)
Faculty of Law, Altinbas University, Istanbul, Turkey
e-mail: leyla.ates@altinbas.edu.tr

M. Harari
Tax Justice Network, Tel Aviv, Israel
e-mail: moran@taxjustice.net

M. Meinzer
Tax Justice Network, Marburg, Germany
e-mail: markus@taxjustice.net

© The Author(s) 2021
I. J. Mosquera Valderrama et al. (eds.), *Taxation, International Cooperation and the 2030 Sustainable Development Agenda*, United Nations University Series on Regionalism 19, https://doi.org/10.1007/978-3-030-64857-2_10

discussion following the Lough Erne Declaration from the G-8 summit of 17–18 June 2013, which called countries to "change rules that let companies shift their profits across borders to avoid taxes" (G8 2013). Ultimately, the IMF defined international tax spillovers as "the impact that one jurisdiction's tax rules or practices has on others" in its landmark 2014 report (IMF 2014).

Moreover, the 2014 report established how a country's corporate tax system may generate macro-relevant effects on other countries via two channels: "base spillovers" and "strategic spillovers" (also see Crivelli et al. 2016; Cobham and Janský 2017). The "base spillover" concept includes changes in taxable profits "in reflection of both real responses (through investment and the like) and profit-shifting responses (affecting, loosely speaking, only where profits are booked for tax purposes)" (IMF 2014). The "strategic spillover" effect refers to "'tax competition' in its broadest sense—most obviously in the potential form of a 'race to the bottom', as countries respond to lower corporate income tax (CIT) rates elsewhere by reducing their own rates" (IMF 2014).

This approach acknowledges that for states, "tax rules and tax rates have become, to a large extent, the currency of tax competition" (Dagan 2018). By maintaining lower statutory corporate tax rates than other states, restricting the scope of or inserting gaps and loopholes into corporate tax rules, pushing down withholding rates in double tax treaties and dispensing with anti-avoidance and transparency policies, jurisdictions unwillingly enable or wittingly incite tax spillovers from other countries. In each of these policy areas, jurisdictions can choose to engage in more or less aggressive tax poaching policies, an approach echoing the notion that "virtually any country might be a 'haven' in relation to another" (Picciotto 1992). As a result, each jurisdiction's policies can be placed on a spectrum of corrosiveness of its corporate tax rules, resulting in a more nuanced picture than the established binary "blacklists" of corporate tax havens (Meinzer and Knobel 2015; Meinzer 2016; Cobham et al. 2015; Lips and Cobham 2018; Mosquera Valderrama 2019).

The focus of this article is on a new empirical legal dataset that makes a novel contribution to cross-border spillover analyses by conducting a transparent legal analysis of a comprehensive set of plausible negative and positive spillover pathways in domestic corporate income tax systems. While extant international tax spillover analyses explore a limited set of spillover pathways or indicators (Lusiani and Cosgrove 2017; Christensen 2018), the new Corporate Tax Haven Index (CTHI) includes 20 key tax spillover indicators under 5 categories and assesses 64 countries' tax systems[2] to identify which policies they should consider for corporate tax reform in order to mitigate cross-border tax spillovers (Tax Justice Network 2019).

---

[2]The list of countries covers all EU-27 member states and the United Kingdom, 12 EU territories (Anguilla, Bermuda, British Virgin Islands, Cayman Islands, Gibraltar, Guernsey, Isle of Man, Jersey, Turks and Caicos Islands, Aruba, Curacao and St. Maarten), 9 African countries (Botswana, Gambia, Ghana, Kenya, Liberia, Mauritius, Seychelles, South Africa and Tanzania) and 14 jurisdictions selected based on their role, established in the research literature, as significantly misaligned with other jurisdictions, and/or anecdotal evidence that the jurisdiction may be playing an important role in international corporate taxation (Andorra, Liechtenstein, Monaco, San Marino,

This article particularly aims to highlight international corporate tax spillovers pathways in the 27 European Union (EU) member states' domestic tax laws, regulations and documented administrative practices, especially in the context of developing countries. As such, out of the 64 countries assessed by the CTHI, the article will focus on the 27 EU countries and compare them to the 4 lower-income countries and lower middle-income countries covered by the CTHI (Gambia, Liberia, Tanzania, Ghana and Kenya), all of which are in the African region and will be referred to in this article as "developing countries".

The article limits its scope to domestic tax rules and practices that may create negative spillovers.[3] It is based on CTHI data and indicators, which categorise domestic negative spillover into two categories. Section 10.2 of the article discusses the "lowest available corporate income tax rate" (LACIT) indicator, consisting of the first category of negative spillovers. From the widely used "highest statutory corporate income tax rate", it derives through legal analyses the lowest rate for active business income available to subsidiaries of large multinationals. Section 10.3 of the article discusses "loopholes and gaps", the second category of the CTHI comprising seven indicators. It analyses the availability of elements within this category such as preferential tax regimes, sector-specific carve outs of the corporate tax rate base, tax rate concessions, tax holidays and economic zones.

The negative spillover analysis of EU member states' regulations is of particular importance to developing countries. In 2008, as an essential means for combating cross-border tax evasion and to strengthen the fight against money laundering, the EU Economic and Financial Affairs Council (ECOFIN) introduced the standard of good governance in tax matters to be adopted in all international agreements with third countries without prejudice to their respective competences (Council of the European Union 2008). In 2010, as part of its communication to the European Parliament, the EU Commission stated that "the EU is seeking from all countries and in particular its partner countries, agreement on the basic cooperation principles of good governance in the tax area (transparency of the tax system, exchange of information and fair tax competition) that its Member States have already achieved" (European Commission 2010). Nonetheless, as our analysis will show, the EU rules and practices have so far failed to achieve fair tax competition for EU member states and for non-member countries. In fact, the current rules contribute to unfair tax competition in a way which harms developing countries the most. Given that the EU has already added texts regarding standards of good governance in tax matters to several trade, strategic and economic partnership agreements (Mosquera Valderrama 2019) and both parties to these agreements are bound to follow the agreement,

---

Switzerland, Singapore, USA, China, Hong Kong, Panama, Bahamas, Taiwan, United Arab Emirates, Lebanon, Macao).

[3]The positive spillover categories and the third category of negative spillover indicators of the CTHI on a country's tax treaty network and withholding rates are outside the scope of this article. For an article related to the positive spillovers categories, see Ates, L., Harari, M. and Meinzer, M. (2020). Positive spillovers in International Corporate Taxation and the European Union. Intertax, 48:4, 389–401.

developing countries can use the standard of good governance in tax matters to demand EU countries take concrete measures on fairer tax practices by eliminating the negative spillovers emanating from their countries.

Furthermore, Article 208 of the Lisbon Treaty on the Functioning of the European Union, which entered into force on 1 December 2009, requires the EU to take into account "the objectives of development cooperation in the policies that it implements which are likely to affect developing countries" (EU 2008). Tax and transfer systems in developing countries are, in general, far less effective at reducing poverty and inequality than those of developed ones. If spillovers from corporate tax rules reduce the tax revenues from direct and progressive corporate income taxes in developing countries, poverty may be exacerbated by shifting the tax mix onto more indirect, regressive types of taxes (Lustig 2018; McNabb and LeMay-Boucher 2014). Considering the vital role of domestic resource mobilisation in achieving the Sustainable Development Goals (Crivelli et al. 2016), both the standard of good governance in tax matters and Article 208 of the Lisbon Treaty can be used as policy tools for developing countries in negotiating their tax matters with EU member states.

10.2   LACIT

The LACIT indicator derives from law-based corporate tax rates built on a transparent legal analysis of the corporate income tax framework of jurisdictions.

Several studies have identified a range of negative spillover effects as states compete to offer lower corporate income tax rates (Devereux et al. 2008; Klemm and Van Parys 2012; Crivelli et al. 2016). Moreover, these studies also point out a discrepancy between statutory corporate tax rates and the legally documented lowest corporate tax rates available in a jurisdiction (Abbas and Klemm 2013). To address this issue, the CTHI calculates a jurisdiction's LACIT differently from existing datasets of statutory corporate income tax rates.

The LACIT indicator is determined by three steps, only the first of which relies on (top) statutory corporate income tax rates for 2018[4] as reported in the Organisation for Economic Co-operation and Development (OECD) tax database (OECD 2019), or in the KPMG Corporate Tax Rates Table and International Bureau for Fiscal Documentation (IBFD) Tax Research Platform for jurisdictions not covered by the OECD (KPMG 2019; IBFD 2019).

In the second step, the CTHI reviews the statutory rates and corrects these if necessary. Corrections are made if there are lower corporate income tax rates available according to the size of the business, the economic sector in which the

---

[4]The CTHI was launched on May 2019, and it took into account the 2018 tax rates for country assessments. The rates will be refreshed every 2 years with each edition of the CTHI.

business operates[5] or the subnational divisions (states/cantons/communes) where the business is tax resident.[6] In this regard, the CTHI adjusts Germany, Italy and Portugal's statutory tax rates due to the rates offered in their subnational regions. For example, the statutory corporate tax rate of Portugal is calculated by adding the general corporate tax rate of 21% to a state surtax of 9% and a local surcharge of up to 1.5% of the taxable profit (OECD 2019). But given that 102 municipalities out of the total 304 municipalities in the country do not impose the local surcharge of up to 1.5% (IBFD 2019), the CTHI ignores this statutory rate for this indicator and sets 30% as the lowest available corporate income tax in Portugal.

In the third step, the CTHI analyses, and adjusts if necessary, the tax rates if treatment differs in any of the following ways: distribution or retention of profits, selection of a particular type of company, sourcing profits from inside or outside the jurisdiction (territorial tax regimes) or upon issuance of unilateral tax rulings. Several cases of adjustment to the EU member states' statutory tax rates are particularly relevant to this matter.

For example, Malta, with a statutory corporate income tax rate ordinarily reported at 35% (IBFD 219), operates a full imputation system. This system ensures that almost all tax paid is refunded upon distribution of profits and thus a much lower corporate income tax rate applies.[7] As a result of Malta's imputation system, the CTHI sets Malta's LACIT at 5% and not at the often reported statutory rate of 35%. A similar result can be achieved when the tax is imposed only upon distribution. For example, in both Latvia and Estonia, the profits of resident companies are taxed only upon distribution (IBFD 2019). Thus, given that a company which chooses not to distribute its profits does not pay any corporate income tax, the CTHI assesses Latvia's and Estonia's LACIT at zero.

Over and above these, the statutory corporate tax rates of Belgium, Luxembourg, Ireland and Netherlands have been adjusted based on findings from the state aid

---

[5]For more details on the economic sector treatment, see Sect. 10.3.4 on "Sectoral Exemptions".

[6]However, differing corporate income tax regimes with lower rates which are available in a specifically designated economic zone or in a subnational region is disregarded for this indicator as the CTHI analyses and assesses it in the tax holidays and economic zones indicator under the loopholes and gaps group; see Sect. 10.3.5.

[7]KPMG notes on Malta: "A fundamental pillar of Malta's tax system is its full imputation tax system which completely eliminates the economic double taxation of company profits. Shareholders in receipt of dividends are entitled to a tax credit equal to the tax borne on the profits out of which the dividends are paid. Since the tax rate of 35% applicable to companies is also the highest tax rate in Malta, shareholders will not suffer any additional tax on the receipt of dividends. Where the shareholder's tax on the dividend is lower than 35%, the amount by which the tax credit exceeds the tax on the dividend will be refunded to the shareholder if the shareholder includes the dividend in his tax return. Upon a distribution of profits by a company registered in Malta (i.e. a company resident in Malta or a non-resident company with a branch in Malta), its shareholders may claim partial tax refund. The most common tax refund is of 6/7ths, i.e. 30% (6/7ths of 35%) of the taxable profits. Where no double taxation relief has been claimed, the effective tax suffered in Malta on distributed profits will be 5%. Malta's tax refunds system is applicable to both resident and non-resident shareholders in respect of the tax borne on profits derived from both domestic and international activities" (KPMG 2018).

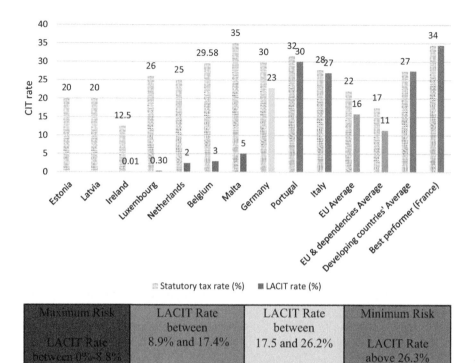

Fig. 10.1 Statutory rate v. LACIT (most misleading jurisdictions and average of regions)

investigations by the European Commission. For example, in Luxembourg, based on a binding agreement with the Luxemburg tax administration, the ENGIE Group was found to have been paying 0.3% instead of 26% corporate income tax on its profits. This rate is based on the commission's conclusion on 19 June 2018 that two sets of tax rulings issued by Luxembourg to two companies in the ENGIE Group endorsed an inconsistent treatment of the same transaction both as debt and as equity and enabled the Group to avoid paying any tax on 99% of the profits generated by two of its subsidiaries (European Commission 2018). The rulings artificially lowered ENGIE's tax burden, and for about a decade, the Group's effective tax rate on these profits in Luxembourg was less than 0.3% (European Commission 2018). Because Luxembourg does not publish all tax rulings online, it is impossible to check if similar arrangements remain in place today. Unless proven to the contrary, the CTHI assumes therefore that large multinational companies can enter into tax deals with Luxembourg tax administrations lowering their corporate income tax rate to 0.3% on recorded profits.

Figure 10.1 provides a summary of the deviations between the statutory corporate tax rate and the LACIT. Estonia, Latvia, Ireland and Luxemburg offer a zero or almost 0% lowest available corporate income tax which is much lower than the statutory tax rate of 20, 12.5, 20 and 26%, respectively. Similarly, the Netherlands, Belgium and Malta offer 5% or less, which is also much lower than the statutory tax rate of 29.58, 35 and 25%, respectively. France is the best performer with its highest tax rate (34%) identical to the LACIT.

The data reveals three important aspects of EU corporate tax policy that are relevant for spillovers impinging on the domestic revenue mobilisation efforts of developing countries. First, the discrepancy between the statutory corporate income tax rates and the LACIT is high in the EU (the EU average statutory tax rate was 22% in 2018 (European Commission 2019) compared with an average LACIT of only 16%). In comparison, the developing countries' average statutory tax rate is much higher, 27%, with no gap whatsoever between their statutory and LACIT rates. This suggests that the EU is engaging in a hidden race to the bottom in corporate tax rates, among others, through the backdoor of secretive and dubious tax rulings. Second, when combining the EU-controlled dependencies, the average LACIT falls even further to 11%, reinforcing the notion of an indirect tolerance or acceleration of the race to the bottom in corporate taxation. This suggests that the EU's insistence on good governance in tax practices is hypocritical. Third, the steep gap between the LACIT rates of EU members and its dependencies on the one hand, and developing African countries on the other hand, suggests substantial tax spillover risks emanating from the EU's relatively lower rates, which may entice inward profit shifting and lead to base erosion in developing countries.

10.3 Loopholes and Gaps

Comparison of the EU member states and developing countries' results across the seven indicators comprising the "loopholes and gaps" category is revealing. As shown in Fig. 10.2 and explained in more detail below, developing countries perform better on average than EU member states on the indicators for capital gains taxation, sectoral exemptions, fictional interest deduction, foreign investment income treatment and patent boxes. On the other hand, developing countries have higher haven scores on average for two indicators: loss utilisation, which assesses the availability of unrestricted loss carry-forward and loss carry-backward, and tax holidays and economic zones.

10.3.1 Foreign Investment Income Treatment

This indicator assesses whether a jurisdiction includes worldwide capital income in its corporate income tax base and if its domestic law grants unilateral tax credits for foreign tax paid on certain foreign capital income. The types of capital income included are interest, royalty and dividend payments from a related or independent company.

In the current international tax setting, the problem of overlapping tax claims (double taxation) of source and residency countries are addressed in unilateral and/or

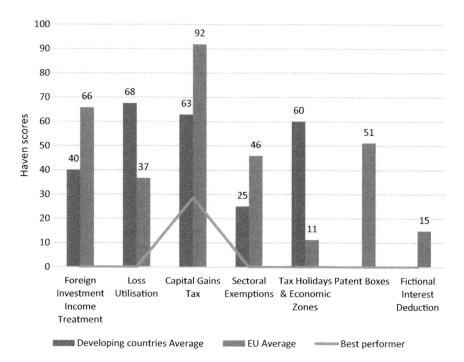

Fig. 10.2 Comparison of loophole and gap indicators for developing countries and EU member states

bilateral ways. In most cases, it is a myth that bilateral treaties are needed to provide relief from double taxation (Dagan 2000). The home countries of investors or multinational companies usually offer unilateral relief from double taxation to support outward investment. They do this primarily through exempting foreign income from tax liability at home (the exemption method) or granting credit for the taxes paid abroad on the taxes due at home (the credit method). There is a third mechanism called "deduction" which is sometimes used to offer relief from double taxation. However, the deduction method does not offer full relief from double taxation. It allows the deduction of any taxes paid abroad from foreign income (e.g. as a business expense) before including this income in the domestic tax base.

Where countries, especially capital exporting ones, refrain from providing unilateral relief or only provide deduction of foreign taxes from the domestic tax base, they contribute to the problem of double taxation and thus indirectly exert pressure on capital importing countries to conclude bilateral treaties with the other country. However, bilateral treaties are expensive to negotiate and often impose a cost on the weaker negotiating partner which is frequently required to concede lower tax rates in return for the prospect of more investment (Neumayer 2007; McGauran 2013; Hearson 2016). In turn, these treaties can expose capital importing countries to negative spillovers.

In addition, with more than 3500 double tax treaties currently in operation, the system has become overly complex and permissive, encouraging corporations to engage in profit shifting, treaty shopping and other practices at the margins of tax evasion. This is the context in which the CTHI reviews unilateral mechanisms to avoid double taxation in the first place. However, not all such mechanisms are equally useful.

When using a unilateral exemption mechanism to exempt all foreign income from liability to tax at home, the country of residence may force other jurisdictions to compete for inward investment by lowering their tax rates (IMF 2013). Because investors or corporations will not need to pay any tax back home on the profit they declare in the foreign jurisdiction (source), they will look more seriously at the tax rates offered. This encourages countries to reduce tax rates on capital income paid to non-residents, such as withholding taxes on payments of dividends and interest.

In contrast, a unilateral tax credit mechanism does not incentivise the host countries of investments to lower their tax rates (IMF 2013). A tax credit system requires that income earned abroad must be taxed at home as if it was earned at home, unless it has already been taxed abroad. In the latter case, the effective amount of tax paid abroad on the income will be subtracted from the corresponding amount of tax due at home. Therefore, for an investor the tax rate in a host country is no longer relevant to her investment decisions. Countries wishing to attract foreign investment will not feel compelled to lower their tax rates in the hope of increasing their stock of foreign investment.

Thus, a jurisdiction that provides no unilateral relief, or only deducts foreign tax paid or effectively exempts foreign income from domestic taxation (through a territorial tax system, exemptions for specific payments or specific legal entities, deferral rules and zero or nil tax rates), creates a pathway for substantial negative spillover effects. On the other hand, a jurisdiction that grants a unilateral tax credit for some or all types of capital income payment scenarios limits the possibility for negative spillovers.

All EU member states promote negative spillovers by creating pathways through their treatment of foreign investment income. As a result of the EU's Parent-Subsidiary Directive (Council Directive 2011), member states must either implement the exemption method or allow a unilateral credit for taxes levied on the level of the subsidiary and lower-tier companies to eliminate economic double taxation of cross-border intercompany dividends (Kofler 2012). Other than Ireland, all member states implement the exemption method. While some member states restrict this negative spillover pathway only to cross-border intercompany dividends (Bulgaria, Denmark, Germany, Greece, Poland and Portugal), others, including Ireland, create negative spillover pathways for other income scenarios as well. Several states create substantial risk by providing no unilateral relief and/or deduction for foreign tax paid and/or effectively exempting foreign income from domestic taxation for all income scenarios (Czech Republic, Estonia, France, Latvia, Luxembourg, Malta, Netherlands, Romania and Slovakia). Other member states limit the risks of negative spillovers by incorporating three income scenarios into their legislative frameworks (Belgium, Cyprus, Hungary, Ireland and Spain) or by introducing only two such treatments (as in the cases of Austria, Croatia, Finland, Italy, Lithuania, Slovenia and Sweden).

Compared with EU countries, three (Tanzania, Gambia and Ghana) out of the five developing countries covered by the CTHI received zero haven scores as they only allow for unilateral tax credits. Kenya, however, exempts foreign investment income in the form of dividends from its corporate tax base, and Liberia exempts such income in all three forms (dividends, royalties and interest). Given the incentive that tax exemption of foreign income provides for ruinous tax wars and negative spillovers, the fact that none of the EU countries receive zero tax haven scores indicates the significant risks for negative spillovers they create, including towards developing countries.

10.3.2   Loss Utilisation

The loss utilisation indicator looks at whether a jurisdiction provides loss carrybackward and/or unrestricted loss carry-forward for ordinary and trading losses.

The basic rationale behind the loss carryover rules is income averaging. Annual tax accounting systems are a main feature of modern income taxation. Income tax is calculated and charged on the income earned in the preceding fiscal year, which consists of 12 consecutive months. However, this system involves an intrinsic unfairness: "taxpayers whose incomes fluctuate from year to year should receive tax treatment equivalent to those with stable incomes" (Romano and Campisano 1981). To eliminate this intrinsic unfairness, countries provide tax relief on profits to reflect losses. Losses may be carried forward and set off against future profits and/or carried backward and relieved against profits in earlier or subsequent years.

However, companies might use losses as an aggressive tax planning tool by increasing or accelerating tax relief on their losses. Unrestricted loss carry-forward and backward thus enables profit shifting, investment round tripping and corporate (re)structuring for tax avoidance purposes (OECD 2011).[8] To avoid abuse of such provisions by multinational companies, jurisdictions generally place limits on the time and value of loss carry-forward rules (OECD 2011). On the other hand, a loss carry-backward provision has more severe impacts on reducing government budgets

---

[8]For example, the use of artificial losses to minimise tax has been a core element of Apple's tax strategy in Ireland. In 2015, the artificial inflation of debt and a multibillion-dollar purchase of Apple's own intellectual property generated billions in recognised losses for Apple's subsidiary in Ireland (Coffery 2018). In other words, Apple Ireland borrowed heavily to purchase Apple's intellectual property from an Apple subsidiary tax resident in Jersey (which applies nearly zero tax). As a result, Apple Ireland had billions in deductible interest payments, billions in deductible intellectual property purchase expenses and billions in capital allowances, enough to write off all profits from European sales for years. Similarly, Apple's offshore entity in Jersey earned billions from the sale of intellectual property and interest repayments which went untaxed (Christensen and Clancy 2018).

and is more difficult to administer than carry-forward provisions (OECD 2011). Thus, a jurisdiction that provides loss carry-backward or unrestricted loss carry-forward rules creates pathways for negative spillovers.

To varying degrees, all EU member states other than Estonia, Latvia, Poland and Portugal promote negative spillover risk through loss utilisation rules. While Ireland and Sweden create substantial risk by providing loss carry-backward and unrestricted loss carry-forward, some member states reduce the risk only slightly by introducing a limitation to loss carry-forward while permitting unrestricted loss carry-backward (as in the cases of France, Germany, the Netherlands and the United Kingdom). Other member states have not introduced loss carry-backward at all. However, they still create risk by applying unrestricted loss carry-forward rules (Austria and Malta) or restricted loss carry-forward rules but not for up to 5 subsequent years and without an annual ceiling such as a fixed monetary ceiling and/or a percentage of taxable earnings for subsequent years.

Compared with EU countries, developing countries' average haven score for this indicator is significantly higher (68 as opposed to 37 for EU countries), predominantly due to the relevant policies of Kenya and Tanzania. In Kenya, losses for every sector can be carried forward without an annual ceiling for at least 9 years, and backward, allowing companies from the petroleum exploration industry to reduce their tax bill, for example, through unfavourable intra-group trades. The fact that developing countries allow for a more flexible loss utilisation policy indicates the risks for revenue losses in developing countries as well as for negative spillovers. The reasons for the higher risks of developing countries' loss utilisation policies likely lie in the lack of coverage of their potential negative consequences to date.

10.3.3   Capital Gains Taxation

This indicator measures the extent to which a jurisdiction taxes corporate capital gains arising from the disposal of domestic and/or foreign securities (i.e. shares and bonds). As such, it assesses the lowest available tax levied on corporate capital gains, applicable to large for-profit corporations which are tax resident in the jurisdiction.

By purchasing and holding assets through intermediary companies in jurisdictions with no or low capital gains taxation, the corporate income tax and capital gains tax systems of any jurisdiction can be easily circumvented. Therefore, the availability of jurisdictions with low or no capital gains taxation jeopardises the tax base of other jurisdictions and creates negative tax spillover effects similar to those of the LACIT indicator.[9] The lower these rates become, the greater this spillover effect becomes. For example, the Paradise Papers revealed how US Yale University had contracted with offshore law firm Appleby to invest US$100 million in India, thereby avoiding the payment of capital gains tax in both India and Mauritius

---

[9]See Sect. 10.2.

(Yadav 2017). Not long after, in 2016, India successfully renegotiated its double tax treaty with Mauritius to require from 2017 onwards taxation of capital gains at the source (i.e. in India at Indian tax rates) and no longer in the residence jurisdiction of the investor (i.e. Mauritius nil capital gains tax). This change resulted in a steep decline of equity direct investment from Mauritius in India in subsequent years (Chowdhary 2019).

Twenty EU member states offer a zero or almost 0% lowest available corporate capital gain tax rate (Belgium, Cyprus, Czech Republic, Estonia, Finland, Germany, Greece, Ireland, Italy, Latvia, Lithuania, Luxembourg, Malta, Netherlands, Portugal, Romania, Slovakia, Spain, Sweden and the United Kingdom). In contrast, out of the five developing countries, only Kenya offers the lowest available capital gains tax rate of 0%. This is because an exemption applies for domestic securities with shares listed on the Nairobi Securities Exchange and gains from the disposal of foreign securities are not taxable in Kenya because of its territorial tax system. Gambia is the best performer among both the EU and the assessed developing countries with a lowest available corporate capital gain tax rate of 25%. In light of this, the fact that the vast majority of EU countries taxes capital gains at zero or almost 0% is striking and provides yet more profound evidence for the negative spillover risks they pose to other countries.

10.3.4 Sectoral Exemptions

This indicator analyses provisions where companies engaging in a specific activity are accorded a tax rate that is lower than the lowest available corporate tax rate usually applicable by default to any economic activity, without being subject to cost or expenditure requirements. If the lower rate is zero, the CTHI considers the exemption "full", and otherwise, the lower rate will constitute a "partial" exemption.[10] Lower rates and narrower tax bases are treated as equivalent.

The CTHI focuses on tax reductions that are available to corporations that merely engage in a specific economic activity or are licensed or registered under a specific regime. These incentives are particularly harmful because it is much easier for multinational corporations to allocate profits to a tax-exempt company if the exemption regime does not ensure that the exemption applies to income resulting from domestic economic activity. By contrast, cost-based incentives are meant to ensure

---

[10]This indicator potentially overlaps with the indicator of LACIT, and the categorisation depends on the question of degree. If a country has these reductions or exemptions in enough sectors (four or more full exemptions, or eight or more partial exemptions), it is considered also under the LACIT, which has a higher weighting in the CTHI. Likewise, if a country has a 0% statutory tax rate, then any sector or activity would also have a 0% tax rate, resulting in a haven score of 100 (highest tax avoidance risk). In addition, this indicator excludes cases of exemptions resulting from a patent box regime or exclusively relating to capital gains. These are covered in Sects. 10.3.6 and 10.3.3, respectively.

that the tax incentive applies only to companies effectively engaged in the domestic economy, by investing in fixed assets, hiring employees or supporting research and development.

Indeed, the IMF differentiates between these two types of incentives and indicates the harmfulness of profit-based as opposed to cost-based incentives. In its 2014 report, the IMF emphasises that cost-based incentives "[. . .] may generate investments that would not otherwise have been made [. . .]", whereas profit-based incentives tend to "[. . .] make even more profitable investment projects that would be profitable, and hence undertaken, even without the incentive" (IMF 2014). Moreover, incentives providing full tax exemptions often create an additional risk factor, in cases where non-taxable companies are not required to submit tax returns or other regulatory filings.

Among the EU member states, only Lithuania, Poland, Romania, Slovakia and Sweden pose almost minimum levels of negative spillover risk. Estonia and Latvia create maximum risk by effectively applying permanent exemptions in all economic sectors,[11] whereas the risk profiles of other jurisdictions lie somewhere between these.

Out of the 64 researched jurisdictions, 10 jurisdictions apply no or zero corporate tax, 5 others present permanent exemptions in all economic sectors and a further 4 jurisdictions apply a wide range of harmful exemptions covering several economic sectors. Together, nearly 30% of the assessed jurisdictions offer widespread profit-based tax exemptions in all or nearly all economic sectors. Among these 19 jurisdictions, more than 70% are EU member states (Estonia and Latvia) or EU-dependent jurisdictions (UK dependencies of Anguilla, Bahamas, Bermuda, British Virgin Islands, Cayman Islands, Guernsey, Isle of Man, Jersey, Turks and Caicos Islands and Montserrat and the Netherlands' dependency of Aruba).[12]

An important finding from Fig. 10.3 is that profit-based exemptions are most widespread in passive investment sectors and the related banking and insurance sector. Furthermore, European Union members are most responsible for offering these. In both real estate and financial investment, 48% of EU countries offer full exemptions and 19% offer partial tax exemptions, whereas among the five developing countries only 30% present full exemptions and 10% partial exemptions. In the banking and insurance sector, a similar mismatch between EU countries and developing countries can be observed (EU27, 22% full exemptions, 15% partial exemptions; developing countries, 0% full exemptions, 20% partial exemptions). The widespread exemption of these types of activities results in spillover risks faced by

---

[11]Estonia's and Latvia's LACIT is zero because of the retention/distribution adjustment we are making in step 3 of the LACIT calculation (discussed under LACIT in Sect. 10.2). Since both countries' LACIT is zero, this applies to all economic sectors.

[12]Among the non-EU jurisdictions, the United Arab Emirates applies no or zero corporate tax; Monaco and Mauritius effectively apply permanent exemptions in all economic sectors; the Lebanon, Panama and Singapore apply a very wide range of harmful permanent exemptions, covering several economic sectors.

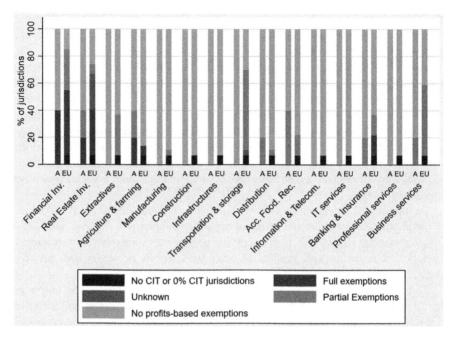

Fig. 10.3 Frequency of sectoral tax exemptions in 15 economic sectors (2 investment and 13 active business sectors) in 5 African (A) developing countries and 27 EU member states. Source: Author's own analysis based on CTHI data (The data presented in Fig. 10.3 was collected for CTHI 2019 but was adjusted subsequently. This adjustment was made because the limited coverage of tonnage tax regimes in the IBFD database became evident after consulting other legal data sources and domestic laws. This led to adjustments in sectors affected by such regimes (principally transportation and storage and business services). Moreover, the mere existence of a tonnage tax regime is now considered a partial exemption in the transportation and storage sector, in line with the treatment of other alternative regimes in Haven Indicator 5 of the CTHI) and based on Millán-Narotzky et al. (2020), with support from Lucas Millán-Narotzky and Miroslav Palanský

developing countries not only directly through profit shifting and asset management relocation but also indirectly by facilitating financialisation processes.

10.3.5 Tax Holidays and Economic Zones

This indicator assesses whether and to what extent a jurisdiction provides time-bound or geographically confined incentives consisting of a tax rate that is lesser than the lowest available corporate tax rate usually applicable in this jurisdiction. These include temporary tax holidays, partial exemptions on corporate income tax and capital gains tax and special tax incentives (temporary or permanent) given to

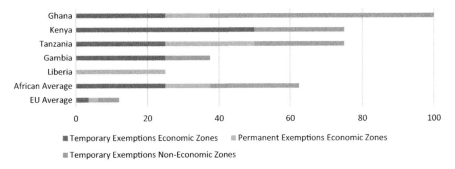

Fig. 10.4 Tax holidays and economic zones' subcomponents

companies located in designated economic zones.[13] Similar to the preceding indicator, only "profit-based" tax exemptions are assessed because of their particular relevance to negative spillovers (IMF 2015).

Geographically confined tax incentives are usually granted as part of a country's goals to attract FDI, develop disfavoured or rural regions or certain sectors, increase government revenues, encourage skills upgrading and innovation and improve the productivity of domestic enterprises (Zeng 2010). However, the available evidence shows that tax incentives are often ineffective in attracting new greenfield FDI, especially in developing countries (Klemm and Van Parys 2012). Investment climate surveys for low-income countries show that tax incentives do not exert a decisive influence on investment decisions. Rather, investors are more interested in good infrastructure, an educated labour pool, the rule of law and macroeconomic stability. Evidence already suggests that providing geographically confined tax incentives imposes pressure on policymakers to provide the same benefits to other geographic areas, increasing revenue loss and social distortions (Keen and Mansour 2009). Moreover, free trade zones may be vulnerable to illicit activity and be abused through transfer pricing strategies given typically weak enforcement of financial regulations, lack of transparency and inadequate customs control (FATF and EGMONT 2013; FATF 2010).

Among EU member states, only France poses maximum risk by temporarily offering one partial and three full exemptions in non-economic zones and a full exemption followed by a partial exemption for companies in economic zones (IBFD 2019), whereas the other member states pose almost minimum risks, except Lithuania. Lithuania has several economic zones where a standard tax inventive regime temporarily applies a full exemption followed by a partial exemption for qualifying companies which is accessible pursuant to the criteria established separately for each economic zone (IBFD 2019).

As presented in Fig. 10.4, compared with EU countries, developing countries have on average considerably higher haven scores on this indicator. In Kenya,

---

[13]An economic zone is commonly defined as a delimited area that is physically secured and has a single administration, separate customs area and streamlined procedures (Rao et al. 2008).

Ghana and Tanzania in particular, special tax incentives in a limited geographical area—such as in free ports, export processing zones and special economic zones—or special tax holidays available over a set period of time result in high haven scores. Ghana, for example, offers several time-bound tax holidays that reduce the statutory corporate income tax rate of 25% significantly; as such, rural banks, tree crops and venture capital financing companies are all taxed at 1% for the first 10 years, while cocoa by-production processing, fisheries and cash crops are taxed at 1% for the first 5 years.

As part of their efforts to attract foreign direct investment from foreign companies, developing countries offer a wide range of high-risk profit-based tax incentives conducive to lower tax revenues and spillover risks. African countries on average offer three profit-based tax incentives, such as economic zones and tax holidays, for every cost-based tax incentive. In comparison, European countries on average offer a near one-to-one ratio of tax incentive types, indicating a greater awareness in the EU of the risks profit-based tax incentives represent (Meinzer et al. 2019).

10.3.6 Patent Boxes

This indicator measures whether a jurisdiction offers preferential tax treatment for income related to intellectual property rights (e.g. patent boxes). A preferential tax treatment for intellectual property rights usually takes the form of either special cost-based tax incentives or profit-based tax incentives (e.g. lower tax rates). For this indicator, the CTHI only considers profit-based patent box regimes.

A patent box regime provides tax privileges for highly profitable businesses and enables cross-border profit shifting into these tax regimes, undermining the tax bases of jurisdictions elsewhere. The available evidence indicates that promises to spur innovation, tax revenues and growth through the introduction of patent boxes have failed to materialise. In contrast, available evidence suggests that patent box regimes are effective only in raising multinationals' share prices (CPB 2014; Guenther 2017; Gaessler et al. 2018).

While patent boxes in theory could increase tax revenues,[14] the positive effects of an individual country's policy are likely to be eroded by the responses of other governments, which may include even more aggressive and corrosive tax policies. For many years, patent boxes have been used by multinational corporations to avoid taxation by shifting profits out of the countries where they do business and into a foreign country with a patent box regime, where the profits are taxed at very low levels or not at all. Research indicates that such profit shifting leads to misattribution

---

[14]Although a report published by the Centre for European Economic Research in 2013 claims that "In the larger of the countries, that have significant innovation bases, it is more likely that IP [intellectual property] boxes will lead to significant revenue losses. Empirical evidence that simulates the Benelux and UK IP Boxes finds that the increase in IP income locating in the countries is insufficient to outweigh the lower tax rate" (Evers et al. 2013).

of economic activities, resulting in productivity slowdown (Guvenen et al. 2018). It also enables multinational companies to monopolise the market, while companies that lack the scale of the multinational corporations will be disadvantaged simply because they do not have the resources available to establish global structures which can allow them to avoid tax (Hwang 2018). Thus, a jurisdiction that has a patent box regime potentially creates a substantial negative spillover risk. When the jurisdiction makes this regime available with OECD nexus constraints that allow taxpayers to benefit only if they can link the income that stems from the intellectual property to expenditures incurred (OECD 2015), it might reduce negative spillovers. However, the modified nexus approach allows artificial increases of qualifying expenditures (Sanz Gomez 2015) and requires using the arm's length price to determine related party acquisition costs (OECD 2015). Given the difficulty in determining an appropriate arm's length price for intellectual property and related royalty payments, this might lead to only a small reduction in negative spillovers, if any (Etter-Phoya et al. 2020).

Fifteen member states of the EU provide patent box regimes. At the time the CTHI research was conducted, nine member states failed to apply OECD nexus constraints (Belgium, Cyprus, Hungary, Ireland, Italy, Luxembourg, Malta, Netherlands, Portugal, Spain and the United Kingdom),[15] whereas two of them operate under the OECD constraints (France and Slovakia). Since the patent box regimes of two member states (Greece and Lithuania) have not been subjected to annual monitoring by the EU (Council of the European Union 2018), the CTHI considers their spillover risk as unknown.

Comparing the haven scores of EU member states to those of the developing countries studied (see Fig. 10.2) is illuminating. None of the five developing countries applies a patent box preferential tax regime at all (haven scores of zero). As a result, it is evident again that the responsibility for creating the negative spillover risk through such regimes lies primarily with EU countries.

10.3.7 Fictional Interest Deduction

This indicator measures whether a jurisdiction offers fictional (notional) interest deduction to lower corporate income taxes.

Many tax systems around the world offer tax advantages for corporations to finance their investments by debt. As opposed to dividends, which are not deductible and are paid to shareholders after tax has been paid, interest payments on loans are

---

[15] Although these member states have replaced their regimes with a new regime which is available only with OECD nexus constraints, the grandfathering rules enable companies who entered the regime earlier to continue benefitting from the old harmful patent box regime until 31 December 2020 or 30 June 2021 (Council of the European Union 2018). Since the preferential regime has been available as of May 2019, the CTHI concludes this pathway is available for the purposes of this indicator.

one of the many deductible costs a company can make for corporate tax purposes. The evidence indicates that this tax advantage for debt financing, known as debt bias, creates significant inequities, complexities and economic distortions (Chan 2011).

To mitigate the different tax treatments of debt and equity financing and to reduce the level of debt bias, some countries have introduced a fictional interest deduction regime. The term "fictional interest deduction" refers to fictitious interest expenses that companies and sometimes also permanent establishments are entitled to calculate annually on the amount of their total equity and deduct for tax purposes, in the same way that interest on loans is tax deductible. The amount that can be deducted from the taxable base is equal to the fictitious interest cost on the adjusted equity capital.

However, adopting a fictional interest deduction regime to neutralise the debt bias has significant drawbacks. The idea behind the fictional interest deduction regime is to apply an artificial interest deduction. Not surprisingly, such a fictitious vehicle may be vulnerable to tax abuse by multinational companies. And indeed, soon after the fictional interest deduction regime was introduced in Belgium, multinational companies used commonly applied techniques of abuse. Through double dipping, companies end up receiving two tax benefits: the tax deduction of interest paid on a loan and fictional interest deduction based on the capital increase with the funds made available by the loan. The latter includes artificially increasing equity through specific intra-group reorganisation (Peeters and Hermie 2011).

Additionally, other countries may decide in response to fictional interest deductions to lower their tax rates in an attempt to lure more multinationals to invest. This accelerates the race to the bottom in corporate taxation. Thus, a jurisdiction with a fictional interest deduction regime potentially creates a substantial negative spillover risk.

Among the 64 countries researched, only EU member states (with the exception of Liechtenstein) apply a fictional interest deduction rule. Belgium was one of the first countries to introduce a fictional interest deduction regime in 2005, and since then, other countries like Italy, Cyprus, Malta and Portugal have followed suit (Council of the European Union 2018; Hebous and Klemm 2018), albeit Italy has just abolished this pathway via its 2019 Budget Law (Deloitte 2019).

Similar to the precedent indicator on patent box regimes, not even one of the five developing countries allows for a fictional interest deduction rule, and several European countries in particular are responsible for the potential negative spillover risk towards other countries.

10.4   Conclusions and Recommendations

When a jurisdiction introduces a low statutory tax rate and restricts the scope of or inserts gaps and loopholes into its corporate tax system, it increases the likelihood of negative spillovers. The CTHI reviews a comprehensive set of negative and positive tax spillover indicators and assesses 64 countries' international corporate tax systems. Then, it converts this qualitative data into numerical data through a coding strategy.[16] Each indicator is given a score between 0 (no harmful impact, zero corporate tax haven attributes) and 100 (full corporate tax haven attributes). The CTHI takes the average of these indicator scores to reach the Haven Score that points to the potential of a jurisdiction's tax system to create spillovers.[17] When we compare the average haven score of all EU member states with the developing countries' average haven scores, the following conclusions can be drawn for negative spillover indicators:

First, the EU average LACIT rate (16%) is much higher than the average of 27% among developing countries. However, the negative spillover risk considerably increases when the EU and their dependencies are considered as a whole (11%). This suggests that the EU member states bear more responsibility for the "race to the bottom" in corporate taxation than developing countries (Etter-Phoya et al. 2020). Second, the EU average haven score for loopholes and gaps category (46) is higher than the average for developing countries (35). Nonetheless, out of the seven indicators included in this category, the EU scores considerably better than developing countries (11 vs. 60) for tax holidays and economic zones. This finding should be carefully considered by developing countries' governments, predominantly in light of available evidence suggesting the ineffectiveness of geographically confined tax incentives in attracting foreign direct investment, especially in developing countries (see Klemm and Van Parys 2012).

Overall, our analysis demonstrates that while the EU's level of responsibility for creating negative tax spillover risks is similar to that of OECD countries, it greatly exceeds the level of risk created by developing countries. As our evidence shows, EU member states should reform their tax systems in order to mitigate the negative spillover effects of their domestic tax rates and rules, both domestically, within the EU and externally, especially towards developing countries. By improving their haven scores in the two categories analysed in this article, EU member states could help achieve its Sustainable Development Goals by reducing the erosion of public revenues and supporting domestic resource mobilisation.

---

[16]To measure the intensity of spillover risks for the LACIT and capital gain taxation, the CTHI calculates a country's lowest available rate as a percentage of the highest observable corporate income tax rate of a democracy in order to determine the extent of tax avoidance risks which undermine democratic choices elsewhere. This rate is 35% in the case of India for 2018. Then, the CTHI subtracts this number from 100. For example, when a jurisdiction has 25% as the lowest available rate, the haven score would be 100 minus the percentage of 25–35, i.e. 28.6. In the worst-case scenario, a country without income taxation has 0% LACIT, and the haven score of this country would be 100. That means this jurisdiction has the highest tax avoidance potential.

[17]It then combines the haven score with a quantitative component of the Global Scale Weight attributed to each jurisdiction that is based on an assessment of the size of each jurisdiction's share of the global total of foreign direct investment. The CTHI value, which determines a ranking, is calculated by multiplying the cube of the haven score with the cube root of the Global Scale Weight. The final result is divided through by 100 for presentational clarity. For the ranking of researched jurisdictions, see Tax Justice Network (2019).

Acknowledgements The writing and research carried out for this chapter were part of the Combating Fiscal Fraud and Empowering Regulators (COFFERS) project (2016–2019). The COFFERS project unfolds as EU tax authorities transition to a new era in tackling tax abuse based upon policy innovation at the international and national levels. The COFFERS project has received funding from the European Union's Horizon 2020 research and innovation programme under grant agreement n. 727145. Special acknowledgement to Burcak Bal Yalcin, Lucas Millán-Narotzky and Miroslav Palanský.

References

Abbas, S. M. A., & Klemm, A. (2013). A partial race to the bottom: Corporate tax developments in emerging and developing economies. *International Tax and Public Finance, 20*, 596–617.

Ates, L., Harari, M., & Meinzer, M. (2020). Positive spillovers in international corporate taxation and the European Union. *Intertax, 48*(4), 389–401.

Chan, N. T. L. (2011). *Excessive leverage—Root cause of financial crisis*. Retrieved March 31, 2019, from https://www.bis.org/review/r111215g.pdf

Chowdhary, A. M. (2019). *Mauritius: India cracks down on a major tax evasion route*. Retrieved June 26, 2020, from https://www.taxjustice.net/2016/05/24/mauritius-india-curbs-a-major-tax-evasion-route/

Christensen, B. M. (2018). *Stemming the spills: Guiding framework for undertaking national tax spillover analyses*. Retrieved August 30, 2019, from https://actionaid.org/sites/default/files/stemming_the_spills_online.pdf

Christensen, M. B., & Clancy, E. (2018). *Exposed: Apple's golden delicious tax deals. Is Ireland helping apple pay less than 1% tax in the EU?* Retrieved August 30, 2019, from https://www.guengl.eu/content/uploads/2018/06/Apple_report_final.pdf

Cobham, A., & Janský, P. (2017). *Global distribution of revenue loss from tax avoidance: Re-estimation and country results*. UNU-WIDER Working Paper. 2017/55. Retrieved May 21, 2019, from https://www.wider.unu.edu/sites/default/files/wp2017-55.pdf

Cobham, A., Janský, P., & Meinzer, M. (2015). the financial secrecy index: Shedding new light on the geography of secrecy. *Economic Geography, 91*, 281–303.

Coffery, S. (2018). *Economic incentives: What apple did next*. Retrieved May 21, 2019, from http://economic-incentives.blogspot.com/2018/01/what-apple-did-next.html

Council Directive. (2011). *2011/96/EU of 30 November 2011 on the common system of taxation applicable in the case of parent companies and subsidiaries of different Member States [2011] OJ L 345*.

Council of the European Union. (2008). *2866th council meeting economic and financial affairs*. 8850/08 (Presse 113), 22–23 (Press Release 14 May 2008). Retrieved March 25, 2019, from https://www.consilium.europa.eu/ueDocs/cms_Data/docs/pressData/en/ecofin/100339.pdf

Council of the European Union. (2018). *Code of Conduct Group (Business Taxation): Overview of the preferential tax regimes examined by the Code of Conduct Group (Business Taxation) since its creation in March 1998*. Retrieved March 25, 2019, from http://data.consilium.europa.eu/doc/document/ST-9639-2018-REV-2/en/pdf

CPB Netherlands Bureau for Economic Policy Analysis. (2014). *A study on R & D tax incentives: Final report*. Luxembourg: Office for Official Publications of the European Communities.

Crivelli, E., De Mooij, R., & Keen, M. (2016). Base erosion, profit shifting and developing countries. *FinanzArchiv: Public Finance Analysis, 72*(3), 268–301.

Dagan, T. (2000). The tax treaties myth. *New York University Journal of International Law and Politics, 32*, 939–996.

Dagan, T. (2018). *International tax policy: Between tax competition and cooperation*. Cambridge: Cambridge University Press.

Deloitte. (2019). *Changes to tax incentives under 2019 budget law.* Retrieved September 2, 2019, from https://www.taxathand.com/article/10903/Italy/2019/Changes-to-tax-incentives-under-2019-budget-law

Devereux, M. P., Lockwood, B., & Redoano, M. (2008). Do countries compete over corporate tax rates? *Journal of Public Economics, 92,* 1210–1235.

Etter-Phoya, R., Lima, S., & Meinzer, M. (2020). Tax base erosion and corporate profit shifting: Africa in international comparative perspective. *Journal on Financing for Development, 1(2),* 68-107.

EU. (2008). *Consolidated version of the treaty on European Union [2008] OJ C115/13.*

European Commission. (2010). *Communication from the Commission to the European Parliament, the Council and the European Economic and Social Committee, Tax and Development: Cooperating with Developing Countries on Promoting Good Governance in Tax Matters.* COM (2010)163 final (21 April 2010).

European Commission. (2018). *Press release—State aid: Commission finds Luxembourg gave illegal tax benefits to Engie; has to recover around €120 million.* Retrieved August 30, 2019, from https://europa.eu/rapid/press-release_IP-18-4228_en.htm

European Commission. (2019). *Data on taxation.* Retrieved August 30, 2019, from https://ec.europa.eu/taxation_customs/business/economic-analysis-taxation/data-taxation_en

Evers, L., Miller, H., & Spengel, C. (2013). *Intellectual property box regimes: Effective tax rates and tax policy considerations.* Retrieved October 7, 2019, from http://ftp.zew.de/pub/zew-docs/dp/dp13070.pdf

FATF, & Egmont Group of Financial Intelligence Units (EGMONT). (2013). *Money laundering and terrorist financing through trade in diamonds.* Retrieved June 26, 2020, from http://www.fatf-gafi.org/media/fatf/documents/reports/ML-TF-through-trade-in-diamonds.pdf

Financial Action Task Force (FATF). (2010). *Money laundering vulnerabilities of free trade zones.* Retrieved June 26, 2020, from http://www.fatf-gafi.org/media/fatf/documents/reports/ML%20vulnerabilities%20of%20Free%20Trade%20Zones.pdf

G8. (2013). *Lough erne G8 leaders' communiqué.* Retrieved June 15, 2017, from https://www.gov.uk/government/publications/2013-lough-erne-g8-leaders-communique

Gaessler, F., Hall, B. H., & Harhoff, D. (2018). *Should there be lower taxes on patent income?* Retrieved May 21, 2019, from https://papers.ssrn.com/sol3/papers.cfm?abstract_id=3216471

Guenther, G. (2017). *Patent boxes: A primer.* Retrieved May 21, 2019, from https://fas.org/sgp/crs/misc/R44829.pdf

Guvenen, F., Mataloni, R. J. Jr., Rassier, D. G., & Ruhl, K. J. (2018). *Offshore profit shifting and domestic productivity measurement.* Retrieved October 17, 2019, from https://www.minneapolisfed.org/research/wp/wp751.pdf

Hearson, M. (2016). *Measuring tax treaty negotiation outcomes: The Actionaid tax treaties dataset.* Retrieved August 30, 2019, from https://core.ac.uk/download/pdf/46172854.pdf

Hebous, S., & Klemm, A. (2018). *A destination-based allowance for corporate equity.* IMF Working Paper. Retrieved December 27, 2018, from https://www.imf.org/en/Publications/WP/Issues/2018/11/08/A-Destination-Based-Allowance-for-Corporate-Equity-46314

Hwang, A. (2018). *Thinking outside the (patent) box: An intellectual property approach to combating international tax avoidance.* Retrieved October 17, 2019, from http://rooseveltinstitute.org/wp-content/uploads/2018/05/Thinking-Outside-the-Patent-Box-final.pdf

IBFD. (2019). *Tax research platform: Country surveys, country analyses, country key features.* Retrieved May 9, 2019, from https://research.ibfd.org/

IMF. (2013). *Issues in international taxation and the role of the IMF.* Retrieved October 11, 2019, from http://www.imf.org/external/np/pp/eng/2013/062813.pdf

IMF. (2014). *Spillovers in international corporate taxation.* Retrieved June 26, 2014, from http://www.imf.org/external/np/pp/eng/2014/050914.pdf

IMF. (2015). *Current challenges in revenue mobilization—Improving tax compliance.* Retrieved October 11, 2019, from https://www.imf.org/external/np/pp/eng/2015/020215a.pdf

IMF. (2019a). *IMF survey: IMF connects dots in spillover analysis of major economies.* Retrieved October 11, 2019, from https://www.imf.org/en/News/Articles/2015/09/28/04/53/socar090211b

IMF. (2019b). *Spillover reports.* Retrieved October 11, 2019, from https://www.imf.org/en/Publications/SPROLLS/Spillover-Reports#sort=%40imfdate%20descending

Keen, M., & Mansour, M. (2009). *Revenue mobilization in Sub-Saharan Africa: Challenges from globalization.* Retrieved June 26, 2020, from https://www.imf.org/external/pubs/ft/wp/2009/wp09157.pdf

Klemm, A., & Van Parys, S. (2012). Empirical evidence on the effects of tax incentives. *International Tax and Public Finance, 19*, 393–423.

Kofler, G. (2012). Indirect credit versus exemption: Double taxation relief for intercompany distributions. *Bulletin for International Taxation, 66*(2), 77–89.

KPMG. (2018). *Malta's tax system.* Retrieved August 30, 2019, from https://home.kpmg/mt/en/home/insights/2018/08/malta-tax-system.html

KPMG. (2019). *Corporate tax rates table.* Retrieved August 30, 2019, from https://home.kpmg/xx/en/home/services/tax/tax-tools-and-resources/tax-rates-online/corporate-tax-rates-table.html

Lips, W., & Cobham, A. (2018). *Who will feature on the common EU blacklist of non-cooperative tax jurisdictions?* Retrieved June 9, 2018, from https://www.researchgate.net/publication/326126153_Paradise_lost_Who_will_feature_on_the_common_EU_blacklist_of_non-cooperative_tax_jurisdictions

Lusiani, N., & Cosgrove, M. (2017). *A strange alchemy: Embedding human rights in tax policy spillover assessments.* Retrieved August 30, 2019, from https://papers.ssrn.com/abstract=3218597

Lustig, N. (2018). Fiscal policy, income redistribution, an poverty reduction in low- and middle-income countries. In N. Lustig (Ed.), *To equity handbook: Estimating the impact of fiscal policy on inequality and poverty.* Washington, DC: Brookings Institution.

McGauran, K. (2013). *Should the Netherlands sign tax treaties with developing countries?* Retrieved May 28, 2019, from https://www.somo.nl/wp-content/uploads/2013/06/Should-the-Netherlands-sign-tax-treaties-with-developing-countries.pdf

McNabb, K., & LeMay-Boucher, P. (2014). *Tax structures, economic growth and development.* ICTD Working Paper 22. Retrieved June 26, 2020, from https://opendocs.ids.ac.uk/opendocs/bitstream/handle/20.500.12413/10253/ICTD_WP22.pdf

Meinzer, M. (2016). Towards a common yardstick to identify tax havens and to facilitate reform. In P. Dietsch & T. Rixen (Eds.), *Global tax governance—What is wrong with it, and how to fix it.* Colchester: ECPR Press.

Meinzer, M., & Knobel, A. (2015). *EU tax haven blacklist—A misguided approach?* Retrieved April 19, 2016, from www.taxjustice.net/wp-content/uploads/2015/09/EU-tax-haven-blacklist-a-misguided-approach.pdf

Meinzer, M., Ndajiwo, M., Etter-Phoya, R., & Diakité, M. (2019). *Comparing tax incentives across jurisdictions: A pilot study.* Retrieved June 26, 2020, from https://www.taxjustice.net/wp-content/uploads/2018/12/Comparing-tax-incentives-across-jurisdictions_Tax-Justice-Network_2019.pdf

Millán-Narotzky, L., Meinzer, M., & Palanský, M. (2020). *Who benefits from tax exemptions? Evidence of incentives for financial rents and environmental destruction.* TJN Working Paper.

Mosquera Valderrama, I. J. (2019). The EU standard of good governance in tax matters for third (non-EU) countries. *Intertax, 47*, 454–467.

Neumayer, E. (2007). Do double taxation treaties increase foreign direct investment to developing countries? *Journal of Development Studies, 43*, 1501–1519.

OECD. (2011). *Corporate loss utilisation through aggressive tax planning.* Paris: OECD.

OECD. (2015). Countering Harmful Tax Practices More Effectively, Taking into Account Transparency and Substance, Action 5 - 2015 Final Report, OECD/G20 Base Erosion and Profit Shifting Project. Paris: OECD Publishing.

OECD. (2019). *OECD statistics: Table II.1. Statutory corporate income tax rate.* Retrieved August 30, 2019, from https://stats.oecd.org/

Peeters, B., & Hermie, T. (2011). *Notional interest deduction: The Belgian experience.* Retrieved March 31, 2019, from https://www.tiberghien.com/media/ACTL%20seminarie_Bernard&Thomas.pdf

Picciotto, S. (1992). *International business taxation. A study in the internationalization of business regulation.* Electronic Re-Publication ed. Retrieved April 26, 2019, from https://taxjustice.net/cms/upload/pdf/Picciotto%201992%20International%20Business%20Taxation.pdf

Rao, K., Pitigala, S., Hoverter, M., & Gauthier, JP. (2008). *Special economic zones performance, lessons learned, and implications for zone development.* Retrieved October 18, 2019, from http://documents.worldbank.org/curated/en/343901468330977533/pdf/458690WP0Box331s0April200801PUBLIC1.pdf

Romano, R., & Campisano, M. (1981). Recouping losses: The case for full loss offsets. *Northwestern University Law Review, 76,* 709–744.

Sanz Gomez, R. (2015). *The OECD's nexus approach to IP boxes: A European Union law perspective.* WU International Taxation Research Paper Series No. 2015-12. Retrieved June 26, 2010, from https://ssrn.com/abstract=2589065

Tax Justice Network. (2019). *Corporate tax haven index (CTHI) 2019 methodology.* Retrieved June 4, 2019, from https://www.corporatetaxhavenindex.org/PDF/CTHI-Methodology.pdf

Yadav, S. (2017). Paradise papers: Yale University turned to offshore firm to enter India via Mauritius. *The Indian Express.* Retrieved June 25, 2020, from https://indianexpress.com/article/india/paradise-papers-yale-university-india-investment-appleby-mauritius-black-money-mhrd-4928983/

Zeng, D. Z. (2010). How do special economic zones and industrial clusters drive. In D. Z. Zeng (Ed.), *China's rapid development? Building engines for growth and competitiveness in China: Experience with special economic zones and industrial clusters.* Washington, DC: World Bank.

Chapter 11
Conclusion

Wouter Lips

This book has been a collaboration between 20 authors who are all working on issues that link taxation with development and emancipation in the Global South in all sorts of different capacities. Together, we have offered ten chapters that explore four relevant themes: global tax governance and developing countries, external assistance for tax capacity building, tax incentives and attracting sustainable investment, and harmful and helpful tax practices for sustainable development. The book paints a picture of the difficulties countries in the Global South face when they participate in international tax relations, whether bilateral or multilateral, but each chapter also highlights opportunities for how the international community can do better in this regard.

In this concluding chapter, we as editors reflect on the lessons this book offers. The nature of edited volumes is that they offer a broad range of chapters on a given topic. As such, this chapter is not the conclusion of a carefully laid out argument, that we now neatly wrap a bow around, but rather a summary of the common ground between the contributors. We also purposefully refrain from offering specific advice to any developing country or developing countries as a category. We feel this is not our place as we advocate country-specific and country-owned solutions. We also don't want to perpetrate the myth that developing countries all share similar interests or development paths, as in modernization-type theories of development, with regard to taxation.

Nevertheless, there are returning themes throughout the chapters: issues that are important, things whose absence obstructs and whose improvement advances the nexus between taxation, development, and developing countries' revenues. Topics that tax practitioners, development professionals, and academics all should

W. Lips (✉)
Ghent University, Ghent, Belgium
e-mail: wouter.lips@ugent.be

© The Author(s) 2021
I. J. Mosquera Valderrama et al. (eds.), *Taxation, International Cooperation and the 2030 Sustainable Development Agenda*, United Nations University Series on Regionalism 19, https://doi.org/10.1007/978-3-030-64857-2_11

recognize as indispensable for improving fair, balanced, and sustainable international taxation.

We wish to highlight five of those key issues that we believe are paramount in moving tax relations between high-income countries and the Global South, and their respective tax subjects, towards a more just outcome: data, transparency, inclusiveness, home-grown policies, and eradicating double standards. All chapters in this volume touch upon at least several of these topics. Summarizing them in the conclusion leads us to the lessons we ourselves, and hopefully you as a reader— whether you have read all chapters back to back or made a curated selection according to what concerns your interests, can take away from this volume.

11.1   The Importance of Data

Three chapters in this book make use of novel datasets, in which the authors themselves were involved in creating those sets. Chapter 10's use of the *Corporate Tax Haven Index* is a reaction against what the authors argue are the biased and incomplete characteristics of official blacklists by governments or international organizations. The *Global Tax Expenditures Database* from Chap. 9 remedies the lack of systematic reporting on tax expenditures, even though these can account for a significant part of government revenues. CIAT's *BEPS Monitoring Database* which forms the basis for Chap. 3 was created to transparently monitor in which ways their members implemented the BEPS minimum standards.

Good quality data is a prerequisite for good policy. This is certainly true for tax policy in developing countries. Developing countries often do not have access to the granular, centrally collected and high-quality data that, for example, the OECD offers to its members. The lack of high-quality economic statistics on taxes in developing countries is well-recognized issue (for more elaboration, see Prichard 2016). The same goes for donor policy. The OECD Development Assistance Committee only introduced a specific code for aid towards domestic resource mobilization (DRM) in its development statistics in 2015. This meant that although aid for DRM was an agenda item in the UN financing for development policy conferences since the early 2000s, specific data was unavailable which in turn makes it hard to coordinate.

Data is not only important for policy design; it also empowers developing countries in international negotiations. In a timeframe of less than 5 years, developing countries have, on paper, become partners on equal footing in the BEPS Inclusive Framework (IF). The two-pillar reform efforts on taxing the digitalized economy (OECD/G20 Inclusive Framework on BEPS 2020)—that are ongoing at time of writing—are enormously complex, however. It is strikingly hard to anticipate what consequences the reforms BEPS IF countries are signing up to will entail. Without access to good quality economic and tax-related data, it is next to impossible.

11.2 The Importance of Transparency

Transparency is a second thread running through this book. This applies to both government policy and taxpayer transparency. Taxation is at the foundation of societies' social contracts, and transparency is an important feature of that. It increases tax certainty, increases trust in the fairness and performance of the tax system, and holds governments accountable. Transparency also was one of the key elements of the G20-led OECD reform programs on exchange of information and BEPS (OECD/G20 Inclusive Framework on BEPS 2020).

The sixth and seventh chapter in this book both tackles the issue of tax incentives. Tax incentives can be performant tools for attracting foreign investments but can quickly tip over into preferential tax advantages or even harmful tax regimes. Both chapters mention the importance of transparency to ensure these incentives stay cost-effective and fair. Arguments in the same vein are made in Chap. 9 on tax expenditures. High-income governments are not off the hook in the context of developing countries though, as Chap. 10 shows how preferential tax regimes can have negative spillovers in the Global South. All these chapters mention a myriad of reform suggestion for their respective topics. But the common ground here is that increased transparency might not automatically result in better government policy but in almost all cases is a necessary condition for improvement.

On the other side of the social contract is taxpayer transparency. Ensuring every taxpayer is treated equally and that people can't evade or avoid paying taxes is just as important for improving trust in the tax system. The OECD's programs on automatic exchange of financial information and multinational country-by-country reporting are important multilateral milestones in this regard. Yet, many developing countries—despite being part of those programs—are not yet sharing and receiving this information (OECD/G20 Inclusive Framework on BEPS 2020). This is mostly due to reciprocity requirements and a lack of technical capacity to meet those. The fourth chapter on improving donor coordination considers the current assistance for improving transparency in developing countries through these programs. The fifth chapter's main concept of Medium-Term Revenue Strategies can be an important tool for coordinating donor efforts to develop the necessary capacity to step into these exchange systems. Moreover, donor governments could consider foregoing reciprocity for a set period of time while allowing developing countries to use the resulting revenues for meeting the necessary conditions for reciprocity.

11.3 The Importance of Home-Grown Policies

The previous paragraph already mentioned taxes as the heart of the social contract. What follows from this is that national tax policies should follow the preferences of countries and not just be an implementation of blueprints that are considered acceptable internationally. This is not at odds with countries learning from each other at the regional or multilateral level or with the sharing of best practices but emphasizes that tax policy should ultimately follow a specific country's needs. This is especially important in the context of developing countries where a power relation vis-à-vis high-income countries, who are also aid donors, unavoidably exists.

Country ownership is an important consideration when donors provide external assistance in tax matters. Donor-driven reform is a plausible trap; whether due to information asymmetry, conditionality, or any sort of other interests that are involved. Chapters 4 and 5 deal with these matters of how to design technical assistance programs with respect to country ownership. The recently introduced concept of Medium-Term Revenue Strategies is one potential tool that can help in this regard. The same goes for policy coherence, as envisaged in Chap. 4, to ensure development objectives and tax policy are in line aids with producing assistance programs that match a partner country's needs. This also holds true for the interaction between investment treaties and taxation, which Chap. 8 investigates. Investment treaties, especially those providing arbitration, can constrain or even undermine a country's efforts to pursue its optimal tax policy.

A more radical, but nonetheless worthwhile, exploration of homegrown policies in Chap. 2 is the case studies on unitary taxation with formulary apportionment and destination-based cash flow taxes in African countries. The author agrees that neither is a panacea nor easily implemented. However, contemplating alternatives to the transfer pricing system in which developing countries have had no say in designing should be a viable option to them. Similarly, the first chapter problematizes the power imbalances in international tax negotiations and how this leads to biased outcomes (in their case, the transactional profit split method). The takeaway here is that what might be good for international tax governance as a whole and provides stability is not necessarily what's best for developing countries.

11.4 The Importance of Eradicating Double Standards

"Do as we say, not as we do" is practically a cliché for when someone wants to criticize development practices. But there are instances where even well-meant and evidence-based advice to developing countries leaves a slightly sour taste because high-income countries themselves don't apply it.

The two Chaps. 6 and 7 on tax incentives are nice examples of this. Well-designed tax incentives can be an important tool for developing countries to attract sustainable investment. But they have to be transparent and monitored because they can quickly become ineffective and thus a drain on a country's finances. Or they can lead to a harmful competitive dynamic. There are few people who would argue these points, including the policy officials in high-income countries or international institutions working with developing countries on tax matters. Yet compare this with the negative spillovers generated by the tax conduct of high-income countries, as explained in Chap. 10, and one can quickly see how this relates to the "do as we say" cliché.

Another more sinister example are blacklists imposed by high-income countries, such as the EU's list of uncooperative jurisdictions. This list has been criticized extensively for listing certain countries while failing to apply their own criteria to EU countries (Lips and Cobham 2017; Lomas 2017). Chapter 10 again exposes this double standard by showing how high-income countries' tax regimes themselves provide a harmful dynamic to developing countries.

Less obvious, but nonetheless important, are the double standards that come along with aid and technical assistance from tax reform. Donor-funded reforms are often held to high standards, for example, the medium-term country-wide consensus on tax reforms as the ideal in Medium-Term Revenue Standards (see Chap. 5). On the one hand, this is understandable since donors should want their funds to be well spent. But on the other, donor countries themselves often do not adhere to those same standards they expect from developing countries.

Ultimately, this is symptomatic of an international tax system whose principles were designed in a colonial context. These have of course been altered over the years, but the biases towards residence, and thus high-income countries, are still in place (see Chap. 1). Advise towards improving developing countries tax systems, without recognizing this fact, places the burden of adjustment solely on developing countries. Eradicating certain obvious double standards is one way to help improve fair and sustainable tax relations between countries.

11.5 The Importance of Inclusiveness

Finally, a last common thread throughout this volume is the importance of inclusiveness. In order to achieve a fair, sustainable, and equal outlook on taxes in the context of sustainable development, developing countries have to become truly equal partners at the negotiating table. For a long time, the lack of participation was symbolized by the institutional divide between the more inclusive United Nation's Committee of Experts on Tax Matters and the OECD as the dominant institutional forum on tax governance.

On paper, the creation of the BEPS Inclusive Framework is a huge step forward in this regard. It formally hosts 137 member countries, actively works with regional organizations such as ATAF (OECD/G20 Inclusive Framework on BEPS 2020), and helps developing countries with technical implementation through the Platform for Collaboration on Tax (2019).

In practice, however, observers note that participation for developing countries is still difficult. This is due to both practical reasons, for example, language barriers, personnel costs or technical capacity (Mosquera Valderrama 2018; Mosquera Valderrama et al. 2018), and power imbalances. The latter means that high-income countries voices carry more weight due to their economic size. Our first chapter examines the consequences of these imbalances in detail within the context of transfer pricing regulations. It is visible in other domains too, however. One example would be the digital economy negotiations that basically come down with trying to find an agreement between the USA and France (as a leader of European countries on this issue). Developing countries, with India at the front, have tried to steer the negotiations towards their preferences in a common G24 statement (G24 Working Group on Tax Policy and International Tax 2019). The options they put forth have not been included into the OECD texts, however.

At the time of writing, the final compromise has not been reached yet, and it is difficult to predict what the impact of the proposals will be (Hearson 2019). Yet, serious criticisms remain on how developing countries' interests are not being served by the BEPS IF. Instead, they risk being drawn into whichever compromise can appease the game between great powers (Christians 2019). A place at the table clearly does not guarantee inclusive participation. If we want to further develop countries' interests, then we should continue to scrutinize this process and dare to question its legitimacy when appropriate.

11.6   To Conclude

We want to conclude with one final remark. From a narrow perspective, tax relations between countries can sometimes look like a zero-sum game. After all, income that is taxed by one country cannot be taxed by another if every country respects the foundational tax principle that double taxation should be avoided. This perspective is made explicitly in the political economy literature on tax but is equally present in law research, and it is also echoed by policy officials. It implies that making international taxation more equitable inevitably means that high-income countries must give up some revenue. This perspective is not false per se and is surely part of the explanation for why it is so difficult to change established tax norms. It also helps explain why the UN has been and to a large degree still is marginalized as a forum for international taxation. But viewed from a broader perspective, that includes development policies, this perspective is misguided as a foundation for policy.

High-income government should allow development departments to be part of their taxation policies with developing countries. All too often tax policy with development countries is decided in finance departments without consultation with development departments. Establishing disadvantageous tax treaties or blocking progress in international tax negotiations on one hand while delivering official aid for development on the other simply is incoherent and counterproductive from a national perspective. A similar argument can be made from an international perspective. The international community has decided that development is part of its responsibilities. The Millennium Development Goals and Sustainable Development Goals are testament of this. This is not only for moral reasons but also because development is a public good for the international community. Development leads to better government capacity which leads to more stable environments for security and economic opportunities. Taxation is part of this, and for these reasons, the needs of developing countries should be an element in revising international tax principles.

References

Christians, A. (2019). *OECD Secretariat's unified approach: How to get things on a truly equal footing*. Retrieved September 11, 2020, from ICTD website: https://www.ictd.ac/blog/oecd-secretariat-unified-approach-equal-footing/

G24 Working Group on Tax Policy and International Tax. (2019). *Proposal for addressing tax challenges arising from digitalisation*, pp. 1–8.

Hearson, M. (2019). *The OECD's digital tax proposal: Untangling the impact of 'Pillar One' on developing countries*. Retrieved September 21, 2020, from ICTD website: https://www.ictd.ac/blog/the-oecds-digital-tax-proposal-untangling-the-impact-of-pillar-one-on-developing-countries/

Lips, W., & Cobham, A. (2017). *Paradise lost—Who will feature on the common EU blacklist of non-cooperative tax jurisdictions?* Retrieved from Open Data For Tax Justice website: http://datafortaxjustice.net/paradiselost/

Lomas, U. (2017). *EU accused of tax blacklist hypocrisy*. Retrieved September 10, 2020, from Tax-News website: https://www.tax-news.com/news/EU_Accused_Of_Tax_Blacklist_Hypocrisy_75952.html

Mosquera Valderrama, I. (2018). Output legitimacy deficits and the inclusive framework of the OECD/G20 base erosion and profit shifting initiative. *Bulletin for International Taxation, 72*(3), 1–11.

Mosquera Valderrama, I., Lesage, D., & Lips, W. (2018). *Tax and development: The link between international taxation, the base erosion profit shifting project and the 2030 sustainable development agenda.*

OECD/G20 Inclusive Framework on BEPS. (2020). *Progress report July 2019–July 2020.*

Platform for Collaboration on Tax. (2019). *PCT progress report 2018–2019.*

Prichard, W. (2016). Reassessing tax and development research: A new dataset, new findings, and lessons for research. *World Development, 80*, 48–60. https://doi.org/10.1016/j.worlddev.2015.11.017.

Printed by Printforce, the Netherlands